THE REICH'S ORCHESTRA
The Berlin Philharmonic
1933-1945

THE REICH'S ORCHESTRA

The Berlin Philharmonic
1933-1945

Misha Aster

mosaic press

Library and Archives Canada Cataloguing in Publication

Aster, Misha, 1978-
Reich's orchestra 1933-1945 : the Berlin Philharmonic & national
socialism / Misha Aster.

Includes bibliographical references and index.
ISBN 978-0-88962-913-4

1. Berliner Philharmoniker--History. 2. Music and state--Germany--
History--20th century. 3. National socialism and music--Germany--
Berlin. 4. Music--Political aspects--Germany--Berlin--History--20th
century. I. Title. II. Title: Berlin Philharmonic & national socialism.

ML28.B5B4724 2010   784.2'094315509043   C2010-901547-9

Published by Mosaic Press, offices and warehouse at 1252 Speers Road, Units
1 and 2, Oakville, Ontario, L6L 5N9, Canada and Mosaic Press, 40 Sonwil Dr,
Cheektowaga, NY14225, U.S.A.

Copyright © 2012 Misha Aster
Designed by Keith Daniel
ISBN 978-0-88962-913-4
eBook 978-0-88962-949-3

We acknowledge the financial
support of the Government of
Canada through the Canada Book
Fund (CBF) for this project.

Nous reconnaissons l'aide finan-
cière du gouvernement du Canada
par l'entremise du Fonds du livre
du Canada (FLC) pour ce projet.

Mosaic Press in Canada:
1252 Speers Road, Units 1 & 2
Oakville, Ontario
L6L 5N9
Phone/Fax: 905-825-2130
info@mosaic-press.com

Mosaic Press in U.S.A.:
c/o Livingston, 40 Sonwil Dr
Cheektowaga, NY
14225
Phone/Fax: 905-825-2130
info@mosaic-press.com

www.mosaic-press.com

Contents

Dedicated to Dr. Igor Kuchinsky, "Witness of History"
(1908-1945-2006)

Acknowledgements

The realisation of this book is a singular testament to the determination and generosity of Walter Küssner, a man whose keen mind is matched only by the nobility of his immense heart. From his colleagues at the Stiftung Berliner Philharmoniker, it is an honour to offer thanks to Gerhard Forck for his enthusiastic support, and for the benefit of his practical and intellectual guidance; to Frau Intendantin Pamela Rosenberg, whose active embrace of this project gave impetus to its critical final stages; to the Orchestervorstand of the Berlin Philharmonic, Peter Riegelbauer and Jan Diesselhorst; and to Frank Kersten, *Kaufmännischen Direktor* of the *Stiftung Berliner Philharmoniker*. Special thanks must also be reserved for Frau Jutta March, passionate gatekeeper of the Philharmonic Archive, Klaus Stoll and Rudi Watzel.

Further, I should like to express my gratitude to the circle of academic colleagues who offered constructive review of my work-in-progress: Albrecht Dümling, Dr. Sophie Fettauer, Dr. Heinz von Loesch; and above all to Professor Wolf Lepenies for his gracious reception of this effort, and his munificent words of introduction.

This project began as a conversation, many, many years ago. That one talk precipitated countless more, the most precious of which, with witnesses of the very history written about in these pages. For their kindness and candidness, I am indebted to Johannes Bastiaan and his devoted wife, to Erich Hartmann, and to the remarkable Gerta Taschner. Thanks also to Enrique Sanchez Lansch for his thoughtful diligence, and to the probing mind of Michael Abramovich.

Turning a few ideas and diffuse paragraphs into a book is, under the best of circumstances, no easy task. The distinct particularities of this unique endeavour, however, magnified the complexities at least hundredfold. I owe deepest gratitude to Dr. Stephan Meyer, who was willing to take a chance, and to Tobias Winstel of Random House/ Siedler Verlag for his faith, tact, and foresight; to Jan Schleusener for his smiling meticulousness through a thankless task; and to Reinhard Lüthje, for delivering my words into the language of their source.

It is an honour on this page to recognise the influence of several great people who instructed, inspired, and shaped the perspectives dwelling herein: to Mr. Jim Volk, Mario di Paolantonio, Professors Valentin Boss and Peter Hoffman, and Rabbi Edward Goldfarb, with thanks and admiration. And finally, to Soula, for her unwavering support, and to my greatest teachers, my parents, for their love.

Introduction

The Berlin Philharmonic Orchestra was founded in 1882 as an independent, self-governing musical association in which the musicians were shareholders—a sort of orchestral co-operative. Over the following fifty years, the orchestra became world-renowned, and toured throughout Europe. In 1933, with the Nazis' rise to power, the Berlin Philharmonic, in grave financial difficulty, was bought out by the German State. The musicians became civil servants under direct authority of Goebbels' Ministry of Public Enlightenment and Propaganda (*Reichsministerium für Volksaufklärung and Propaganda*, abb. RMVP). For the next twelve years, the orchestra served as Nazi Germany's flagship cultural ambassador, touring internationally both before and during the Second World War, providing musical accompaniment for a plethora of public events from the Nuremberg Rallies, to the opening of the 1936 Olympic Games, to Hitler's birthday.

There has never been a book written on the subject of the Berlin Philharmonic during the Third Reich, in any language. This book represents the first comprehensive study of the relationship between Hitler's regime and its musical crown jewel. It is intended neither as a book on music history, nor as an analysis of Nazi aesthetics. Indeed, music plays but a minor role in this work. Rather, as my title dares to suggest, *The Berlin Philharmonic: 1933-1945* is an historical case study whose goal is to mount a comprehensive, systematic, factual account of the relationship between two collective entities: the Berlin Philharmonic Orchestra and the Nazi State.

This relationship is set forth as a meeting of autonomous powers—the Berlin Philharmonic orchestra *and* the Third Reich, not 'during', 'with', 'under' or some other subordinate conjunction. The following pages purport an investigation of a community which practiced music and politics in dialogue with a regime which, on a broader scale, practiced the same. Through primary documents, one can see the ways in which the regime used the orchestra and the orchestra used the regime. The Nazi regime's patronage afforded the Berlin Philharmonic innumerable privileges unique among German cultural institutions. The orchestra accepted these benefits with a combination of gratitude, apprehension and vindication. As the musicians attempted to balance their exceptional status with a degree of artistic and organisational autonomy, tensions between ideological principle, legal jurisdiction, personal taste, and pragmatic regulation, revealed profound contradictions at the heart of the Nazi State. Though the malevolent 'Nazi' influence can never be dismissed from the equation, of equal importance is the recognition that there was a functional logic to the organisation of the orchestra and its development 1933-45. Models of funding and management structure were erected during the Third Reich, many elements of which still remain integral to the Berlin Philharmonic Orchestra's organisation to this day.

The relative paucity of research on this subject is surprising considering the Berlin Philharmonic's renown and its unique status in the constellation of National Socialist cultural policy. General histories of the Nazi period in Germany referenced in preparation of this manuscript include Eberhard Jäckel's *Hitler's Weltanschauung* (1972), Michael Burleigh's *The Third Reich: A New History* (2000), and the first two instalments of Richard Evan's Third Reich trilogy, *The Coming of the Third Reich* (2004) and *The Third Reich in Power* (2005). Jäckel, Burleigh, and Evans, respected historians all, offer political histories from a range of interpretive perspectives, and include some elaboration of Nazi cultural policy, discussion of the Goebbels-Göring rivalry, reference to Philharmonic conductor Wilhelm Furtwängler, and limited mention of the Berlin Philharmonic story. In relation to the latter topics however, each accepts conclusions from other secondary literature, serving to perpetuate a variety of common misconceptions this book attempts to rectify.

Timothy Mason's *Sozialpolitik im Dritten Reich: Arbeiterklasse und Volksgemeinschaft* (1979) as well as Gerhard Hirschfeldt and Wolfgang J. Mommsen's *Der »Führerstaat«: Mythos und Realität; Studien zur Struktur und Politik des Dritten Reiches* (1981) provide a helpful intellectual tool for unlocking the tangled Berlin Philharmonic-Nazi State relationship with the elucidation of 'intentionalist' and 'functionalist' interpretations of the regime's activities. 'Intentionalism' argues Nazi ideology, as articulated principally in Hitler's *Mein Kampf*, the writings of Alfred Rosenberg, and other key documents, defined a program of political action, of which Nazi government policy can be understood as a systematic execution. 'Functionalists' argue that despite the ideological avowals of the regime's ministers and functionaries, the complexity of governing Germany forced pragmatic compromise which tempered, mitigated, even marginalised the actual presence of National Socialist dogma in many areas of State jurisdiction,. Both schools acknowledge the largely bureaucratic nature of administration adopted by the State as a means of implementation and control. The Philharmonic case clearly illustrates the tensions between these two powerful trends.

The Berlin Philharmonic receives mention in several of the important histories of music in Nazi Germany: Fred K. Prieberg's *Musik im NS-Staat* (1982), Michael Mayer's *The Politics of Music in the Third Reich* (1991), Erik Levi's *Music in the Third Reich* (1994), and Michael Kater's *The Twisted Muse: Musicians and their Music in the Third Reich* (1997). Prieberg was a pioneer in the field, and his exhaustive research, particularly his *Handbuch der deutschen Musiker, 1933-45*, is an invaluable reference source. Levi offers a narrative through the period, which reads well, but is scantily referenced. He makes claims about the Berlin Philharmonic which my research has been unable to substantiate. Mayer draws much from Prieberg, while Kater, as his title indicates, looks mostly at individual cases. Kater does important service by illustrating how qualitative considerations were still paramount in determining musical careers in Nazi Germany, but does not withhold moral condemnation of those who prospered under the regime.

Fierce polemics invariably revolve around the figure of Furtwängler. In the historiography of the Third Reich, few figures at once encapsulate the ethical mire of the historical experience while capturing the imagination as an ideal of the romantic artist quite like the great conductor. The Furtwängler case arouses passions among musicians, scholars, and amateurs which transcend differences in opinion. Among the scholarly voices, Prieberg and Kater are particularly vicious in their exchanges. Their disagreement extends beyond divergence in their moral evaluation of Furtwängler, his character and his actions; it regularly descends into bitter chastisement of the other's methodologies, even calling into question their respective qualifications and competence. Though in tone hardly becoming of civilised debate, the dispute between Prieberg and Kater is illustrative of the emotionally-charged atmosphere surrounding this powerful personality.

For my part, I have attempted, to the greatest extent possible, to steer clear of 'taking sides' (to borrow the title of Ronald Harwood's challenging if not entirely historically reliable 1995 dramatisation of Furtwängler's de-Nazification trial) on the conductor's ethics. My purpose is rather to focus on the role of Furtwängler not as an autonomous historical actor, but in relation to the Berlin Philharmonic Orchestra. To this extant, Pamela Potter's contribution to National Socialist Cultural Policy (ed. G. Cuomo, 1995), entitled "The Nazi 'Seizure' of the Berlin Philharmonic, or the Decline of a Bourgeois Musical Institution," is, to my knowledge, the only academic article relating directly to this research subject.

From available material relating to the Berlin Philharmonic during the Third Reich, the two themes of Furtwängler and the fate of the orchestra's Jewish musicians have vastly overshadowed consideration of other aspects of the Philharmonic's general culture and development 1933-45. Furtwängler is a topic unto himself, and the subject of numerous scholarly and popular biographies, including Prieberg's *Kraftprobe* (1986), Shirakawa's *The Devil's Music Master* (1992), and Haffner's *Furtwängler* (2003), not to mention an industry of documentary films and even theatre plays. Naturally, the conductor played a decisive role in Philharmonic affairs during the period, but his influence can be overstated, and should not obscure the individual choices, predicaments, experiences, artistic and political lives of the orchestra's roughly one hundred members, of whom Jewish players represented less than 5% in 1933. By contrast, the personal memoirs of Furtwängler's secretary, Bertha Geissmar, *Musik im Schatten der Politik oder Tatstock und Schaftstiefel* (1945) is a lively and accessible account touching in detail on the Philharmonic's transition from the 1920s to 1935. The author herself being Jewish however, Geissmar places inordinate weight on the anti-Semitic character of the early Nazi years, without reflecting on the policy's remarkably limited impact on the Berlin Philharmonic. The book contains numerous anecdotes of meetings and events key to understanding what took place during those years, but her view is told in first person narrative, very much coloured by a Furtwängler-positive lens, and is occasionally less than factually rigorous. It also only covers until her emigration to England in 1935.

Erich Hartmann's book *Die Berliner Philharmoniker in der Stunde Null* (1996) is a valuable personal reflection on the experience of 1944-46 from inside of orchestra. Hartmann, a *Kontrabassist* in the Berlin Philharmonic from 1943, provides important information as to the fate of specific orchestra colleagues, and paints a unique portrait of the atmosphere within the orchestra 'in der Stunde Null'. The life of the orchestra during the war, however, especially through its closing stages, was not representative of the orchestra's broader Third Reich experience, and Hartmann, having only joined in late 1943, had only limited appreciation of orchestra's special development under the Nazis.

Hartmann's book is one of a handful of reference materials generated by the Berlin Philharmonic itself. *Einhundert Jahre Berliner Philharmonisches Orchester: Darstellung in Dokumenten* (1982), is the standard history of the orchestra exhibited in documents. Complied by veteran Philharmonic violist Peter Muck, the three volumes represent the most exhaustive work ever written on the Berlin Philharmonic, and is cited extensively in all other writing on the subject since 1982. With respect to the 1933-45 period, Muck's selection is judicious, rather reflecting musical as opposed to organisational or political developments, and placing misrepresentative emphasis on examples of protest. Gerassimos Avgerinos, a timpanist in the Philharmonic, wrote and self-published two books in 1972, *Künstler Biographien*, an encyclopaedia of every musician ever to play in the Berlin Philharmonic, and *Das Berliner Philharmonisches*

Orchester: 70 Jahre ein GmbH. Avgerinos' source references are sadly sparse, but the encyclopaedic information cited in both books is extremely helpful, and seemingly remarkably accurate.

A principal reason for the relative obscurity of this book's theme in the historiography has been the assumed scarcity of documentary material. Between November 1943, and January 1944, the Berlin Philharmonic lost both its administrative offices and its musical home, the Alte Philharmonie, to Allied bombing raids. With the destruction of these facilities, the bulk of the orchestra's primary correspondence, files, and documents were believed lost. The Bundesarchiv (including the former American-directed Berlin Document Centre), housing most of the papers salvaged from Goebbels' RMVP, is the single largest source of surviving documentary material pertaining to the orchestra. Systematically working through the archive, one can reconstruct a vivid impression of the lines of bureaucratic communication between the Berlin Philharmonic administration and secretaries of the RMVP, as well as the tone and language thereof.

The Geheime Staatsarchiv (Berlin-Dahlem) concentrates primarily on the pre-1933 period, with therefore somewhat limited coverage of this project's theme. Important within its collection, however, are documents from the Preussische Finance and Interior ministries concerning the search for a satisfactory funding formula for the Berlin Philharmonic in the late 1920s and early 1930s, establishing precedents for events after 1933.

The archive of the Berlin Philharmonic Orchestra itself is rather small, reconstructed after 1945 predominantly from donations from former orchestra musicians or their families. The collections of personal photographs offer private views of tours, travel and concerts. Several dozen files include inherited official documents such as *Uk-Stellung* confirmations, declarations of Aryan status, visa applications, travel plans. The archive also contains some post-war musicians lists which are useful in cross-reference with other materials.

Private collections represent the greatest treasure uncovered by the research of this book. Access to the personal archives of former Philharmonic members Johannes Bastiaan, Carl Höfer, and Heinz Wiewiorra have provided a wealth of insight into the orchestra's internal life: *Rundschreiben, Reisepläne, Vorstand* memos, documents not previously included in systematic research on the subject. This material also offers effective counter-balance to the bureaucracy-heavy files in the Bundesarchiv. Whereas the Bundesarchiv catalogues correspondence between Berlin Philharmonic administration and the RMVP, the musicians' collections trace communication within the orchestra, and between the orchestra's administration and its musicians. Cross-referencing these sources, one begins to chart the bi-directional flow of information and power.

Primary documents drawn from the aforementioned archives, form this book's skeletal structure. For this reason, despite attempts at comprehensiveness, there are, admittedly, gaps where, rather than succumb to speculation, I simply submit to an open question mark and the hope this work might stimulate subsequent research to uncover more evidence. At the same time, by using all the documentary material available, it is my hope the following pages can unveil original sources to further scholarly review, while offering casual readers a unique taste of the troubling, at times shocking, at others even humorous, state of 'normalcy' in this historical milieu.

The issues are dealt with in a text arranged thematically rather than chronologically. Individual chapters are devoted to 1) the evolution of the Philharmonic's organisational structure; 2) profiling the orchestra musicians as a musical and political community; 3) examining the orchestra's variable financial conditions; 4) reviewing the array of venues in which and audiences for whom the Philharmonic performed; 5) discussing the artistic and political constraints on Berlin Philharmonic programming, including both victimised and celebrated composers, conductors, and performers; and 6) a final chapter highlighting the orchestra's international touring activities as a synthesis of previous issues, crystallising the Philharmonic's precarious duality of propagandistic service and artistic accomplishment. A final epilogue deals with the orchestra's immediate post-war state of affairs. The aim of 'spiralling' through history, chapter for chapter, in this way is to generate a matrix of parallel narratives, layering themes, offering a cumulative impression of the historical actors and their troubling times.

The Berlin Philharmonic's experience during the Third Reich traced a truly exceptional case of privilege—an existence "in a glass bubble," as it was once described, under the protection of Furtwängler and the patronage of Goebbels. Simultaneously, the orchestra's experience acutely typified the ambivalent condition of Germany during the Nazi years, stretched between desperation, fear, naivety, ambition, reticence, and opportunism. Perhaps in the past, the moment was not right for the telling of this story. Certainly in the case of the Berlin Philharmonic, that colossus—Herbert von Karajan—with his personal history closely bound to the mysteries of the Third Reich, emblemised Germany's moral ambiguities towards its Nazi experience—and those of the institution which he led. Doubtless, during von Karajan's tenure, discussion of the Berlin Philharmonic and the Third Reich was not encouraged in the halls of the Philharmonie. But now, almost two decades after the great maestro's passing, over fifty years from the death of Wilhelm Furtwängler, six decades since the war unleashed by Berlin flooded back upon its perpetuators, in time for the Berlin Philharmonic's 125th anniversary, a persistent curiosity lurks. It is my hope this book can illuminate a few corners, shake a few myths, and encourage further inquiry into this important history, in all its fascinating, troubling, and moving complexity.

Chapter One

Road to the Reich's Orchestra

THE BERLIN PHILHARMONIC ORCHESTRA is a musical community born of rebellion. In 1882, a band of disgruntled musicians from the so-called *Bilse'chen Kapelle* broke away from its autocratic masters to form an independent collective, quickly rising to one of Europe's most celebrated orchestral ensembles. Its proud, defiant, ambitious character determined its progressive constitution, and typified its unique brand of music-making. Even as great conductors Hans von Bülow, Arthur Nikisch, Richard Strauss and Wilhelm Furtwängler assumed prominent positions of musical responsibility vis a vis the orchestra, their status extended only to the degree of directorship of the orchestra's principal concert series, the *Philharmonischen Konzerte*, but never abrogated the Philharmonic musicians' collective sovereignty .

From 1903, the orchestra evolved further, formalising its self-governing character into a legal cooperative entity, a G.m.b.H., in which each active musician was a shareholder (up to fifty-six musicians, based upon seniority; retired members were compelled to sell their shares to younger colleagues). The orchestra elected a committee of three delegates, called the *Vorstand*, for renewable three year terms to act as general representatives and administrators. Institutional operations, from rehearsal schedules to concert programming, legal affairs to budgetary matters, were all managed through the Chairman, also known as the *Geschäftsführer* (or Business Manager), and two alternates of the *Vorstand*. Autonomous, the orchestra chose its own business relationships, and entered contractual agreements with various concert agencies, tour promoters, and concert halls, as equal partner.

1

Over time, however, the excitement of emancipation wearied under the weight of institutional expansion and financial instability. The First World War did nothing to diminish the orchestra's musical achievements, but post-war inflation brought financial struggle. Through the 1920s the situation grew increasingly dire. The circle of musicians who had earlier broken away, were forced to return to a system of patronage for survival.

In its increasingly desperate quest for financial subvention through the 1920s, and recognising their largest patron, the City of Berlin's, limited means, the Berlin Philharmonic sought to secure government support from beyond the municipal level by capitalising on its international reputation, playing a nationalist card, presenting itself as a 'German orchestra', for all Germany and to the rest of the world.[1] This move reflected the orchestra's sense of self-importance, but also resonated well with the Berlin politicians who were keen to offload the financial burden of the orchestra, while loathing to jeopardise the viability one of the city's cultural gems.[2]

The contention of the Berlin Philharmonic's cultural significance to the German Reich as a whole was a tricky gambit, due to a number of factors. First, subsidising elite cultural institutions during times of severe unemployment, hyper-inflation, and social strife did not play well on either the right or the left of the political spectrum. Second, cultural propaganda in other European countries was not a priority of the German central government in the 1920s, and the case for attracting cultural tourism to Germany was ineffectual.[3] Furthermore, the pure subjectivity of such claims made it difficult to make political hay. While the orchestra did tour and broadcast, it was problematic for State politicians to justify investing in a local, particularly a Berlin, institution, on the basis of critical appraisals and artistic reputation. Finally complicating matters was the fact the State government (or *Reich*) had no ministry expressly responsible for cultural affairs, making tailoring arguments to the political interests of specific departments extremely challenging. The situation was a jurisdictional nightmare. The official line of the central government was clear: responsibility for cultural institutions was a provincial and municipal matter.[4] The Land (or Province) of Prussia, meanwhile, was equally steadfast:

During its residence in Berlin, the orchestra serves exclusively the cultural life of the capital city. Its tours of Germany are not limited to the territory of Prussia. On its foreign tours, the orchestra exemplarily represents the general condition of culture in Germany as a whole.[5]

Nevertheless, with persistence from both the orchestra and municipal officials, State Interior, and Prussian Science, Art and Education ministries eventually agreed, on account of its "national significance,"[6] to entertain the possibility of subsidising the Berlin Philharmonic.

On May 23rd, 1929, a meeting was convened by Berlin Deputy Mayor Gustav Böss in the city hall to discuss a reorganisation of the Berlin Philharmonic Orchestra.[7] The Reich and Land of Prussia were prepared to invest in the orchestra, but required a measure of institutional accountability, a feature lacking in the funding formula to date. As controlling mechanism over the orchestra's financial direction, an *Arbeitsgemeinschaft* (association) was created that would ensure stable funding from the City of Berlin, Land, and Reich in exchange for a controlling interest in the Berlin Philharmonic GmbH. The share values held by City, Land and Reich would be proportional to their subsidy contributions and total 51% of the GmbH base capital of RM 114 600.[8] Though Prussia was reluctant to commit to the arrangement immediately, it was expected the Land would assume its place in due course.[9]

A series of interlocking contracts were drafted binding the Reich, City, and eventual Land, together into a working partnership or *Arbeitsgemeinschaft*, defining the terms of entry of the *Arbeitsgemeinschaft* into the Berlin Philharmonic Orchestra GmbH, and detailing the relationship between majority and minority shareholders within the GmbH.[10] The preamble read:

> The objective of the enterprise is the formation of an orchestra ensemble for common musical-artistic purposes and the promotion of art in Berlin and abroad.[11]

Under the terms of the agreement, the *Arbeitsgemeinschaft* would fulfil the long-desired guarantee of financial solvency for the Berlin

Philharmonic Orchestra, even in event of deficit.[12] In exchange, the musician-shareholders would cede controlling interest to the *Arbeitsgemeinschaft* by virtue of majority votes within the GmbH shareholders group (*Gesellschaftterversammlung*) and a 13-member supervisory board *Aufsichtsrat* comprising seven representatives of the City and two of the Reich, with the remaining four voices elected from among the members orchestra. Additionally, the orchestra was required to perform up to 32 popular, afternoon, and chamber music concerts per season in service of the City at venues around Berlin. Finally, the orchestra was committed, "upon request of the members of the working partnership and with the approval of the supervisory board, to perform at special events of the City of Berlin and of the Reich government, in full attendance, at no additional fee."[13]

These measures amounted to a radical transformation of the proudly independent Berlin Philharmonic. After 47 years, it appeared the self-governing musical cooperative would, under financial duress, negotiate itself out of existence. Nevertheless, the orchestra accepted the terms proposed by the *Arbeitsgemeinschaft* for a number of reasons. First and most importantly, the promise of financial stability, a commitment which represented for the musicians both short-term relief and long-term security. Secondly, the agreement represented a victory for the orchestra in its crusade to convince the Reich, and the Land, of its extraordinary regional and national significance. This concession established the scale of financial support the orchestra required, and offered a powerful precedent for future negotiations. Thirdly, the *Arbeitsgemeinschaft* agreed to retain the GmbH structure—an acknowledgement of the musicians' traditional rights within the institution and promise of at least partial continued, even if only cosmetic, autonomy. And finally, it was understood and legally enshrined by the parties of the *Arbeitsgemeinschaft*, that its purpose of the agreement was the stabilisation of Philharmonic funding—that the intent was supportive, not an interference in the orchestra's artistic direction. Occasional ceremonial employment and periodic use for local, socially-beneficial cultural programming were accepted as reasonable conditions of public patronage.[14]

After an intense period of negotiation, correspondence, and legal drafting, by fall 1929, it appeared the matter had been settled.[15]

Then, suddenly in September, the global stock market crashed, and the Reich withdrew. Despite support from many within the Reich Interior Ministry,[16] the shaky condition of the government, combined with a recurrence of jurisdictional clashes and political agendas doomed repeated attempts to revive the process over the following months and years.[17]

Meanwhile, the financial situation of the Berlin Philharmonic deteriorated rapidly. Debts mounted, salaries went unpaid. Orchestra *Vorstand* Lorenz Höber was reduced to begging at every government office, at every level; Berlin magistrates in turn directed desperate letters to Prussian and State ministries. The orchestra survived on what the municipality could provide, and on the help of a small circle of private patrons.[18] State subsidies sporadically trickled in, but were erratic, a fraction of the commitments under the *Arbeitsgemeinschaft* plan.

The State radio broadcaster (*Berliner Funk-Stunde A.G.*) emerged as a potential partner for the Philharmonic, but could only offer to cover a small portion of the orchestra's inflating deficit (though greater than the Reich's entire subsidy) with a contract for a series of concert transmissions.[19] The appointment of Adolf Hitler as Chancellor on January 30th, 1933 did nothing to improve the Berlin Philharmonic's fraught situation.

On February 7th, 1933, Berlin Deputy Mayor Dr. Heinrich Sahm wrote yet another letter to the Reich Interior Ministry, expressing hope that a common solution to the Philharmonic crisis might be found in 1933.[20] Over the weeks following a change of winds was slow, but noticeable. In principle, the Reich Interior Ministry still did not support orchestras, but by mid-March exceptions were being mentioned in official correspondence:

> Aside from the Philharmonic Orchestra in Berlin [...] State subsidy in the coming year will be provided only to the Silesian Philharmonic in Breslau, in regard to its exceptional geo-political significance, and the National Socialist Reich Symphony Orchestra [NSRO].[21]

No longer a political hot potato, the arguments the orchestra had asserted for years regarding its German national significance were now being recognised, even underlined by the new National

5

Socialist government. Though the Breslau Orchestra and the NSRO were certainly not among the Berlin Philharmonic's typical artistic peers, under the new regime, the orchestra was honoured to be grouped alongside other musical symbols of national significance amid a radical redefinition of cultural policy.

One of the first major developments in the sphere of cultural policy after Hitler came to power, was the creation of the Ministry of Popular Enlightenment and Propaganda (the *Reichsministerium für Volksaufklärung und Propaganda* or RMVP), under the direction of Berlin *Gauleiter* and Hitler stalwart, Joseph Goebbels. With a wide-ranging mandate, the new ministry did not directly control, but influenced areas ranging from school education to sports training to radio programming to funding for the visual arts. Though not so named, the RMVP represented a facet frustratingly absent from previous Weimar governments—a ministry responsible for culture. The RMVP soon became a player in the ongoing Berlin Philharmonic saga.

The national and international stature of the Berlin Philharmonic clearly appealed to Goebbels, who, deeply schooled in the biases of National Socialist ideology, saw culture not only as an expression of national character, but as an essential key in the conditioning of it. Moreover, the Berlin Philharmonic projected the very best of German musical culture to the rest of the world. Though the orchestra officially remained Interior Ministry jurisdiction, with the 1933 government changeover, Goebbels saw his RMVP as a significant stakeholder in its direction.

On March 23rd, 1933, secretaries from the RMVP and Reich Interior Ministry met to discuss possibilities for cooperation in support of the Berlin Philharmonic. As the RMVP had no independent operating budget at the time, there was little Goebbels' representatives could offer. Still, it was agreed the matter would be pursued at higher levels: "A protocol for sharing working responsibilities [for the BPhO] with the Propaganda Minstry, will be prepared for presentation to the Herr Reichskanzler." [22]

During the following weeks, matters developed quickly. The Berlin Philharmonic's principal conductor, Wilhelm Furtwängler turned to Goebbels for help in keeping the Philharmonic afloat. This offered Goebbels the chance to make his intentions clear: "Herr Dr. Goebbels, following his meeting with Dr. Furtwängler, plans to assume responsibility for the Philharmonic orchestra within his own ministry," reported Berlin municipal officials.[23]

The Interior Ministry, however, balked. Cooperation was one thing, but wresting complete authority in an area of rightful jurisdiction was most certainly another.[24] At a meeting convened by the Reich Interior Ministry on the 8th of April, 1933, the game of political poker was played out. Attending were secretaries of the Reich Interior, Finance and Propaganda Ministries, as well as two Berlin Magistrates, Prussian Finance and Interior Ministry representatives, and Furtwängler.[25] It was quickly established that despite the Berlin Philharmonic's deep financial difficulty, Prussia could make no support guarantees; simultaneously, the City of Berlin was also looking to extricate itself from the orchestra's over-reliant position. With contributions dwindling from other sources, the state broadcasting authority, the *Reichs-Rundfunk-Gesellschaft*, had become the Berlin Philharmonic's largest subsidising partner.

The Propaganda Ministry presented a written guarantee of security for the orchestra. The Interior Ministry countered with a proposal to almost double its subsidy, from RM 65 000 to RM 120 000. It was resolved that the *Reichs-Rundfunk-Gesellschaft*, which, though unrepresented at the meeting, answered to the Propaganda Ministry, should increase its support from RM 75 000 to RM 155 000. With this, Berlin Mayor Wilhelm Hafemann seized his chance, suggesting that with such new-found magnanimousness, the Reich alone should take full control of the orchestra's future.[26] The meeting was adjourned on this note, with the stakes ever climbing.

Rather than improving the situation of the orchestra however, these political shenanigans made its situation much worse. The City of Berlin put a fixed limit on its yearly subsidy and cut off the taps to further emergency needs.[27] Philharmonic *Vorstand* Lorenz Höber wrote dispondently to the Reich Interior Ministry, praying "that it would not be the interest of the government, to sit idly and watch the Berlin Philharmonic disintegrate."[28] The Interior Ministry replied, instructing Höber to ask the Propaganda Ministry for assistance. The RMVP responded by saying they had no money,[29] directing Höber back to the Interior Ministry.[30] Berlin city officials were themselves stonewalled by their State-level colleagues and not prepared to offer more help.[31] It was truly a bureaucratic nightmare. Still trying to function, the Berlin Philharmonic went on tour, using the opportunity once more to play its nationalist card:

> The Berlin Philharmonic Orchestra GmbH begs the Reich Ministry of the Interior to ensure the orchestra does not collapse, particularly during this time while it is touring, and earning unparalleled artistic praise— especially in France.[32]

Inadvertently, the Philharmonic was making Goebbels' case for him. By the time the orchestra returned from its tour, the Propaganda Ministry had essentially won its jurisdictional struggle with the Interior Ministry. Goebbels personally secured from the Reich Finance Ministry the necessary cash to cover the orchestra's immediate debts and budgetary deficit,[33] and negotiations were commenced to formalise a long-term relationship between the Berlin Philharmonic and the RMVP. An decidedly cheered Höber wrote: "Now the only question is how our company [the GmbH] should be integrated into the Ministry."[34]

In this context, Höber was certainly thinking of the *Arbeitsgemeinschaft* precedent of 1929, suggesting the RMVP "enter into the GmbH, and by mutual contract between the GmbH and the Reich, guarantee the company's long-term security."[35] The *Arbeitsgemeinschaft* model, which first introduced the notion of the State entering as partner into the GmbH, provided the basis for the ultimate resolution of the orchestra's status. The negotiating position for the orchestra remained much the same as in 1929: agreeing to sacrifice a degree of autonomy in exchange for financial security, yet wishing to retain its independent corporate character. As then, the State's agenda was control, primarily budgetary, but this time as part of a larger vision of cultural politics.

Also, in contrast to previous negotiations, in 1933, the State held all the cards; without municipal or regional officials at the table, the Philharmonic was alone and vulnerable; and Goebbels was not interested in a partnership, simply control. In the *Arbeitsgemeinschaft* agreement of 1933 it was not the RMVP, as originally suggested by the orchestra, but the Reich government, represented by the RMVP, which entered into to GmbH, and not as share-holder partner, but as monopolist. Isolated and desperate, the orchestra had little choice. The musicians of the Berlin Philharmonic agreed to sell the entirety of their principal asset—their GmbH—to the Reich. Therewith, they converted themselves from shareholders into civil servants.

It was still several months before formal matters were concluded, and time after that before a stable financial framework was in place,[36] but on June 30th, 1933 arrived the first memo from Berlin Philharmonic *Vorstand* Lorenz Höber to the RMVP signed off "Heil Hitler."[37] The Reich's orchestra was coming.

On November 1st, with Hitler's personal blessing, the Berlin Philharmonic was officially pronounced a *Reichsorchester*.[38] On January 15th, 1934, eighty-five members of the Berlin Philharmonic sold their shares in the *Berliner Philharmonisches Orchester GmbH* to the German Reich.[39] The City of Berlin transferred its RM 3 000 share gratis. By the end of February, 1934, the Reich controlled 100% of the GmbH.[40] A report by Lorenz Höber expressed the orchestra's tremendous sense of relief, tinged with a new kind of uncertainty:

> The conversion of the Philharmonic into a State enterprise has fundamentally transformed the organisation's structure. The orchestra members, until January 1934, its owners and shareholders, are now employees of the company. In transferring their shares to the Reich, the musicians gave up their earlier self-directing, self-governing rights [...] Nevertheless, the orchestra is not simply content to have its existence guaranteed; it is the orchestra's wish to engage with the Ministry to serve it in future. In thanking the Ministry for the security it has offered in exchange for the orchestra's shares, the orchestra hopes for a lively cooperation [with the Ministry].[41]

The crucial figure in the marriage between the Berlin Philharmonic and German Reich was Wilhelm Furtwängler. Furtwängler was a celebrity in Germany, an icon, revered by musicians and patrons, known widely even outside artistic circles. Born to an upper-class Berlin family, he was accustomed to circulating among the cultural and political elite. Relationships to important people, irrespective of their ideological persuasions, were completely natural to Furtwängler. To express his concerns, he never resisted contacting the highest officials—even when their names were Hitler and Goebbels.

Both Goebbels and Hitler esteemed Furtwängler highly, as a musician and as a man, and Furtwängler felt comfortable calling upon them on personal or professional matters. He had a particularly close relationship with Goebbels, who referred to the conductor frequently in his diaries. "Yesterday morning; long talk with Furtwängler in the garden at Wahnfried [Bayreuth]," wrote Goebbels in 1936, "He confided all his concerns, sensibly and intelligently. He has learned much and is completely with us. I will help him where I can, particularly with the [Berlin] Philharmonic Orchestra."[42]

The degree to which Furtwängler was truly 'with' the Nazis, or simply used personal and political cunning to trick Goebbels into granting concessions for acts of dissidence, is a matter of extensive, heated debate, but is not the principal concern here.[43] In the case of the Berlin Philharmonic, Goebbels identified the orchestra as a tremendous instrument for cultural propaganda, and crafted a clever strategy for harnessing it by putting the Philharmonic in employ under his direct supervision. Procedurally, Goebbels could comandeer the vehicle, but functionally, Furtwängler held the keys. From Furtwängler's point of view, Goebbels offered security for the orchestra, and pre-eminent status for himself. As Gerhard von Westerman, a man who worked intimately with the conductor from 1939 to 1945 later reported: "Furtwängler frequently sought to make use of his influence with Goebbels—and often succeeded."[44]

Furtwängler first conducted the Berlin Philharmonic in 1917.[45] He assumed a formal position in relation to the orchestra as successor to Arthur Nikisch in 1922. From that time on, he and the orchestra developed an intense, successful musical partnership. Always somewhat distant, Furtwängler's feeling towards the orchestra was not so much one of compassion, as a sense of self-important responsibility—he would protect the interests of the orchestra because the orchestra was his instrument, an expression and reflection of himself. The orchestra's democratic tradition was of little regard in this way, but so long as the results were benevolent, Furtwängler's motivation hardly mattered. With his instrument desperately floundering, however, Furtwängler took it upon himself to save the orchestra.

In its fifty-one year history up to 1933, the Berlin Philharmonic had never had either an artistic director or an *Intendant*. Historically, the Philharmonic's principal conductors were not contracted to the orchestra at all, but to the producer of the *Philharmonische Konzerte*, the *Konzertagentur Wolff & Sachs*. In fact, Hans von Bülow and Arthur Nikisch were only de-facto musical leaders of the Berlin Philharmonic through their direction of the orchestra's main concert subscription series. In 1924, Furtwängler became the first conductor directly associated with the Berlin Philharmonic, elected by the orchestra's membership as principal conductor.[46]

In 1929, in conjunction with the *Arbeitsgemeinschaft* negotiations, Furtwängler was offered a contract with the Berliner Philharmonischen Orchester GmbH, naming him *Dirigent* (conductor) for the period of ten years. His salary of RM 50 000 per year, plus RM 15 000 for "expenses" committed him to thirty concerts with the orchestra per year, within which Furtwängler's 'Philharmonischen Konzerte' were identified as the "artistic highlights".[47] In addition, Furtwängler was to be consulted on all other programming matters, held a veto right over new orchestra members, could request early retirements, determine orchestra seating arrangements, and approve the selection of any managing director.[48] These were all unprecedented compromises to the orchestra's democratic tradition. Though beyond his conducting duties Furtwängler's role was envisaged as purely consultative, the 1929 contract set some significant precedents.

The reasons for the tremendous concessions to Furtwängler were at least three fold. First, the nature of political and bureaucratic relations required the City and Reich to request a single, chief interlocutor. In the new *Arbeitsgemeinschaft* arrangement, City and Reich were integrated into the institutional structure. The orchestra *Vorstand* could represent the musicians, but an executive authority was needed to preside over all three shareholding groups. More importantly, both the City of Berlin and its Philharmonic Orchestra feared losing Furtwängler. The conductor was not short of alternatives, including positions in Vienna and New York, offering lucrative options to simply walk away.[49] The orchestra feared without his name, their meagre funding would dry up, subscriptions would dwindle, and the ensemble would disappear. City officials feared a terrible loss of prestige with Furtwängler's departure and the threat of the orchestra's attendant demise. Sweetening the pot for him, the 1929 contract spoke of an eventual position for Furtwängler with a Berlin opera house as well.[50]

The final reason was personal, having to do with Furtwängler's own sense of might and responsibility. Furtwängler was a vainglorious and, despite his own protestations, an intensely political being. He held the strongest position in negotiating with the orchestra and the *Arbeitsgemeinschaft*—and that predominance appealed to him. He realised the orchestra's degree of dependency, and did nothing to dispel it. That the orchestra respected and trusted Furtwängler made their concessions easier to stomach, but these feelings were immaterial—the orchestra had no choice. By contrast, in choosing to commit to Berlin, Furtwängler further strengthened his dominating position vis a vis the orchestra, promising "that in the future, whenever in the world one speaks of the Philharmonic Orchestra, Wilhelm Furtwängler will also be named, and conversely, that the name Wilhelm Furtwängler should always remain inseparable from that of the Philharmonic."[51] These ambitions did not perish with the aborted *Arbeitsgemeinschaft* plan.

On August 1st, 1933, well before negotiations on the proposed Reich takeover had been completed, Furtwängler wrote to the members of the Berlin Philharmonic:

> Gentlemen! The Führer and Reich's government have given me assurance that the Berlin Philharmonic will, under all circumstances, be protected. Herr Reichsminister Goebbels has tied this assurance to a guarantee of my absolute leadership in all artistic and personnel matters of the orchestra. Because of this, I expect that all agitation within the orchestra in future be allayed. No decision can be made without me and my consent. My 12 year association with you, gentleman, must serve as assurance, that all measures undertaken by myself, are made only in the orchestra's best interest.[52]

In his letter, Furtwängler appealed to the orchestra to trust his leadership not only in artistic, but also in personal and political matters—that he would assume responsibility for he orchestra's well-being, and expect full compliance from the musicians with his judgement. This again represented a major departure from the Berlin Philharmonic's tradition of democratic decision-making and self-administration. Though much ground had already been conceded in the 1929 contract negotiations, Furtwängler's "absolute leadership" was not the government's condition, but his own. It implied not simply reserving a consultative role, or even asserting a veto right, but demanded an official submission of effective control. At once the orchestra was being asked from one side, the government, to sacrifice possession of its collective identity (the GmbH); on the other side, Furtwängler was insisting upon an unconditional surrender of executive authority. Parallel to the Reich's take-over, Furtwängler was orchestrating a Philharmonic reorganisation of his own.

With his plan in 1933 to reconstitute the Berlin Philharmonic as an organ under his own supervision, Furtwängler was proposing something entirely new, both for the orchestra, and for himself. As "Führer" of the orchestra, Furtwängler was assuming an administrative as well as musical position at the head of a large cultural institution. With this concentration of power, he set to establish an organisational structure that would at once manage the daily running of the orchestra, insulate him from administrative duties, and suit the financial and political accountability needs of the government. Furtwängler proposed two key allies in this restructuring: Lorenz Höber, *Orchestervorstand* since 1923, whom Furtwängler trusted and felt he could rely upon, and the conductor's long-time personal secretary, Berta Geissmar.

Lorenz Höber shared the first stand of the Berlin Philharmonic's viola section with his brother, Willi. He had been elected *Orchestervorstand* one year after Furtwängler's arrival in Berlin, seeing the orchestra as its chief organiser and administrator through the tumultuous decade leading up to Hitler's arrival. As *Vorstand*, Höber was responsible for all areas of the Philharmonic's financing, legal affairs, contractual agreements, artistic planning, relationships with government, as well as internal orchestra matters such as scheduling and services. While acknowledging that in recent years the management of the Philharmonic had perhaps suffered a few *Schönheitsfehler* (or superficial mistakes)[53], Furtwängler supported retaining Höber in the orchestra's reformed structure. Principally, the conductor foresaw the *Orchestervorstand* running the orchestra office, responsible for concert bookings and travel arrangements, while maintaining the internal orchestra housekeeping.[54]

Meanwhile, Furtwängler wished Geissmar to manage the artistic planning. Bertha Geissmar first met Furtwängler in 1915, when he succeeded Arthur Bodanzky as *Hofkapellmeister* in Mannheim, Geissmar's hometown. From a well-to-do family, she organised Furtwängler's correspondences, contracts, expenses, concert programming and travel arrangements first in Mannheim, then in Berlin when the conductor was chosen as successor to Arthur Nikisch as conductor of the *Philharmonischen Konzerte* in 1922. From 1922 to 1933, Geissmar was Furtwängler's private secretary, not a member of the Berlin Philharmonic's administration.

With the reorganisation of the Philharmonic after the Nazi ascendancy however, Furtwängler took the opportunity to press for a staff position for Geissmar with the title *Chefsekretariat* (Chief Secretary), therewith transferring the expense of her employment to the orchestra.[55] He submitted a RM 10 000 per year salary demand on her behalf. Further cementing his case, Furtwängler played the jealousy card, reporting to Goebbels' RMVP that the Propaganda Minister's arch-rival, Hermann Göring, had given him a secretary at the Staatsoper (where Furtwängler had been installed by the latter as *Operndirektor*), along with a title as *Staatsrat*. Offering a blackmailing *coup de grâce*, Furtwängler reminded the RMVP that his seventy to eighty appearances with the Philharmonic accounted for over half the orchestra's yearly earned revenues.[56]

Despite Furtwängler's well-crafted practical, financial and political arguments for integrating Geissmar into the Philharmonic's administrative structure, the RMVP was extremely sceptical about the plan.[57] The reason: Berta Geissmar was Jewish.

The degree of anti-Semitic fervour in Germany in the early years of the Nazi regime was virulent, and Geissmar's background was widespread knowledge in the musical community. She stood irrationally and unreasonably accused of masterminding conspiracies, of manipulating Furtwängler's choice of soloists in favour of Jewish musicians, and of promoting Jewish influence within the Philharmonic. Leading the charges, Gustav Havemann, a Berlin violinist, pedagogue, and convinced Nazi, who quickly impressed himself on the Nazi bureaucracy delivering repeated threats to root her and her influence out of Germany.[58]

Nonetheless, Furtwängler stood by his secretary, and though she was banished from official acknowledgement as member of the orchestra administration, did, at least for a time, manage to get the Philharmonic to pay her salary.[59] Eventually Furtwängler engaged another secretary, a Frau Freda von Rechenberg, whom Geissmar recalled as "…pure Aryan." While Rechenberg served as Furtwängler's representative in dealing with the authorities, it was hoped Geissmar could continue working behind the scenes.[60] She remained a contributor to the orchestra's management until the spring of 1935, but, under the accumulation of accusations and pressures, finally left Germany, initially for America, then settling in London as secretary to Sir Thomas Beecham. Rechenberg remained Furtwängler's secretary, with no direct affiliation to the Philharmonic, to the end of the conductor's life.

In 1933-34, however, Geissmar was an important cog in Furtwängler's plan to restructure the Berlin Philharmonic under his leadership. Leading the Philharmonic implied a burden of official responsibility beyond what he was prepared to assume alone. In addition to Höber and Geissmar, Furtwängler must have been mindful of insistence from the government upon some Nazi Party representation in the new management of their musical acquisition. It is not clear if the installation of Dr. Rudolf von Schmidtseck as "Representative and Advisor" of the Berlin Philharmonic in September, 1933 was the initiative of Goebbels, RMVP bureaucrats, or of Furtwängler himself.[61]

Geissmar's account of the introduction of *Unser Schutznazi* ("our protection-Nazi") is ambiguous. She suggests von Schmidtseck "was introduced to Furtwängler, and shortly thereafter, with the concession of the administrators of the Berlin Philharmonic, pronounced the orchestra's 'Commissar'."[62] Whom she meant by the 'administrators' of the orchestra is not clear since the orchestra's power structure at the time was in persistent flux. Moreover, the comment does not necessarily preclude the possibility von Schmidtseck's arrival was in fact welcome.

Clear is that Furtwängler required a delegate to work with Höber and Geissmar in the daily operations of the orchestra. Furthermore, it would seem from their subsequent work together, von Schmidtseck was someone Furtwängler trusted.[63] Also, from the pattern of future hiring, even if the creation of the position had not been his choice, Furtwängler held considerable influence over candidates and appointments.[64] Finally, von Schmidtseck's appointment was deemed provisional by the RMVP,[65] suggesting he was not their unanimous selection.

Little is known about Dr. Rudolf von Schmidtseck.[66] During the 1933-34 season he conducted seven concerts with the Berlin Philharmonic Orchestra.[67] He was a member of the NSDAP.[68] As Furtwängler defined his role, von Schmidtseck was responsible for finances, personnel, contracts, correspondence with the RMVP and other government and Nazi agencies, discipline within the orchestra and its administration, and, as a member of the NSDAP, for matters of ideological nature within the organisation.[69]

While Furtwängler was willing to offer such apparently gross concessions to Nazi Party influence through von Schmidtseck, his actions regarding Nazi organisational and ideological interference in the affairs of his orchestra suggest official lip service.[70] There is no evidence von Schmidtseck was responsible for ideological agitation or initiator of ideologically-motivated activity within the orchestra during his tenure.

Furtwängler further established that von Schmidtseck was to act "as my personal delegate responsible for all occasions when I am otherwise indisposed (at official functions etc.)"[71] Evidently, Furtwängler already had a notion of absenting himself from certain official occasions, likely also those with overt Party associations. While these arrangements did not spare the Berlin Philharmonic from such appearances, in engaging von Schmidtseck, or capitalising on his appointment, Furtwängler had arranged for a Nazi decoy—an apparently benign front to do the regime-toting 'dirty work' without threatening either the orchestra's musical interests or his own supremacy.

Von Schmidtseck was appointed *kommissarischen 1. Geschäfts-führer* of the Berlin Philharmonic Orchestra on a provisional contract explicitly binding him to Furtwängler.[72] Though the contract was subject to renewal at the end of 1934,[73] this did not occur. When Furtwängler resigned from his position with the Berlin Philharmonic in December, 1934,[74] von Schmidtseck was immediately suspended from duty, never to return.[75]

The successful conclusion of negotiations concerning the absorption of the Berlin Philharmonic GmbH into the Reich in January, 1934, naturally, lead to a number of key changes in the structure and management of the orchestra. Borrowing from the *Arbeitsgemeinschaft* model, an *Aufsichtsrat* or administrative board was assembled, constituting an executive committee with authority over all areas—artistic, budgetary, contractual, and in terms of personnel.[76] With the general assembly dissolved (the GmbH consisted of only one shareholder—the State), the Reich was not obliged to share direction with any other group, including the orchestra itself. In 1934, the *Aufsichtsrat*, chaired by State Secretary Walter Funk from the RMVP,[77] consisted of Funk, State Secretary Pfundtner from the Interior Ministry, *Ministerialdirektor* Dr. Erich Greiner of the RMVP, *Ministerialrat* Joachim von Manteuffel from the Reich Finance Ministry, *Ministerialrats* Dr. Eugen Ott and Otto von Keudell, also from the RMVP, and, as lone orchestra representative, Lorenz Höber.[78] This last member, a cosmetic concession to the orchestra.[79]

Whereas Furtwängler's guarantees from Goebbels were predicated on personal favour, this *Aufsichtsrat* committee represented an authority in legal terms above Furtwängler's claim to "absolute Führung". While Furtwängler's interest was in retaining a degree of independence for the Berlin Philharmonic from the government, his aim was not preserving the orchestra's communal structure, but rather assuring his own power over a superlative musical instrument. The *Aufsichtsrat*, meanwhile, was less interested in the orchestra's artistic standard per se, or in satisfying Furtwängler's ambitions, than in fulfilling a mandate to reform the Berlin Philharmonic to meet the government's needs as an effective and efficient cultural ambassador for the Reich. Another political battle was brewing.

On March 10th, 1934, *Ministerialdirektor* Greiner invited representatives of the Reich Treasury, Reich Finance Ministry and Philharmonic *Aufsichtsrat* Chairman, State Secretary Funk, to a meeting in the offices of the RMVP, where he presented his concept for the new structure of the Berlin Philharmonic.[80] The plan called for limiting Furtwängler's position vis-a-vis the orchestra to "Conductor of the orchestra" who, "for an agreed fee, should be contracted to a specified annual number of concerts with the Philharmonic in Berlin and abroad."[81] This amounted to a scaling back of the conductor's role to his status prior to the 1933 reform process—a musical figure-head with little substantive organisational authority.

In addition to defining the role of Furtwängler, the plan established two additional administrative posts, an artistic director (also second conductor) and "an experienced business manager."[82] Both positions represented entirely new advents, introducing a level of professional administration not previously existent in the orchestra's management. For these positions, von Schmidtseck, closely linked to Furtwängler, was deemed neither a viable artistic leader, nor a competent administrator. As artistic director and alternate resident conductor, Greiner projected a conductor along the lines of Carl Schuricht[83], a respected musician who, though posing no direct threat to Furtwängler, would offer a counterweight to Furtwängler's dominance.

More important than the artistic post however, was the installation of a business director, or *kaufmännischer Geschäftsführer*, who would be responsible for the orchestra's financial and commercial affairs, as well as for the significant coordination issues with the State ministries."[84] This figure would replace Höber, and was viewed by the Ministry as an "extremely important appointment."[85] Taking the *Geschäftsführung* out of the hands of the orchestra and inserting a professional administrator was not merely a question of managerial competence, but also decisive in determining the future shape of the organisation.

After the Nazi seizure of power, business practices, organisational protocols and institutional structures did not change over night.

Reforms, pragmatic, legal, and ideological, required implementation. The term was *Gleichschaltung*, and its practice was a harmonisation of government and public institutions with the tenets of National Socialism. This implied not simply an application of racial policies, but the firm entrenchment of hierarchical power structures in accordance with the "Führer principle", and a dutiful accountability to the Führer, the Party and the Fatherland.

The Berlin Philharmonic was to be no exception. What Greiner and the RMVP sought in a *kaufmännischer Geschäftsführer* was a man to oversee the process of *Gleichschaltung*, an experienced, responsible NSDAP member with a clear head for business, who could effectively manage both the business affairs of the Philharmonic and act responsively to the demands of the government.

When presented with the plan two days later, Furtwängler, naturally, opposed the installation of a managing director, citing the the qualities of Höber and Schmidtseck as adequate to filfull the proposed position's duties.[86] Disregarding these protestations, a process was set in motion by the RMVP to find the right man.

Within the bureaucratic system of the Third Reich, there was no set procedure of application or calls for tenure for contracts or appointments. Personnel departments of the various ministries essential functioned by way of bureaucratic cronyism—with little procedural transparency, applications were solicited by connection or personal reference, with appointments made either unilaterally by department heads, or in the case of the Philharmonic, by consensus of the *Aufsichtsrat*. The Third Reich, however, was a treacherous climate—a regime born in the spirit of vengeance. Opportunism, acrimony, suspicion and greed infected every aspect of society; with respect to political appointments with the Berlin Philharmonic, intrigue always hovered in the background.

In the spring of 1934, the RMVP considered a number of candidates in its search for a *kaufmännischer Geschäftsführer* for the Philharmonic. A Herr Müller[87], whom Furtwängler described as "very nice,"[88] was presented, but soon fell out of contention. Furtwängler's voice was still influential, if not formally entrenched. A Herr Sellschopp from Lübeck surfaced briefly as a candidate for the "special trustee of the Ministry," but refused to work under von

Schmidtseck.[89] Herr Paul Wehe, according to his references was not only "an outstanding businessman and organiser,"[90] but "a faithful and absolutely reliable Party member [...] an honourable man of exemplary mentality and utmost conscientiousness."[91] Despite seemingly excellent business and political credentials (NSDAP member since 1930),[92] Wehe was also not offered the job. Von Schmidtseck, almost certainly acting on Furtwängler's behalf,[93] expressed unspecified reservations.[94]

The day of this decline to Paul Wehe, another candidate was introduced to Furtwängler, one who faired better in the conductor's estimation.[95] Karl Stegmann had no apparent background in music. He came from manufacturing, his family dealing in textiles.[96] In addition to strong character and business references ("outstanding accounting knowledge and experience"[97]), Stegmann arrived with one considerable advantage: having worked the previous year for the *Deutsche Arbeitsfront* or German Labour Front (despite its name, a Nazi-sponsored anti-labour organisation), Stegmann was experienced in *Gleichschaltung* operations. Specifically, he had been involved in the "liquidation" of the Central Employment Agency, a trade union organisation.[98] In this process, he was responsible for a complete financial audit of the "Marxist" agency's records, for exposing irregularities and abuses to the authorities, and overseeing the transferal of the agency's assets to the State.[99] Stegmann was identified as a "National Socialist through and through," and a member of the SA (Stormtroopers).[100] Furthermore, "he understands how to deal with difficult people."[101] The RMVP had their man. Karl Stegmann was appointed *kommissarischen 2. Geschäftsführer* of the Berlin Philharmonic Orchestra on a probationary basis,[102] on June 1st, 1934.[103] He remained for almost eleven years.

Two years after his appointment, Stegmann faced another, far more serious assessment when, on the basis of an anonymous denunciation, his Nazi Party membership was revoked.[104] The charge: Stegmann stood accused of formerly belonging to a druid lodge. He wrote an impassioned plea to the Party, attempting to reaffirm his ideological credentials. He reminded Party officials of how, since his hiring by the Propaganda Ministry in 1934, he had "continually sought opportunties to work for Nazi interests."[105] Stegmann appealed to the RMVP and to his benefactors on the *Aufsichtsrat* to intercede on his behalf.[106] In February 1937, Walter Funk, Berlin Philharmonic *Aufsichtsrat* chairman and soon-to-be-appointed *Reichswirtschaftsminister* contributed a petition on his behalf. In it, Funk not only lauded Stegmann's administrative services to the Berlin Philharmonic, but confirmed that in Stegmann's "special assignment" with the orchestra, Funk had come to know an "honourable and convinced National Socialist." The letter also categorically implied that despite exemplary service, should his Party membership be revoked, Stegmann could not be retained with the Philharmonic. "It would be a great blow to the organisation," wrote Funk in Stegmann's defence, "to lose him."[107]

Stegmann was fortunate; the *Gauleiter* of Berlin happened to be his de-facto boss, Goebbels himself. His appeal made its way up the chain of command all the way to the chancellor's desk. On May 31st, 1938 arrived the news that Stegmann, "despite previously belonging to a Lodge, may remain a member of the NSDAP. Signed, Adolf Hitler."[108]

The extent of Stegmann's Nazi fervour in the course of his duties with the Berlin Philharmonic is difficult to ascertain.[109] There are no internal Philharmonic documents relating to directives of a distinctly invasive or ideological nature. In such a politicised environment, from documents such as applications and appeals, it is problematic distinguishing conviction from bravado, ideological persuasion from professional opportunism. Ultimately, in the case of his denunciation, it was Stegmann's professional competence that saved him, rather than an exhibition of his Nazi credits. The greater implication, however, was clear—without Nazi credentials, neither Stegmann, nor anyone else, would be eligible to hold administrative office with the Philharmonic.

In June, 1934, with the crucial position of *kaufmännischen Geschäftsführer* filled, Greiner sought to "swiftly push forward with the reorganisation and restructuring of the orchestra."[110] On the 18th of June, 1934, the new *Gesellschaftsvertrag* or constitution of the *Berliner Philharmonischen Orchesters GmbH* was ratified by a "special meeting of the shareholders."[111] Ratification was purely a matter of formality since the members of the orchestra had already sold their voting shares to the Reich. Though statues remained on paper concerning voting majorities and requirements for quorum at annual general meetings,[112] by virtue of its monopoly, the Reich could impose its will legally, and unilaterally.

The terms of the new orchestra constitution divided the organisation into three organs: the *Geschäftsführung* or Administration, the *Aufsichtsrat* or Board of Directors, and the general shareholders, with power concentrated in the first two.[113] The *Geschäftsführung* consisted of two managers who represented the company internally and externally.[114] Though in principle this pyramidal structure mirrored *Führerprinzip* ideas of hierarchic, top-down organisation, the actual power stream flowed inversely. The Reich, as represented by the RMVP, was lone shareholder. The RMVP reserved the right to approve appointment to the *Aufsichtsrat*; the *Aufsichtsrat* in turn held control over appointment to the *Geschäftsführung*, with explicit permission of the RMVP and Goebbels' stamp of approval.[115] The Administration was indeed beholden to the *Versammlung der Gesellschafter*, in this case, the Reich. In essence, the new constitution served to codify the Reich's relationship with itself.

The two-manager system represented an unorthodox variation from *Führerprinzip* ideas; it was a type of cohabitation between Furtwängler and the State bureaucracy. Von Schmidtseck filled the role as artistic director and *2. Dirigent* as Furtwängler's deputy. Originally, Greiner and the *Aufsichtsrat* had envisioned the post as a much more robust counterweight to Furtwängler, rather than his ally.[116] Stegmann, as *kaufmännischen Geschäftsführer* (also known as *2. Geschäftsführer*), meanwhile set to work restructuring the orchestra's business model and harmonising its critical relationship with the government. In so doing, he was presumably given ample opportunity to exercise his lauded gift for "working with difficult people."[117]

As long as Furtwängler remained optically, if not officially, leader of the orchestra, however, the arrangement was unstable. While the organisation could be reformed to meet the new criteria of institutional management, the orchestra as a musical community, and its programming, remained outside the grasp of the State bureaucracy—firmly in the hands of the orchestra's chief conductor.

Conflicts of agendas were apparent in many areas: budgeting, finances, engagements, and programming. In 1934, the RMVP attempted to reign in Furtwängler's autonomy contractually, stipulating an 850RM cap on honoraria for invited guest soloists; "Exceptional cases," the conductor was informed, "will require approval of the *Geschäftsführung*. Engagement of non-Aryans is under all circumstances forbidden."[118] The degree to which Furtwängler wished to hire soloists for more money, or to engage non-Aryans, was immaterial. These new bureaucratic efforts clashed with Furtwängler's primary bone of contention: political interference in his sphere of interest. This was a provocation. As 1934 wore on, both sides grew frustrated, on one hand with the lack of progress in completing the *Gleichschaltung* process in relation to the Philharmonic, on the other hand, the personal and principled defence of artistic freedom. The break came in December 1934.

On March 12th, 1934, Furtwängler conducted a Philharmonic concert including the premiere of Hindemith's *Mathis der Maler Symphony*. The piece offered a preview of the composer's full-length opera set to open at the Berliner Staatsoper under Furtwängler's baton in the winter of 1934. Paul Hindemith, a Berlin resident, had a long-standing relationship with the Berlin Philharmonic, both as composer and a performer.[119] He dedicated his *Variationen für Orchester* to Wilhelm Furtwängler and the Berlin Philharmonic in honour of the orchestra's 50th anniversary in 1932.

Reception of the *Mathis der Maler Symphony* in 1934, however, was stormy. This may have had to do with a clash between the composer's progressive musical language and reactionary Nazi aesthetic tastes, but primarily, the subject of Hindemith's opera on which the symphony was based, with its central theme of art and freedom, was a highly sensitive matter. Politically, the opera could be interpreted as an act of dissent. In July, 1934, word arrived definitively that performance of *Mathis der Maler* at the Staatsoper would not be permitted.[120] Angered by yet another affront to his authority, over the following months Furtwängler appealed to his high connections, including Hitler, Göring, and Goebbels, in an attempt to see the ban lifted,[121] but to no avail.

On December 4th, 1934, in an act as much of political theatrics as ethical principle, Furtwängler tried to call the regime's bluff. He submitted to the government a formal request for immediate termination of his duties as *Operndirektor* of the Staatsoper, as conductor of the Philharmonic, and as vice-president of the *Reichsmusikkammer*.[122] Though the direct catalyst for this dramatic act was not his problem (the Staatsoper was Göring's protectorate), a day later, Goebbels accepted Furtwängler's resignations, urging him to contact the Ministry to clarify the legal and financial details.[123] On one hand a forceful blow to the regime's prestige, Furtwängler's departure also opened the door for Goebbels' ministry to finally complete their work on the reorganisation of the Philharmonic undisturbed. Within days, Furtwängler's associate, von Schmidtseck was suspended from duty.[124]

Furtwängler's resignation came as a shock to the Berlin Philharmonic and to its audiences, in Berlin and abroad. In the days following, 350 of the approximately 1000 subscribers to the *Philharmonischen Konzerte*, some of whom patrons dating back to the days of Hans von Bülow,[125] cancelled or returned their subscriptions.[126] The orchestra descended into a state of crisis. The musicians trusted Furtwängler to lead them through their transition from fragile orchestral cooperative to *Reichsorchester*, then he abandoned them. Some felt betrayed, others admired his stance as a symbol of resistance. Furtwängler's *Abschiedsbrief* (farewell letter) to the orchestra, concluding "…It is not easy to take leave of a partnership of almost two decades, with all our collective achievements. The time we were able to work together, I shall never forget"[127] left a decidedly ambivalent impression.

After all they had been through, the orchestra appeared on the brink of disintegration. Stegmann wrote to the chairman of the orchestra *Aufsichtsrat*, Walter Funk reporting on conditions:

> We fear that following Dr. Furtwängler's depature, even if not immediately then in the long term, the best artists of the orchestra will also leave, diminishing the ensemble's reputation, and resulting in the loss for Herr Reichsminister Goebbels of one of his best instruments of cultural propaganda abroad."[128]

Aware of the stakes, the RMVP bureaucracy shifted into damage control, responding both defensively and proactively. On the public relations front, the Ministry was wary of Furtwängler's move being seen as a "moral defeat" for the government.[129] Even under dictatorship, popular opinion played an important role in determining policy. Furtwängler was officially put on 'vacation leave', with the press raising expectations he would return to active performing in the near future.[130]

With respect to the orchestra, despite resigning from his official position, the Philharmonic was promised Furtwängler would be free to return to conduct as a guest as soon as the spring.[131] In the meantime, Karl Stegmann turned to Lorenz Höber whom he remarked, by virtue of his long association with Furtwängler, "maintained the authority" to keep the orchestra together and to provide some artistic guidance.[132] And from his retreat in Munich, the conductor himself continued making his views known.[133]

To fill the programming gap left by Furtwängler's departure and the parallel cancellation of conductor Erich Kleiber, with his own six-concert Philharmonic series, in solidarity,[134] a special meeting was convened on January 2nd, 1935, between Stegmann, Höber and the executive of the *Reichsmusikkammer* (Reich's Chamber of Music), to hammer out a schedule, with artists and contingencies, for the mangled remainder of the 1934-35 season. The *Reichsmusikkammer*, a subsidiary of the *Reichskulturkammer* (Reich's Chamber of Culture), was created by Goebbels as a sort union for composers, musicians, critics and agents. It was a highly politicised organisation, which all persons professionally active in those fields were required to join. Though Goebbels had named Furtwängler vice-president at the organisation's inception (the President was Richard Strauss), now the RMVP believed the *Reichsmusikkammer* would provide the necessary "protecting and supporting hands" for the orchestra during its "presently uncomfortable transition period."[135]

On the organisational front, the new circumstances offered a clear deck in the Berlin Philharmonic's artistic leadership. With Furtwängler out of the picture and the great orchestra listing rudderless, the opportunists seized. Letters came pouring in to the Propaganda Ministry from Nazi-affiliated conductors across Germany, offering to act as Furtwängler's successor. A Friedrich

Jung, Party member, music director of the Berliner Song Society and "a participant [of unnamed description] at the Bayreuth Festival since 1925" wrote to Goebbels directly, requesting a personal meeting to discuss his application for the conducting position with the Berlin Philharmonic.[136] Professor Leopold Reichwein, who claimed to be the "first important German conductor to embrace the National Socialist movement" and was a frequent contributor to the NSDAP's newspaper, the *Völkischer Beobachter*,[137] sent an application to the *Reichsmusikkammer* soliciting work with the orchestra, either on a permanent basis or as guest conductor.[138] Nazi ideologues, both within the Ministry and in the broader German musical community saw this as their chance to claim the orchestra machinery and mould it according to their ideas.

Amid a plethora of competing interests (Furtwängler, Goebbels, the orchestra, the Ministry bureaucrats, the *Reichsmusikkammer*, the Party), in the struggle between ideology and pragmatism for influence over the Berlin Philharmonic, the dubious nature of political practices under the Third Reich again came to the fore. The strongest figure to emerge out of the debacle unleashed by Furtwängler's resignation was a man by the name of Hermann Stange, a conductor of reportedly modest talent (previous *Generalmusikdirektor* in Sofia, Bulgaria and Helsingfors, Finnland), who, by virtue of ambition, connection and persistence, found himself at the head of Germany's foremost musical institution.

In May, 1933, a letter arrived on the desk of Hans Hinkel, *Reichskommisar* for cultural affairs in the Prussian Ministry of Science, Art and Public Education.[139] In it, the author, Hermann Stange, described his accomplishments in two years as GMD of the Royal Bulgarian National Opera in Sofia, from 1930 to 1932. He went on to express his disappointment in finding, upon returning to Germany, no recognition for how successfully he had represented "cultural interests of my Fatherland" abroad.[140] Unemployed, blaming "die jüdische Front," (the Jewish front)[141] Stange found support in the Nazi-sponsored *Kampfbund für Deutsche Kultur*, which he joined in August, 1932, and later that year, the NSDAP itself. Even after Hitler's seizure of power, however, he complained: "Even today, I still must fight for work and recognition." Stange was asking

Hinkel to help find him employment. A meeting between the two men did likely take place sometime after this initial letter.[142]

On the 13th and 14th of June 1933, Stange was at it again, sending virtually identical letters, one to *Ministerpräsident* Göring, the other to *Reichsminister* Dr. Goebbels. Again Stange summarised his credits in Bulgaria, highlighting his desire "to work especially in the interest of German cultural propaganda."[143] Now back in Germany, and firmly committed to the National Socialist cause, Stange appealed to the leaders for a job.[144] The letters were tedious and self promoting, but while invoking ideological rhetoric, did not really suggest genuine Nazi fervour. Conducting Mozart and Humperdinck in place of Italian and Russian classics in Bulgaria, as Stange proudly trumpeted, did not represent the type of radical, if often more refined, cultural propaganda the regime embraced. Likewise, Stange's anti-Semitic rants seem to owe more to his career frustrations, which may in turn owe more to his own mediocrity, than to any deep-seeded feeling of racial superiority.

Stange's gift, however, was persistence. He maintained contact with Hinkel, scouting for posts with orchestras and theatres across Germany.[145] For over a year, he pursued every avenue tenaciously, eventually squeezing his way on to the map. In November, 1934, Stange wrote to Rudolf Hess, *Reichsminister und Stellvertreter des Führers*, claiming to have been referred by Hinkel.[146] After a more abbreviated summary of his Bulgarian activities, Stange got to the point:

> Returning to Germany, I immediately joined with the National Socialist movement, and, based upon my accomplishments abroad (reports of which have been filed with the Propaganda Ministry), sought to continue my career with an appropriate position in my homeland.[147]

For Stange, Nazi Party membership connected directly to his search for a position. He felt entitled to a post in the 'new Germany' as a German who had spent time abroad, and upon returning, had joined the Party. This sense of entitlement or professional advantage among members of the Party was fed by the Nazi's own propaganda. Whether Stange's letters to Hess, or to Göring, or to Goebbels ever made an impression, is unclear. It would seem the breakthrough came via Hinkel, in connection with the "schützenden und fördernden Hände"[148] of the *Reichsmusikkammer.*

When he cut his ties with the regime, Furtwängler not only resigned from his post with the Berlin Philharmonic, but also quit as vice-president of the *Reichsmusikkammer.* Hinkel, meanwhile moved to Goebbels' ministry, was the principal bureaucrat responsible for matters of the *Reichskulturkammer.* With an urgent vacancy on the executive of the *Reichsmusikkammer,* the self-described "Reichskulturwalter"[149] appointed Stange Furtwängler's successor as RMK vice-president in December, 1934.[150] The coupling of the Berlin Philharmonic with the RMK in the wake of Furtwängler's departure, opened the door for Stange to engineer his way back onto a German concert podium.

Stange was not present at the special meeting of Stegmann and Höber with representatives RMK on January 2nd, 1935, yet his presence loomed large. Herr Ihlert, deputising for RMK President Strauss, announced that "at the wish of the Propaganda ministry", the new RMK Vice-President should conduct the first *Philharmonisches Konzerte* since Furtwängler's depature, on January 14th.[151] Stange's diligent behind-the-scenes politicking efforts had evidently paid off. The RMVP's own representative, Karl Stegmann, however, voiced concerns over this move on financial grounds—the critical concert required a high-profile conductor who could pacify nervous patrons. Ultimately, the Hamburg conductor Eugen Jochum was chosen, but it was agreed Stange could conduct subsequent concerts in the orchestra's primary subscription series.[152]

Meanwhile, Stange had contacted Höber independently to inform him that he would not accept second-tier billing.[153] In truth, no conductor on earth would have likely satisfied the Berlin Philharmonic as successor to Furtwängler under such conditions. Still, within days, the orchestra had "adopted a decidedly negative attitude vis a vis Stange." [154] After so much plotting and diligence, however, Stange would not be denied. Employing the contacts of his new office, he further schemed to secure not just a guest conducting position with the Philharmonic, but to fill the official void left by Schmidtseck: on January 21st, 1935, Walter Funk appointed Stange as Schmidtseck's successor the Philharmonic's general manager and its principal conductor.[155] The move once again marginalised Höber, and in the absence of the imposing presence of Furtwängler, to whom von Schmidtseck deferred, effectively appointed Stange sovereign intendant, artistic director, and chief conductor in one.

The term of Stange's initial contract lasted to June 30th, 1935,[156] by which time it was hoped for clarification on Furtwängler's definitive status. The contract was later extended through September.[157] The exact nature of Stange's activities as *1. Geschäftsführer* of the Berlin Philharmonic during his tenure, however, remain unclear. He seems to have attacked his role with vigour, undertaking many initiatives.[158] Rather than fulfilling his ambitions, however, the power of his appointment appears to have only encouraged Stange's propensity for self-promotion.[159] His strategies for the orchestra only alienated the musicians further.

Doubtless prompted by accounts from his former colleagues, Furtwängler wrote a savage denunciation of Stange to Walter Funk from his quasi-exile in Munich, describing Stange as a "Daydreamer with uncontrollable reform ideas [...] someone who almost pathologically aggrandises his own over-estimated abilities and underestimates those of his colleagues."[160] Naturally, it would have been surprising to hear Furtwängler accept anyone as his successor graciously, but in this case, he argued vehemently in defence of the orchestra. From a musical point of view, Furtwängler deemed Stange unfit to conduct the *Philharmonischen Konzerte*, suggesting rather, if necessary, he could be offered concerts in the 'popular' series to prove himself. As a plausible candidate for *Geschäftsführer* position, Furtwängler named Herr von Benda, a producer and conductor with the Rundfunk, who by comparison to the boastful Stange, "should posess the necessary sensitity for complicated musical questions."[161]

Several weeks after Furtwängler's condemnation, in May 1935, Stange's reputation received another blow with an investigation into alleged previous membership in the German Socialist Party.[162] According to reports, Stange privately confided once belonging to the SPD to a Dr. Friedrich Mahling of the RMK. Not only was the SPD a political party abhorred by the Nazis, this testimony ran contrary to statements by Stange in his initial solicitation letter to Hinkel, where he wrote explicitly that: "I must mention I have never belonged to any political party" before joining the NSDAP in 1932.[163] Though Stange aggressively denied the charge, this denunciation counted as the third time doubts were cast on his honesty.[164] The network which had brought him to prominence, quickly turned against him.

The sense of triumph Stange must have felt in achieving the prominence he had so long lusted for was also not being taken well by his colleagues: "Through the most childish manipulations," reported Ihlert to Hinkel, "he attempted to undermine my authority [...] Stange behaves with such preposterous vanity he makes himself look ridiculous; for example, he declared to the city authorities that whenever he conducts, the following title must be publicised: vice-president of the *Reichsmusikkammer*, Artistic Director of the Philharmonic Orchestra and General Music Director!"[165]

At this point, the walls began crumbling around Hermann Stange. The orchestra opposed him. The RMK arranged to replace him as vice-president.[166] The press strongly questioned his artistic abilities.[167] Following his complaints to Funk, Furtwängler reportedly took up matters with Goebbels personally.[168] At this stage, Funk and Hinkel had had enough. After publicly acknowledging Hitler as "chief of Reich artistic policy" in February 1935,[169] Furtwängler was sanctioned to return to conducting duties. Though he held no official status with the Berlin Philharmonic again until 1952, Furtwängler's return in April 1935, effectively ended the Stange experiment. By the end of the concert season he had again been marginalised and was eventually replaced.

The Stange experience revealed the limits of bureaucratic imposition in the affairs of the Berlin Philharmonic. While the case of Stegmann showed how government could effectively insert a qualified administrator with a specific mission into a leadership role, the Stange example was a disaster, replete with opportunism and cronyism. The Propaganda Ministry bureaucrats made a mistake in thinking they could treat the Berlin Philharmonic like a private toy, rewarding tenacity, without regard for quality. Invoking ideological catch-phrases and currying favour with well-placed officials could not substitute for professional competence. Granted, so long Furtwängler lurked behind the scenes, Stange, in the eyes of the orchestra, the press and the public, was a lame duck leader. But Stange was architect of his own rise, which at the same time sewed the seeds of his downfall. By relying on the system to reward a sense of entitlement rather than proving himself meritorious in the eyes of his musical peers, Stange could not survive long-term. We cannot know what, if anything, the man himself learned from the experience, but the Ministry decision-makers knew better next time.

The search for a new *1. Geschäftsführer* did not last long. Furtwängler had already identified the man of his choice in his attack on Stange of March 1st, 1935—Hans von Benda.[170] Though he had humbled himself in absolute terms with his pathetic February apology to Hitler and the regime, Furtwängler paradoxically strengthened his position vis a vis the Berlin Philharmonic in his resignation by proving how closely the orchestra's well-being depended on him. Considering the investment the regime was making in the orchestra, there would be no further risks jeopardising one of the Reich's "best instrument of cultural propaganda."[171] If Furtwängler could tolerate Benda, the Ministry could sanction him too.

Though Hans von Benda conducted the Berlin Philharmonic on a few occasions prior to 1935,[172] his principal occupation was as producer of the Concert Division of "Funkstunde Berlin," a division of the State broadcasting authority.[173] Sources conclude Benda was, in all likelihood, a member of the NSDAP.[174] An experienced administrator, his appointment was seen as a stabilising influence. As *1. Geschäftsführer* (business manager) and *Kunstlerische Leiter* (artistic director), he understood his responsibilities to his superiors at the Ministry, "to work together in closest agreement,"[175] while prudently managing the complicated web of Furtwängler relationships—his with the conductor, the conductor with the Ministry, the orchestra with the conductor etc.[176] The situation was a precarious one:

> Dr. Furtwängler himself maintained no official contractual relationship to the orchestra [since his resignation in 1934]. Nevertheless, the tradition of his position vis a vis the orchestra continued, by and large, to reflect his personal wishes.[177]

31

Whereas on occasion over the previous two years, figures had tried to take sovereign control over the institution, there evolved by 1935-36 a fairly stable, if idiosyncratic, structure of parallel spheres and levels of influence. The Propaganda Ministry essentially controlled the legal and budgetary machinery of the institution, installing responsive administrators in the key management positions, thereby securing effective charge of the bulk of programming and internal organisation affairs. Furtwängler, meanwhile, remained the musicians' honourary leader, and in political terms, held the trump card of direct access to Goebbels, who could, in individual cases, dictate terms to the bureaucracy. With no official status with the orchestra, however, Furtwängler was excluded from matters of daily operations, leaving the Philharmonic open to exploitation at the regime's discretion.

In the area of artistic direction, Benda shaped season programmes around Furtwängler's wishes for the ten *Philharmonischen Konzerte*.[178] Furtwängler would, depending on mood and circumstance, conduct six to nine of these concerts, thereby keeping the subscribers and orchestra musicians happy. Outside this series, Benda had a free hand to develop the musical profile of the Philharmonic by his own design. Over the four years of his term, Benda undertook a gradual reform of the concert season by reducing the number of 'popular' concerts, previously numbering up to fifty per year, and replacing them with themed "classical evenings" at the same popular prices. He further reduced the orchestra's reliance on radio and guest performances, but found ways to insert himself into the spotlight by delivering introductory speeches prior to live radio broadcasts of the *Philharmonischen Konzerte* on Monday evenings.[179]

Von Benda and Furtwängler seemed to live a relatively peaceful co-existence until, in May 1939, Furtwängler abruptly petitioned Goebbels for Benda's immediate resignation.[180] This came as a shock to Benda, but appears pre-mediated on Furtwängler's part. Despite obsequious reassurances "that Herr *Reichsminister* Dr. Goebbels will protect and support me,"[181] the case was apparently sealed before Benda even got wind of trouble. Benda's contacts were well-placed bureaucrats, but could do nothing against the whims of higher authorities. The ethos of National Socialist power was a system of mutual exploitation—it did not necessarily prize loyalty. Despite dedicated service both to the orchestra and his Ministry superiors, Benda was expendable; his dismissal just another small concession to maintain Furtwängler's continued cooperation. Furtwängler wrote to Goebbels on the 25th of May 1939;[182] by June 9th, Benda's successor was already in place.[183]

The reason offered for Benda's dismissal was conflict of interest—specifically, Furtwängler's disapproval of his parallel conducting career, primarily with a chamber orchestra composed of members of the Berlin Philharmonic, the *Kammerorchester der Berliner Philharmoniker*, also known as the *Benda Kammerorchester*.[184] Furtwängler ensured that the contract of Benda's successor spelled out manifestly "that the Artistic Director of the Philharmonic will under no circumstances conduct."[185] Benda defended his work with the chamber orchestra, on both artistic grounds—"because I hold a personal love for the German music of the 17th and 18th centuries"[186]—and on political grounds: "because I perceived the advantage of a chamber orchestra of approximately twenty-five members as a useful tool for propaganda abroad."[187]

The facts are various. Benda was not a man above self-promotion, and most certainly did have conducting ambitions which he would not, or could not, set aside after assuming his position with the Philharmonic. Furthermore, the activities of the *Kammerorchester* did indeed conflict with Philharmonic affairs, particularly when the smaller group would go on tour, leaving the Philharmonic staffed with substitute players. This would happen up to four weeks a year.[188] On the other side, Furtwängler had been aware of Benda's conducting work long before recommending him for the *Geschäftsführer* post; both he and the RMVP knew of and condoned the formation of the *Kammerorchester*.[189] In addition, though he did lead the Philharmonic on many occasions, unlike his predecessor, Benda limited himself to secondary concerts, and never during his tenure, conducted the Berlin Philharmonic in the Philharmonie.[190]

Attempting to paint Furtwängler as an unreasonable plaintiff, Benda proposed the thesis "that tension and conflict arose between Dr. Furtwängler and myself only when, aside from assuring Furtwängler's interests, I was also required to protect those of the orchestra and the Ministry as well."[191] He cited numerous examples where Furtwängler's unpredictable and irrational demeanour would undermine months of careful planning. He also chided Furtwängler that despite his assertion as leader of the Berlin Philharmonic, he was perpetually unwilling to conduct the orchestra at official functions or abroad.[192] "In his character and being," wote Benda of Furtwängler, "there is an artist with God-given talent who must not only take, but must also learn to serve."[193]

Ultimately, however, the conflict between Benda and Furtwängler and sudden deterioration of their relationship amounted less to a matter of priorities, difficult personalities, or incompatibility of artistic visions. It came down to a matter of rivalry; the threat to Furtwängler was not Benda himself, but a new conductor who, in 1938, after a successful debut at the Berliner Staatsoper, Benda "assumed as a matter of course" to engage with the Philharmonic,[194] yet towards whom Furtwängler developed an almost pathological aversion. His name was Herbert von Karajan.

A new light on the Berlin conducting scene in 1937-38, von Karajan soon also established connections in high places. Furtwängler saw von Karajan as a weapon levied by powerful interests against him. He, with many others, believed not only the patron of the Staatsoper, Hermann Göring, but also Goebbels himself was behind the plot. Years later, at his de-Nazification tribunal, Furtwängler expressed definitively his suspicion that Goebbels supported Karajan was stoked through Benda's behaviour.[195] Hans von Benda's successor, Gerhart von Westerman later reported that while no direct connection could be drawn between Benda's dismissal and what became known as *der Fall Karajan* (the Karajan Case), it was clear that "Benda had a significant interest in engaging Karajan for the Philharmonic."[196] In the tangled web of mistrust, intrigue and manipulation characterising the times, this mere suspicion was probably enough. Benda's behaviour led Furtwängler to believe Goebbels supported Karajan, therefore, Furtwängler used Goebbels to discharge von Benda.

On August 26th, 1939, Hans von Benda was officially placed on vacation leave for the remaining six months of his contract with the Philharmonic.[197] This fact, rather than an immediate termination of the contract, suggests acknowledgement of the precarious nature of his dismissal. In his letter of notice, Goebbels (writing several months later, delayed, one must assume, by more urgent matters, such as the start of the war) expressed "his thanks for the efforts [...] you have dedicated to the Berlin Philharmonic Orchestra,"[198] leaving his RMVP staff to deal with the mess left behind by executive meddling in bureaucratic affairs. Gerhart von Westerman, *Intendant* of the broadcasting authority in Saarbrücken, almost certainly on the suggestion of Furtwängler,[199] was called for an interview for an unspecified "job opportunity in Berlin"[200] in early June, 1939. An offer was made and general terms and conditions were promptly agreed.[201] Though Westerman began work in Berlin less than three weeks later, formally, Benda was still *Geschäftsführer*.[202] It took another six months for the RMVP to clarify Benda's status and officialise the transition.[203]

In contrast to his predecessors as *1. Geschäftsführer* of the Berlin Philharmonic, Gerhart von Westerman was not a conductor, but a trained composer. A member of the NSDAP,[204] in administrative capacities, Westerman had previously directed the Munich broadcasting authority (1925-35), Berlin's short-wave radio service (1935-38) and the Saarbrücken broadcasting authority (1938-39).[205] Accustomed to a position of stature, and perhaps also aware of the pitfalls encountered by previous occupants of the office, arriving at the Philharmonic, Westerman dictated strong terms: an initial three year contract, a generous RM 1 200 monthly salary plus RM 300 in expenses, six weeks holiday annually, and the title *Intendant*.[206]

This final point was controversial. The nomenclature surrounding the head offices with the Philharmonic had always been imprecise, from Furtwängler's 'official' title, when he still held an official position, through nebulous combinations of *Geschäftsführer* (1. or 2.), *Vertreter* (representative), *Dirigent*, 1. or 2. (conductor), *Leiter* (chief)—*künstlerische* or *kaufmännische* (artistic or business), and *Direktor* (director)—*Generalmusik* or *Verwaltungs*—(General Music or Administrative) between von Schmidtseck, Höber, Stegmann, Stange, and Benda. Though subsequent literature retroactively ascribed *Intendant* to this list[207], Westerman's proposal in 1939 was in fact something new.

The position, as Westerman conceived it, had evolved since the days of *Gleichschaltung* and co-habitation. The *Gleichschaltung* projects were either complete, as in management, programming and structural reforms, or lay dormant, such as questions of racialist policy (see Chapter 2). The orchestra *Vorstand* had been reduced to a rank of purely internal representation.[208] The orchestra's financial relationship with the Reich was stable, and operated fluently under Stegmann's auspices. Furtwängler was no longer an official force, and increasingly unreliable, required discrete consultation on artistic matters, but with care, could be kept at arm's length. The subscribers were content with the orchestra's activities at home, the government was pleased with the orchestra's services abroad. After the drama of the previous decades, it seemed a certain peace had descended on the Berlin Philharmonic. This was acknowledged in the decision to contract Westerman directly with the *Berliner Philharmonisches Orchester GmbH.*, rather than through the Ministry.[209]

What was needed in 1939-40, in Westerman's assessment, was a steady hand to stay the course. This required absolute, if attentive, authority. Recognition as *Intendant* (roughly, General Director) connoted sovereignty in a way previous titles did not. This fact, however, made Goebbels and the RMVP uncomfortable. Westerman insisted on the matter, using a range of arguments. He claimed it would be important to maintain the Intendant title he held with the broadcasting agencies because he feared "anything else would be seen as a step down from his previous positions and might affect his prospects in future."[210] He argued *Direktor* or *Geschäftsführer* would not do justice to his artistic leadership, *künstlerische Leiter* too limiting in regards to his administrative responsibilities.[211] Furtwängler supported the Intendant initiative, ostensibly because of the strong distinction from the *Generalmusikdirektor* title employed by Benda later in his tenure.[212]

After much debate within the RMVP, at the end of June, 1939, Westerman's bid was accepted.[213] Then, in August, upon personally reviewing the new contract, Goebbels suddenly overruled, the Propaganda Minister insisting "such a title [as *Intendant*] can only be bestowned upon a someone who truly performs that leadership function."[214] Evidently, *Führerprinzip* in theory, was more desirable than it in practice. More to the point, *Führerprinzip* was more complicated than a matter of pragmatic authority. In the case of the Berlin Philharmonic, the delineations between practical, political, and symbolic had become so obscured that, while he was amenable to Westerman directing the programming and operations of the orchestra, Goebbels was not prepared to allow Westerman the kind of freedom of a 'truly functioning' *Intendant*. This had nothing to do with Stegmann's position, or even Goebbels' own honorary 'Schirmherr' title. Like Furtwängler's deferential acknowledgement that the Reich's artistic policy "will be determined solely by the Führer and Reich's Chancellor and his appointed ministers,"[215] behind Goebbels' insistence was also a truth—in Nazi Germany, there was only one true hegemony. Westerman could dictate the terms of his appointment, but required a bureaucratic structure for support. The State bureaucracy had the power to legally and organisationally transform an institution, but could be trumped by superior ministers. Furtwängler had the influence to see people hired and fired, but he too could be humbled. Westerman would never be a true Intendant because the regime would always reserve the right to intervene in Philharmonic affairs. Beyond that, however, the Berlin Philharmonic had become a *Reichsorchester*—a symbol of the regime, a symbol of Germany; it could have only one true Führer.

Westerman settled for *1. Geschäftsführer* and *Künstlerische Leiter* titles.[216] He paid careful attention to the legal and financial details of his appointment, putting the RMVP bureaucrats on notice he would not be trifled with.[217] Thereafter, Westerman did indeed prove a steady hand. He further expanded the orchestra's national and international profile, while shielding the musicians from the worst effects of the war.[218] His relationship with Furtwängler remained courteous yet distant.[219] Though he too faced a denunciation through the Party in March 1940,[220] in the professional sphere, the extent of his enthusiasm on behalf of Nazi ideas appears negligible. He was liked by the orchestra. There is no evidence the RMVP or leaders of the government ever overruled him or questioned his judgement. He held his position until the collapse of the Third Reich in May, 1945. Westerman eventually did invoke the *Intendant* title, but it was never officialised. That would only come about in 1952, seven long years after the Führer's demise.

Chapter 2

The Philharmonic Community

In September 1931, the City of Berlin resolved to reduce its budget for culture, forcing Berlin Philharmonic musicians, by way of the City's holding strength in the GmbH, into an immediate 12% wage reduction.[1] This followed on the heels of a 6% wage rollback for all musicians, soloists, and conductors imposed in February of the same year.[2] Within months, however, it was clear, this measure achieved nothing but to further antagonise an already desperate situation.

In addition to its funding of the Berlin Philharmonic, the City of Berlin also subsidized another orchestra, the *Berliner Sinfonie-Orchester* or so-called "Blüthner Orchester", named for the piano manufacturer which founded the ensemble in 1907. By comparison to its more prestigious city neighbour, the *Sinfonie-Orchester* was a local orchestra, performing at community events, playing popular and school concerts. In many politicians' eyes, these activities were more valuable to the public good than the Berlin Philharmonic's elite following and international reputation. Inadvertent rivals struggling for share of an ever-shrinking pool of municipal subsidy, both Berlin orchestras became embroiled in a polarising political debate over the merits, standards and aims of public money for cultural institutions.[3]

For a time in this debate, in the press and among city councillors, it in fact appeared the Philharmonic was losing. But while its renown and quality were regarded with scepticism, even contempt within certain political camps, the Berlin Philharmonic's chief advantage vis a vis the Berliner Sinfonie-Orchester remained its esteemed place in the musical life of Germany. This reputation ultimately earned the orchestra support, if only reluctantly, from offices higher than the city magistrates. As long as the Reich and *State Rundfunk* (broadcasting service) were prepared to support in the Philharmonic in recognition of its quality and national stature, its position would always be favourable to that of the Sinfonie-Orchester.[4]

Finally, in April, 1932, a compromise was hammered out on the municipal level. On April 15th, 1932, following a meeting of the city council,[5] the Deputy Mayor of Berlin, Gustav Böss, wrote to the Reich Interior Ministry advising of a municipal plan to ease both the Berlin Philharmonic's worsening financial crisis, and the city's own:

> For some time now a plan has been under way to absorb some members of the Berliner Sinfonie-Orchester into the Philharmonische Orchester, while guaranteeing the protection of the remaining members of the premier orchestra.[6]

The proposal would see the dissolution of the Sinfonie-Orchester, with a proportion of its members subsumed into the Philharmonic, while modifying the Philharmonic's programming to fill a more socially-active mandate.[7] In so doing, the city could divest itself of one entire orchestra, representing an estimated annual saving of RM 170 000[8], but retain its local social and cultural benefits.

Under the terms of merger outlined at a meeting of the Philharmonic board of directors at the Berlin City Hall on June 4th, 1932, the Berlin Philharmonic would grow from 86 to 105 musicians. By absorbing nineteen musicians, this represented an accession of almost 40% of the members of the former Berliner Sinfonie-Orchester, which comprised only fifty players, by the Philharmonic. The remaining "Blüthner" musicians would be disbursed to other assorted theatre and Kaffeehaus orchestras around Berlin). In addition, the newly constituted Philharmonic Orchestra would be committed to six Furtwängler-led *Volks* or popular concerts per season,[9] plus another twenty-five *Volks* concerts with other conductors, two choral concerts, a chamber music series, and twelve afternoon concerts for school children.[10]

Naturally, these measures, born of political haggling rather than musical concern, were met by the Berlin Philharmonic with grave discontent. Furtwängler in particular, whose supremacy was severely undermined by events, never accepted the merger, or the former Sinfonie-Orchester musicians.[11] For the orchestra, not only did the politically-imposed shaping of season programming subvert its artistic freedom, the forced acceptance of new players was anathema to its self-governing tradition.

Moreover, the plan made little financial sense. By spring 1932, the Philharmonic did not even have enough money to pay the wages of its present members, let alone assume responsibility for up to twenty more.[12] By March 1933, the City of Berlin was disbursing more to the Berlin Philharmonic just to keep the orchestra solvent, than it had saved in the dissolution of the Sinfonie-Orchester less than a year before.[13]

In spite of rancour and protests, the merger went ahead. On September 7th, 1932, in the presence of Furtwängler, Max von Schillings, representing the *Städtische Oper Berlin* (Municipal Opera), to which a number of leftover players would be assigned, and members of the Philharmonic orchestra, an audition was held for musicians of the former Berliner Sinfonie-Orchester; eventually, twenty-three were accepted into the Philharmonic through this humiliating exercise.[14] On October 1st, 1932, the fusion of the two orchestras was made official.[15] On January 27th, 1933, the twenty-three new Philharmoniker purchased their shares in the *Berliner Philharmonisches Orchester GmbH*, and entered the musical cooperative. Three days later, Hitler became chancellor of Germany.

Among the twenty-three new musicians, at least six were confirmed members of the National Socialist Worker's Party (NSDAP), including cellist and former Sinfonie-Orchester *Vorstand*, Fritz Schröder.[16] During the heady days following the Nazi seizure of power, the Party members from the former Sinfonie-Orchester linked with the NSDAP members already within the Philharmonic in a push to transform the organisation in accordance with the ideological principles of the new regime. A report by Fritz Schröder detailed repeated efforts through the spring and summer of 1933 to concentrate power and pursue an ideological agenda:

Factual Report on the Activities of the Berline Philharmonic Orchestra; efforts of NSDAP members to form a political cell rejected by orchestra leadership: [...]

Dr. Furtwängler is attempting to reverse the fusion [of Philharmonic and Blüthner orchestras] through official channels.

Orchestra not pleased with general management, demanding its overdue re-election. Meeting of orchestra representatives at Dr. Furtwängler's home. Previously mentioned wishes are being submitted to Dr. F. for consideration.

Party members who have committed themselves to orderliness are being decried as troublemakers. Dr. Furtw., appears to be misinformed. On the question of the Jews, Herr Dr. Furtw. has spoken to the effect that these should still remain in the orchestra following a consultation and agreement with Herr Reichsminister Dr. Goebbels.[17]

In June 1933, Schröder supplanted long-time Philharmonic member Richard "Excellenz" Wolff as orchestra *Vorstand*, alongside Lorenz Höber. Neither Wolff nor Höber were NSDAP members. Though Schröder's election appears to have been legitimate, the vote was triggered by Wolff's suspension as *Vorstand* by a Berlin magistrate[18], an extraordinary measure of questionable legality engineered through political intrigue with the aide of two other convinced Nazis, trumpet-player Anton Schuldes and cellist Wolfram Kleber.[19] Both Schuldes and Kleber had been musicians in the Philharmonic prior to the Sinfonie-Orchester merger.

By summer 1933, it appeared the orchestra's internal culture was transforming in step with the Nazification of German society. But, in August, Furtwängler approached Goebbels and Hitler himself to discuss the condition of his orchestra. It is unclear whether the facts were linked, but five weeks after the introduction of Rudolf von Schmidtseck as *Geschäftsführer* of the Berlin Philharmonic, on October 19th, 1933, it was announced that, on Hitler's expressed wish, the Berlin Philharmonic was to become a *Reichsorchester*, effective November 1st, 1933. In conjunction with the State's acquiring 100% of the GmbH, the contracts of fifteen members of the orchestra would on that date be terminated.[20] All fifteen named were former Sinfonie-Orchester musicians, including Fritz Schröder. The decision was a matter of cabinet decree, and not open to challenge.[21]

If Furtwängler cut a deal with Goebbels and Hitler, accepting von Schmidtseck's installation and the Reich takeover in exchange for dissolution of the Sinfonie-Orchester merger, cannot be directly ascertained. What is certain is that Furtwängler was behind Hitler's decree. Furtwängler protested the amalgamation of the two orchestras from the beginning, on both musical and financial grounds, and lobbied vigorously for its reversal after the fact.[22] He also rejected the aggressive infiltration of Nazi intrigue into the internal politics of the Philharmonic which coincided with the merger.[23] To a certain extent perhaps an moral stance, Furtwängler's mobilisation to the highest authorities also represented an effort to maintain his own sovereignty over the orchestra in the face of increasing upheaval within its ranks. In frustration, Furtwängler turned to Goebbels and Hitler, and, going over the heads of the Berlin politicians,[24] eventually got his wish.

Just as musicians of the Berlin Philharmonic were enraged by the political machinations that imposed an additional twenty-three musicians into their community in 1932, the fifteen members of the former Berliner Sinfonie-Orchester who were forced to leave the Philharmonic, felt decidedly wronged by political dictates one year later. They collectively retained legal counsel, a Dr. Heyl, and demanded a meeting with the RMVP. Not only were the fifteen musicians unceremoniously fired, but they were also collectively owed almost RM 3 600 in salary,[25] plus payment for their shares in the GmbH.[26] Beyond monetary considerations, many could not believe it was Hitler's intent to throw Party members and war veterans "into the street,"[27] principally while there were "foreigners and Jews" still playing in the Philharmonic. Wrote violinist Walter Neander:

Es ist für einer Deutschen deprimierend, dass ein Kriegsopfer auf die Strasse gesetzt wird, und dass anderseits Ausländer und Juden im Orchester verbleiben [...] Ich bin der festen überzeugung dass diese mir ungerecht dünkende

Handlungsweise gegen den Willen unseres Führers ist, denn ich kann nicht glauben, dass er einen alte Frontkampfer so behandeln lassen würde.

It is depressing for a German that a war veteran should be thrown out onto the street while foreigners and Jews remain in the orchestra. [...] I am firmly convinced that the unjust treatment I have received is against the will of our Führer. I cannot believe that he would treat an old veteran from the front like that.[28]

In their meeting with *Staatsrat* Hans Schmidt-Leonhardt of the RMVP, the question was posed directly "whether the fact that veterans of the front lines and party members are being affected, whereas non-Aryans remain in the orchestra."[29], whereupon, according to Schröder, the *Staatsrat* jumped from his chair furious, and concluded the meeting abruptly. The *Staatsrat*'s account recalled slightly differently:

It is an untrue exaggeration to say that I jumped up at some sentence or another. I only spoke according to my duty. [...] I agreed to present this message about the exclusion of front-line veterans and Party members in contrast to the numerous Jews who remain in the orchestra [to my superiors]; and I have done so.[30]

It is in fact highly unlikely Hitler was aware of the consequences of his merger-reversing degree for several members of his Party. Of course neither he nor Goebbels would have deliberately sought to alienate their supporters, the deal, however, was a concession to Furtwängler. In their estimation, a favour assuring the prominent conductor's cooperation was a priority far greater than nurturing the ambitions of a few loyal followers.

With reinstatement out of the question, legal negotiations between Dr. Heyl and the RMVP over financial compensation dragged on for months. In September, 1934, the RMVP offered the group of fifteen a total of RM 5 000 for their outstanding wages and GmbH shares.[31] Though the terms were accepted, it was another three months before all 15 former members of the Berliner

Sinfonie-Orchester and Berlin Philharmonic Orchestra received a paltry compensation from the Reich of RM 390 each.[32]

But what of those numerous Jews who continued to occupy the ranks of the Berlin Philharmonic, while veterans and Party members were relegated to the streets? In 1933, the Berlin Philharmonic, an orchestra of over one hundred musicians, counted among its ranks a total of four Jewish members: Szymon Goldberg, 1. concertmaster; Gilbert Back, 1. violin; and the two solo-cellists, Nicolai Graudan and Joseph Schuster.

On April 13, 1933, less than ten weeks after Hitler's ascent to power, Berlin *Oberbürgermeister* Wilhelm Hafemann, bearing the title *Staatskommissar zur Wahrnehmung der Geschäfte* called *Orchestervorstand* Lorenz Höber to a meeting wherein he demanded a list of "All Jewish members of Your orchestra with indication of instrument and nationality."[33] Höber agreed, but did nothing. Ten days later, with no response, Hafemann threatened Höber in writing that he expected to receive the list of Jewish Berlin Philharmonic members within three days, or he would make use of "Any necessary means available"[34] to obtain copies of the concerned musicians contracts "so that the question can be reviewed immediately, if and at what earliest date dismissal notices can be issued."[35]

Though anti-Semitic fervour in the wake of the Nazi take-over was rampant, Höber knew he had two things in his favour. First, the law. The Berlin Philharmonic, though high-profile and partially publicly subsidised, was, in April 1933, still a private organisation. The early anti-Semitic laws passed by the Nazi government, such as the *Gesetz zur Wiederherstellung des Berufsbeamtentums* (Law for the Reinstatement of Civil Service), applied only to public institutions such as government branches, universities, *Hochschule*, or state theatres. The Philharmonic, therefore, remained, exempt. Though no astute observer assumed it would end there, in the face of Hafemann's idle threats, Höber at least knew he had time.

Second, Höber, and the Berlin Philharmonic had Furtwängler. Furtwängler and Goebbels had already exchanged barbs on issue of Jews in German cultural life in the pages of the *Deutsche Allgemeine Zeitung*. On April 11th, 1933, Furtwängler wrote:

Art and artists exist to unite, not to separate. At the end of the day, I only recognise one line of separation: the one between good and bad art. Whereas the line between Jews and non-Jews is being drawn with cruel fierceness, even where the stance of the persons concerned on national politics is beyond reproach, the other one, which is so important for our music culture in the long run, that decisive line between good and bad, is being tragically neglected. [36]

Directly beside these comments, Goebbels mounted his rebuttal, apologising most sardonically for any over-zealousness in the drive to root out Jews from German cultural life, callously 'explaining' that for the past fourteen years, the "genuinely German artists," had been condemned to oblivion while Jewish artists such as Bruno Walter, Otto Klemperer and Max Reinhardt hogged the limelight. The initiatives of the Nazis first months in office, therefore, simply represented "a natural reaction" to this fact.[37] "They accuse us of being good politicians but bad friends of the arts," wrote Goebbels in his journal, "The future will prove how thoroughly mistaken they were."[38]

While Furtwängler was limited in his public defence of Jewish musicians, Höber knew he would stand by those in the Berlin Philharmonic to keep zealots like Hafemann at bay. Höber waited until Hafemann's three day ultimatum expired before replying. In his letter, Höber reminded the *Oberbürgermeister* that he had already informed him of "all members of Jewish heritage, as far as I know", but identifying the *halbjüdischen Mitglieder* (half-Jewish members —Höber never used the derogatory *Juden* label), "will present certain difficulties", requiring a little more time.[39] He enclosed the contracts and, significantly, the *GmbH. Gesellschafter Urkunden* of the Jewish musicians, begging Hafemann's indulgence to wait another three weeks until the orchestra returned from tour before a complete list could be delivered.[40]

This game of cat and mouse between Höber, Furtwängler and Nazi authorities and agitators persisted for months. Upon returning from tour with the Philharmonic in May, Furtwängler found a pile of correspondence awaiting him—letters, telegrams, postcards from

Jewish musicians, composers and academics who had, in the interim, been fired, suspended, or threatened, requesting his intervention on their behalf.[41]

The issue of Furtwängler's attitude towards and actions on behalf of Jewish colleagues has been debated extensively elsewhere.[42] In the case of the four Berlin Philharmonic musicians, Furtwängler tried his best to retain his valued first-stand players. In a letter to Goebbels, he offered almost apologetically: "As I already told you in person, in spite of an extremely intensive search, the three [sic] Jews in the orchestra were hired after a tedious audition process as no Aryans anywhere near as good could be found."[43] It is entirely possible, given Furtwängler's statement of recognition for only qualitative and not racial distinctions, he did not even know Gilbert Back was also Jewish; otherwise, one might assume the conductor merely conveniently 'forgot' one of his long-standing first violinist's true identity. That Goldberg, Graudan and Schuster were Jewish was hard to overlook. Furtwängler's statement could also be understood not as political kowtowing at all, but an indication of actual prejudice in the Philharmonic's auditioning procedures.

To Furtwängler, however, the issue was much larger than a question of bias, but ultimately touched upon the limits of political interference in his artistic sphere. He took up the question of the Jewish members of the orchestra again with Goebbels in connection with the Berliner Sinfonie-Orchester merger, financial security for the Berlin Philharmonic through the Reich, his own leadership, and the appointment of an NSDAP *Kommissar* (von Schmidtseck), among other concerns. For him, the issues were all interconnected. Furtwängler seems to have persuaded Goebbels to accept the three or four Jews as part of his pact with the Reich.[44] As with the 'debate' in the pages of the *Deutsche Allgemeine Zeitung*, Furtwängler's stance was more urgent, while Goebbels took the more conciliatory position. The conductor's case did not reject anti-Semitic policy per se, but rejected political interference in his domain. Goebbels saw the matter in larger terms, and was prepared to offer, as he would often over the following twelve years, small concessions in exchange for a greater gain. If it would help keep Furtwängler on board and solidify his grip on the orchestra for use to his own propagandistic ends, Goebbels would call off the dogs on the Berlin Philharmonic's Jewish musicians.

The times, however, were ugly. On April 26, 1933, at a joint concert with the Berlin Philharmonic and the *Nationalorchester Mannheim* (where Furtwängler was once GMD), a number of Mannheim musicians protested violently at "Germans" being made to sit second place to the Philharmonic's Jewish principal players. Though rumours abounded of "dozens" of Jews in the Berlin Orchestra, the fury was specifically directed at Concertmaster Szymon Goldberg, [45] "The concertmaster from Mannheim was by far the inferior musician," recalled Bertha Geissmar, "but he was a Party member and had immediately fallen into step with the new regime."[46] Furtwängler refused to let the concert proceed unless he, and not politics, dictated the seating arrangements. He threatened to cancel the concert altogether if he did not get his way.

In the end, Furtwängler's steadfastness worked. Golberg did sit as concertmaster for the Mannheim performance. But it was not the end of the story. Immediately after the debacle, Furtwängler wrote a strongly worded letter to the *Vorstand* of the Mannheim orchestra articulating his position, using Goebbels' acquiescence as ammunition:

> With regard to the question of contributions of the Jews in the Berlin Philharmonic Orchestra, that is something that does not concern you, but only the government of the Reich, which has taken the Philharmonic Orchestra under its control. The government of the Reich knows well [...] that, in an orchestra, the heights of the German orchestral arts represent not only Germany, but the whole world, and that first and foremost the system of merit must be and remain the final authority.[47]

Szymon Goldberg joined the Berlin Philharmonic in 1929. Born in Poland, he was already a celebrated soloist before coming to the orchestra at the age of nineteen. He regularly performed chamber music with men like Gregor Piatigorsky, Edwin Fischer, and Arthur Schnabel, and later formed important musical partnerships with Lilli Kraus and Radu Lupu. Both Goldberg and solo-cellist Joseph

Schuster followed in long lines of distinguished virtuosi leading the Berlin Philharmonic's string sections, and were featured in numerous solo concertos with the orchestra. Among the orchestra's three concertmasters in 1933 (with Siegfried Borries and Erich Röhn), Furtwängler singled Goldberg out: "He could probably actually be considered the best European Concertmaster of our time."[48]

Once the Berlin Philharmonic became an asset of the Reich at the beginning of 1934, its musicians were officially installed as civil servants. They were therefore subject to the racial laws already in effect for the public service. Once the "Jewish question" in relation to the Philharmonic became a matter of law, rather than accusation, conjecture and rancorous debate, it became considerably more difficult for Furtwängler or anyone else to defend the Jewish members of the orchestra. At the end of the 1933-34 season, Goldberg, along with Joseph Schuster, left Germany. There is no indication this was precipitated by direct political order, the decision to leave rather more likely a response to accumulating nastiness both within the German music community and German society as a whole.

Furthermore, Goldberg at least, appears to have departed in some haste. The Berlin Philharmonic's accounting books, either reflecting the suddenness of his leaving, or perhaps the harsh exit restrictions imposed on émigrés, still showed outstanding debts to Goldberg in 1935,[49] while years later, Goldberg hired legal counsel in America in a property reclamation suit regarding his former home in Berlin.[50] His departure was in public attributed as a *plötzlichen Ausfall* (last minute cancellation).[51] Goldberg was succeeded by Hugo Kolberg. Simultaneously, Tibor de Machula, a Hungarian but whose background check assured "documented Aryan ancestry"[52] was named "successor to the Jew Schuster."[53]

After just sixteen months of Nazi rule, only Graudan and Back remained. In December 1934, Nicolai Graudan's contract was up for renewal. Unlike section players, Berlin Philharmonic concertmasters and solo-cellists signed individual, customised contracts (*Privat-Dienstverträge*) with the orchestra, offering higher salary for fewer services, with consent for independent solo work, "as permitted by the performance schedule."[54] Born in Lithuania, Graudan was both Jewish and a foreign national. He joined the Berlin Philharmonic in 1927, succeeding Gregor Piatigorsky. He was a regular soloist in Berlin and with orchestras abroad, and performed chamber music with Goldberg, Paul Hindemith and Rudolf Serkin, among others. His wife, Joanna Graudan, was also a talented pianist and pedagogue. The story of Graudan's 1934 contract renewal coincided with the period of Furtwängler's resignation, and revealed a strategy of dislodging 'undesirables' effectuated through more subtle means than anti-Semitic lobbying or political dictate.

Graudan's contract was not automatically cancelled in the absence of the conductor's benevolence, but rather renewed"[55] The Ministry, however, denied Graudan a raise comparable to his section-leader colleagues, insisting instead on "an increase in individual performances."[56] Worse than firing, this amounted to professional humiliation—more work for less pay, assigning second-class treatment to a world class musician. By summer, 1935, a bitter Graudan had found another position in England, and requested liquidation of his contract with the Berlin Philharmonic.[57] Permission was granted by the orchestra and Ministry in short order, with Karl Stegmann assuring his superiors, "naturally, we will only select a gentleman who is of Aryan descent"[58] to fill the principal cellist's chair. Illustrating the Philharmonic's exceptional status, within two days of Graudan's resignation from the orchestra, the *Reichsmusikkammer* banned him from all further musical appearances in Germany.[59]

And then there was one. Less than a week after Graudan's departure, *Staatskommissar* Hans Hinkel of the RMVP demanded from Stegmann and the newly arrived *künstlerischer Leiter* (Artistic Director) Hans von Benda, an accounting of the *Gleichschaltung* project as pertained to Jewish elements in the Berlin Philharmonic. Stegmann and Benda reported:

> The only full Jew in our orchestra is Gilbert Back. He has been with the Orchestra since the 1st of October 1925 [. . .] Back is a talented violinist. He has never, not even during the Weimar Republic, stood out or belonged to a political party. His father founded the first German school in Sofia, his brother was an officer in the Austrian army during the World War and was distinguished with the Golden Medal of Bravery. His cousin was an

interpreter in the German Services and was part of the well-known campaign through Persia. Back is an Austrian citizen."[60]

Despite Stegmann and Benda's best efforts to paint Back in a noble and patriotic light, to Hinkel and those of his ilk his religion outweighed his merits as a musician or as a man. In September 1935, the infamous Nürnberg race laws were tabled by Hitler to much fanfare at the *Reichsparteitage*. Shortly thereafter, for the remarkably large sum of about RM 16 000, Back was essentially bought out of his contract.[61] Via Turkey and Paris, he eventually reunited with his former Philharmonic colleagues Goldberg, Graudan and Schuster in America. By the start of the 1935-36 season, the Berlin Philharmonic no longer contained any Jewish musicians.

In addition to the four Jewish members who vacated the orchestra, in 1935, the Berlin Philharmonic also had two members of partly Jewish descent (*Halbjuden* or *Mischlingen* as they were repugnantly termed): eighteen-year veteran solo-cellist Hans Bottermund, a Dane, whose grandmother was Jewish; and Bruno Stenzel, a second violinist for sixteen years, whose Jewish mother came from Hungary.[62] Even though from the start of the 1936-37 season, Philharmonic musicians were required to carry an "Arischer Nachweis" (proof of Aryan-ness),[63] it appears a 'don't ask-don't tell' policy descended on the orchestra. From Goebbels' standpoint, clearly "full Jews" were undesirable among the ranks of Germany's national musical symbol but despite Furtwängler's apparent victory obtaining Goebbels' exceptional agreement over Goldberg, Back, Schuster and Graudan, it took less than two years to see that concession rendered moot. Over the longer-term, Goebbels was willing to live with an indeterminate handful of 'half-Jews' in the Berlin Philharmonic to keep Furtwängler and the remaining orchestra members happy. Fortunately, the Philharmonic careers of Bottermund, Stenzel and perhaps others, outlasted the Third Reich.

In the final extension of anti-Semitic identification, up to four Berlin Philharmonic members had Jewish wives. These cases were: Concertmaster Hugo Kolberg, violinist Richard Wolff, Principal Clarinet Ernst Fischer, horn player Otto Hess.[64] Furtwängler was a great admirer of Kolberg's, engaging him as a frequent soloist and chamber music partner. Kolberg's initial contract was an unprecedented five year offer. The original draft of this contract contained the clause: "This contract is signed with knowledge of the fact that Mr. Kolberg is married to a non-Aryan."[65] This was later deleted, perhaps for the insulting nature of the statement, but perhaps also for the legal loophole the acknowledgement presented should a more stringent application of racialist policy at some subsequent date be applied.

After his move from Frankfurt to the capital in 1934, with Furtwängler's commendation, Hugo Kolberg became a significant figure on the Berlin and German musical scenes. Despite superlative contributions to national musical life, however, Kolberg remained under suspicion. In August, 1938, an internal RMVP memo reported Kolberg had requested five weeks leave to perform a series of concerts in the United States. Rather than seeing this as a propaganda opportunity on which to capitalise, the Ministry feared, because Kolberg was married to a Jewish woman "he intended to be able to use the trip to immediately stay in America permanently."[66] Kolberg was forced to sign a declaration vowing his return. "At the same time," continued the memo, "we have to count on the possibility that he will use the opportunity to make contacts so that he can eventually permanently settle in America."[67] Hans von Benda did not oppose Kolberg's leave request because he perceived he would likely need to be replaced within the next year or two anyhow. Indeed, in 1939, Kolberg did leave the Berlin Philharmonic for America, serving as concertmaster with orchestras in Pittsburgh, New York, Cleveland and Chicago. Twenty years later, Kolberg, meanwhile divorced from his Jewish wife, won a *Wiedergutmachungs* (compensation) claim against the German government, and at the age of sixty, returned to the Berlin Philharmonic for the last five years of his professional career.

Whether and under what circumstances Furtwängler interceded on Kolberg's behalf is not clear. In the case of Ernst Fischer, however, a member of the Philharmonic since before the Great War, the solo-clarinettist manifestly acknowledged his feeling of indebtedness to Furtwängler. As Fischer reported to the conductor's de-Nazification tribunal in 1946: "At the time my Jewish wife and I were gravely threatened. After 1933 Dr. Furtwängler always helped protect us from the campaigns that the Gestapo and government attempted."[68] Fischer and his wife survived safely. Otto Hess expressed similar feelings of gratitude. Richard Wolff, meanwhile, was at first thrown out of the *Reichsmusikkammer* for having a Jewish wife. In his case too, Furtwängler seems to have ensured this measure would have no repercussions.[69] In a cruel twist of fate, Wolff's wife died in 1937, whereupon the RMK promptly reinstated his membership.[70]

It is reported Furtwängler also arranged for the Jewish wives of Philharmonic musicians, those acknowledged at least, to hear concerts in the Philharmonie, even long after Jewish patrons had been barred from attending concerts there.[71] On August 2, 1937, Goebbels wrote in his diary: "There are still some half-Jews in the Philharmonie. I will attempt to get them out. This will not be easy. Furtwängler is trying to retain them with all of his might."[72] Whether these *Halbjuden* were the musicians' wives or others, the news of Jews still in the Philharmonie sparked controversy. In September, 1939, a letter was sent to the RMVP from a woman claiming to be the wife of a Berlin Philharmonic member (the name is indecipherable), complaining vociferously about the presence of Jewish wives at concerts.[73] The Ministry demanded an explanation from the Philharmonic, which Stegmann prepared categorically:

Nach unserer Ansicht wird es sich bei dem Angeber kaum um die Frau eines unserer Orchestermitglieder handelt. Ausserdem sind die Angaben irreführend. Es sind tatsächlich nach dem Austritt unseres 1. Konzertmeisters Kolberg nur noch drei Orchestermitglieder, die jüdische Frauen haben. [Diese Frauen] besuchen den seit langem unsere Konzerte nich mehr, bemühen sich aber zur Zeit bei der Reichskulturkammer und die erlaubnis zum Konzertbesuch. Jedenfalls: im Betieb und auch in den Konzerten treten diese jüdischen Frauen überhaupt nicht mehr auf. Die Geschäftsführung würde, wenn sich irgundwelche Unzu[...] glichkeiten aus dem Verhalten der jüdischen Frauen ergeben würde, selbstverständlich von selbst die notwendigen Schritte unternehmen.

From our perspective, this anonymous trouble-maker

could hardly be the wife of one of our orchestra members. Furthermore the information provided is misleading. As a matter of fact, since the departure of Kolberg, our former first concertmaster, there are only three members of the orchestra remaining who have Jewish wives. [These women] have not attended our concerts for a long time—although they are currently attempting to gain permission from the *Reichskulturkammer*. In any case, at rehearsals and also at our concerts, these Jewish women are not in appearance whatsoever. The management would of course of its own accord take all necessary steps to address this issue, should it prove necessary.[74]

This memo is remarkable for a number of reasons. First, Stegmann casting doubt on the letter's authenticity suggests either an audacious case of forgery for sensational provocation, or some Philharmonic members' wives agitating aggressively yet unbeknownst to the musicians themselves, or worse still, that Philharmonic musicians themselves were playing a two-faced game with their colleagues. Secondly, the admission that Jewish wives were indeed petitioning the authorities for special permission to attend concerts substantiates the notion Furtwängler might, at some stage, have intervened on their behalf. Thirdly, Stegmann's emphatic assurance to the Ministry that all deviations from racialist policy would be quickly and decisively dealt with 'in house' echoes a similar statement issued to Hinkel four years earlier:

> [...] The management will on its own rigorously ensure that the Jewish influence is and remains, as always, completely silenced. Since 1930 no Jews have been accepted in the orchestra, and, of course, in the future they will also not be hired.[75]

These assurances appear in the same memo as the extensive, if ultimately futile, defence of Gilbert Back. Curiously, Stegmann and Benda, both RMVP appointed, NSDAP loyalists, appear to be contradicting themselves, promoting retaining Jewish musicians while promising the expunging of all Jewish influence. Perhaps through sensitive observation they, unlike their Ministry superiors, had acquired an appreciation for the subtlety of Furtwängler's argument—that Jewish musicians could be distinguished from the caricatured image of "Kitsch, tasteless virtuosity;"[76] that good Jewish musicians could be good German musicians too. Perhaps they had developed an appreciation too for, and loathed to disrupt, what Lorenz Höber dubbed the Berlin Philharmonic's *Gemeinschaftsgeist* (communal spirit).[77]

But what of this mythical *Gemeinschaftsgeist*? The fact no Jewish musicians entered the orchestra after 1930 might be noteworthy. It is not clear if this fact, cited by Stegmann and von Benda, was mere coincidence, or if any sort of prejudice played a part in orchestra auditions prior to the Nazis coming to power. The politics of auditions required attendance of all active orchestra members, a minimum two-thirds positive vote, and the approval of Furtwängler.[78] Thereafter came a year's probation period. "Many a good musician," wrote Lorenz Höber of the selection process, "has, despite good effort, failed, if, during the qualifying period, he did not show the qualities that are essential for the orchestra: community spirit, enthusiasm and submission to the will of the collective."[79] Given the importance the members themselves placed on maintaining the orchestra's exemplary musical standards, it is doubtful, even if some individuals held biases, that a general racial prejudice could have infected their selection procedures, a least to a majority extent.

But while the fact of so few Jewish Berlin Philharmonic members might surprise, the Jewish contingent in 1933, registering less than 4% of the orchestra population, already represented a much larger proportion than the Jewish share of German society as a whole. Doubtless, their abbreviated exodus was greeted positively by the Nazis and Nazi sympathisers in the orchestra, even likely the *Geschäftsführung*, who no longer needed to make excuses. By contrast, the reaction of the rest of the orchestra seemed eerily subdued. Within any average community, one would not normally expect the fate of such a small minority to register massive reaction, yet the Berlin Philharmonic claimed to be something exceptional. What of that special *Gemeinschaftsgeist*, it was claimed, that set the Philharmonic apart from other orchestras, particularly as concertmasters and principal players were among the persecuted? The orchestra's internal politics, it would seem, were not naive of the changes in the world surrounding it.

The founding of the Berlin Philharmonic was a political act, and the orchestra always took great pride in its democratic culture. The orchestra elected the executive *Vorstand* by secret ballot, and decision-making functioned in a participatory, consultative fashion. Even after the formal take-over by the Reich, with its ancillary imposition of a management class, the orchestra remained essentially self-governing in internal affairs. Violist Lorenz Höber, who had served as orchestra *Vorstand* since 1922, though replaced in his *Geschäftsführung* capacities, continued to coordinate most internal orchestra activities, including *Dienstpläne* (schedules), *Besetzungspläne* (rehearsal plans), and some travel and accommodation arrangements. Ranging from 97 to 106 players, the rotation of musicians and programme to programme disposition presented a major logistical task. Höber was also ex-officio on the *Aufsichtsrat*, both before and after the transformations of 1933-34. Most importantly, however, the *Vorstand* was the voice of the orchestra to management, and responsible for orchestra discipline. This power is what appealed to Fritz Schröder in his challenge to the *Vorstand* during the Berliner Sinfonie-Orchester merger, an episode which represented just the first in many challenges to the internal politics of the orchestra, initiated from without and within.

In his 1933 attempt to radicalise the political climate of the Berlin Philharmonic community, Fritz Schröder did not act alone. He was abetted by at least two other Philharmonic members, trumpet-player Anton Schuldes[80] and cellist Wolfram Kleber,[81] plus, presumably, several of his Sinfonie-Orchester colleagues. This initial Nazi cluster claimed to operate in the interest of orchestra *Sauberkeit und Ordnung* (cleanliness and order), in the wake of the Nazi rise to power.[82] This innocuous-sounding agenda had a racist dimension, but also bore the pretence of a missionary purpose. As Wolfram Kleber later, under the title *Deutsche Orchestermusiker rufen auf!*, stirringly wrote to his musical colleagues:

> We want to apply ourselves to the sacred matter of our German arts in peace. We seek to prevail and honour the power of our vocation. It is our duty to do so, and thereby to serve the people and the Fatherland [...] The Führer restored to us our honour, and is working for the true peace![83]

Evidently, in the opinion of Kleber, Schröder and Schuldes, the Berlin Philharmonic in 1933 needed a shake-up to instil the right nationalistic and subservient feelings. In 1933, though Schuldes and Kleber had schemed to dislodge long-time *Vorstand* member Richard Wolff, Schröder was elected as his replacement by an apparently free vote. Through more political intervention, this time engineered by Furtwängler, the result was eventually overturned, and within nine months, Schröder was sent packing along with fourteen other former Sinfonie-Orchester members. Schröder's short-lived democratic mandate by the Berlin Philharmonic community, however, set an important precedent.

It is difficult to ascertain the precise number of Nazi Party members in the Berlin Philharmonic between 1933 and 1945. This is partly due to incomplete records, partly attributable to the fact that not all Party-member musicians joined in 1933, rather most enlisting at various times throughout the twelve year period, and partly too by several musicians dying or retiring over those years, rendering their affiliations difficult to trace. With documented certainty, fifteen musicians are known to have belonged to the Party between 1933 and 1945; circumstantial evidence points to another three; a 1946 orchestra musicians' list in the Berlin Philharmonic Archive bearing 'Pg' pencil markings and dates of entry, brings the combined total to over twenty. [84]

Two points of comparison are helpful in this regard: first, unlike many cultural institutions of the Soviet Union, or even in the DDR, joining the Party, though most certainly encouraged, was not required of members of the orchestra. All musicians were forced to join the *Reichsmusikkammer*, itself a highly politicised government organ, as a form of union membership, but Berlin Philharmonic musicians did not need to enlist with the NSDAP to benefit from the regime's largesse. Second, at its most inflated tally, 20% of the Berlin Philharmonic were Nazi Party members. By way of comparison, in 1943 the Vienna Philharmonic had a 42% Nazi Party membership rate.[85] The point, however, is not statistical. The number of Party members is less significant than how those individuals behaved within the orchestra community, and the way the community responded to their presence.

Reasons for joining the Party were various. Naturally, there were those who signed up out of strong ideological conviction. Kleber; Schuldes; violists Reinhard Wolf and Werner Buchholz, a holdover from the Berliner Sinfonie-Orchester; and another violinist, Hans Woywoth, who reportedly came to rehearsal in full SA uniform[86], qualified as believers. These men represented a Nazi 'hard line' which did intimidate colleagues. Other musicians were less extrovert in their political commitment. In the cases of Alfred Graupner, a violinist satirically nicknamed *der Bluthund* ("the Bloodhound")[87], violinist Hans Gieseler, contrabass player Arno Burkhardt, and trombonist Friedrich Quante, as examples, their motives for obtaining NSDAP membership remained obscure; it might have been professional favour, a matter of family security, force, or personal convenience. These men may have been relatively benign Party members rather than true Nazis, but exonerating them does injustice to the vast majority of Berlin Philharmonic musicians who resisted the pressures and temptations of joining the Party.

During the Third Reich, to those with careerist ambitions, enlisting in the NSDAP could at times provide an advantage. Whether his motive, or simply a by-product, this certainly worked for Concertmaster Erich Röhn, who, alone and in his *Philharmonischen-Quartett* with Carl Höfer, Werner Buchholz and Wolfram Kleber, received a great deal of extra-orchestra patronage from the Nazi elite.[88] If Röhn himself was a Party member cannot be documented. Through his close connection to Buchholz and Kleber, two of the orchestra's most active Nazi supporters, however, he must be counted among those "circumstantially" associated with the Party.

Orchestra *Vorstand* Lorenz Höber, meanwhile, was definitively never a member of the Nazi Party. This, in all likelihood, was the reason the government, in 1934, refused him an official place in the reformed Philharmonic *Geschäftsführung*.[89] Still, Höber occupied an esteemed position among the orchestra community, respected for his integrity and organisational skills. With such a profile and vast experience, he was essentially irreplaceable. The thwarting of the attempted Schröder coup, however, did not dull the ambitions of the orchestra's Nazi contingent. In 1937 a Philharmonic memo was circulated, announcing a number of reforms to the orchestra's internal structure. Among the measures, it was announced: "The former *Vorstand* Höber is no longer the deputy of the orchestra but representative of the management; the orchestra's official representative is now the newly elected *Vertrauensrat*; the *Vertrauensrat* chooses a speaker who also oversees operations for the *Arbeitsfront* and the orchestra's representative to the *Reichsmusikkammer*."[90] How exactly these reforms were orchestrated or imposed is not clear. While Höber could not be removed, however, with these changes, he was subjugated to the Ministry-appointed *Geschäftsführung*, while a new executive committee overtook the orchestra's representative role.

The newly formed *Vertrauensrat*, which constituted the official face of the orchestra, consisted of six members: the two *Geschäftsführer* (von Benda and Stegmann at the time), and four elected orchestra representatives. The first four elected members of the *Vertrauensrat* were *Der Bluthund* Alfred Graupner, Wolfram Kleber, Anton Schuldes, and Alois Ederer.[91] Ederer, also a confirmed NSDAP member, perished in a British bombing raid on Berlin in 1943. With the constitution of the *Vertrauensrat* committee, Kleber was named *Betriebszellenobmann* to the *Deutschen Arbeitsfront*, and later appointed by the *Reichsmusikkammer Orchesterobmann*.[92] Another circumstantial Party member suspect and former Berliner Sinfonie-Orchester player, harpist Fritz Hartmann, became the orchestra liaison to the *Reichsmusikkammer*.[93] Höber, as orchestra *Vorstand*, was left with principal responsibility for areas of internal orchestra duties, "including scheduling of rehearsals and auditions, monitoring sick leave, and maintaining employment statistics."[94]

By 1938, therefore, though Höber continued his organisational duties, the Berlin Philharmonic was represented both inside and out, entirely or at least in overwhelming majority, by Nazis. While the *Geschäftsführer* positions were political appointments from outside, the *Vertrauensrat* was a supposedly elected body. How is it a small group of Nazis were democratically chosen to represent a community, the vast majority of which, at least individually, was apparently not of that ideological persuasion? Though documentation is scant, there are several possible answers. First, manipulation: if balloting remained secret, results might have been falsified; if voting became an open procedure, intimidation might have played a role. A second hypothesis would be that only Nazis stood for election. This might have been the case because the nomination process was rigged, or because other orchestra members protested the subjugation of their *Vorstand* Höber, or because a prior general consensus within the community established that men with Party credentials best represented the interests of the orchestra. A third possibility, is that the elections were indeed free and fair and the orchestra democratically chose Nazis to represent them. The truth is probably some combination of these factors.

The Third Reich was a society erected on fear; implicit and explicit intimidation was intrinsic to German daily life, and the musicians of the Berlin Philharmonic were not immune. They were, however, also a politically savvy collective. Since the 1920s, the Berlin Philharmonic had been constantly dealing from a position of weakness, being forced to retreat by multiple governments, patrons, even by Furtwängler, into a series of compromising concessions on its institutional independence, organisational structure, internal make-up, artistic autonomy, and budgetary control. Facing the political ambitions of their Nazi colleagues in the 1930s, it was again a matter of prudence for Philharmonic members to consent to their objectives. Whether this meant not daring stand against them, or not daring to vote against them, a moral compulsion or duress compunction, the reciprocal, however, was also true: in submitting to the Nazis' agenda, orchestra members saw an advantage. The *Gemeinschaftsgeist*, was less some spiritual or mystical bond between inspired musicians, than a very practical aspect of the orchestra's unique body politic. From its inception, the orchestra culture functioned by way of pragmatic consensus-building; in a sense the very definition of a democratic community—even in surrendering to extremists. The prime value remained the superlative performance of music within a creative and secure environment. As with the fate of their Jewish former colleagues, in 1937-38, Berlin Philharmonic musicians had little choice, yet still a choice. In demonstrating deference, and accepting a Nazi face, the Philharmonic could hope to curry favour with the ruling class and to retain the privileges the regime afforded it, preserving its remaining *Gemeinschaftsgeist* values in the process.

Such pragmatic calculations, however, did not lessen the degree of political pressure, or blunt the independent initiative of the orchestra. From 1938 on, perhaps as an indication of the *Vertrauensrat* exercising its new influence, the Berlin Philharmonic received a number of memos and visitors from the NSDAP. On October 26, 1938, orchestra members were called to a meeting where "At the behest of the NSDAP regional authority for Greater-Berlin, the Party's local Education Director Pg. Scheller, will be speaking to us about questions of the national-socialist world view. ATTENDANCE IS MANDATORY!"(emphasis original)[95] On January 16, 1940, at another *Betriebsversammlung*, the Philharmonic received a call from the State spokesman of the NSDAP, *Oberregierungsrat* Prinz Schaumburg-Lippe."[96] As on all such occasions, "The meeting is duty [underlined original], and non-attendance will be permitted only with the express consent of the management."[97] A collective agreement, introduced in 1938, and charting the orchestra members' rights and duties, as well as penalties and fines for disobedience,[98] ensured compliance with attending these meetings.

From 1938 on, *Pflicht* (duty), upon pain of *Ordnungsstrafen* (disciplinary fines), became a prominent part of orchestra correspondence vocabulary.[99] In December, 1938, the musicians of the Berlin Philharmonic, including the concertmasters and solo-cellists (also those off-duty) were compelled to participate in an "oath to the Führer and Reichs-Chancellor."[100] This oath ritual was expected of all public service employees, including the members of the Berlin Philharmonic. It immediately followed, however, a ceremony bestowing a *Treudienst-Ehrenzeichen* (badge of honour for loyal service) upon selected musicians of the orchestra.[101] Apparently, while *Parteigenossen* were automatically awarded the honour, non-NSDAP members had to be in long-standing service of the orchestra to qualify.[102]

In 1939, the RMVP passed a new work and service contract for the Berlin Philharmonic. While the charter first promulgated in 1934 was relatively mild, with no overtly political content, the later revision changed tenor completely:

> 1. The primary responsibility of a member of every orchestra is to help guarantee the lofty artistic purpose its operation to the best of his abilities. The accomplishment

of this purpose requires a conception of duty in the sense of the National Socialist world view from both the leadership and its subordinates. This demands the commitment of an individual member to constant maintenance and improvement of his artistic proficiency and positive integration in the community of the orchestra, the faithful obedience to their musical leaders and other superiors [...] and from the group a strong sense of responsibility with respect to the unwritten laws of German culture."[103]

The following paragraphs included passages such as "No member has the right to criticise the conductor's performance or requirements in any way," and "All execssively loud pre-concert warming up is forbidden," [104] mixed with standard banal clauses carried over from the previous *Dienstordnung* contract.

Surprisingly, though accepted by the Propaganda Ministry, this thoroughly authoritarian document was not drafted by the government, but rather by the orchestra itself. "Following the *Reichsarbeitsblatt* (Reich work regulations) VI, No.14, 1938 [...]" wrote Karl Stegmann to the RMVP submitting the new *Dienstordnung* for approval, "we have written up a special official regulation for our members considering the special issues of service in our orchestra."[105] Stegmann was not in a position to compose and impose such an important document unilaterally. Rather, the "we" in his submission almost certainly refers to the body responsible for orchestra representation—the six-man, Nazi-dominated *Vertrauensrat*, of which Stegmann was a member. The cell which had been bristling for "Sauberkeit und Ordnung" with Fritz Schröder in 1933,[106] eventually got its way.

Despite this barrage of ideological indoctrination, however, the members of the Berlin Philharmonic were not content simply to serve. In 1936, a movement was instigated by cellist Ernst Fuhr and violinist Georg Diburtz, neither Nazi affiliated, to establish a 'Kameradschaft der Berliner Philharmoniker.' The idea was to create an orchestra musicians' association independent of the GmbH which would sponsor collegial activities among the musicians; offer, following the *Wiener Philharmoniker's* 'Goldenen Ring', honours and hospitality to guest artists and dignitaries; and allow the orchestra musicians to control financial assets, such as gifts, donations, bequests, and collected *Hilfsfonds*, outside the realm of the GmbH.[107]

The *Kameradschaft* initiative, particularly the latter aim to independently accrue and administer assets, presented a firm challenge to the hegemony of the RMVP. It was a dangerous game, the fact of which the orchestra veterans Fuhr and Diburtz were surely cognisant. Even before the plan reached the Ministry, Benda and Stegmann expressed stern reservations.[108] To tame the impression of an orchestra 'breakaway' faction, Diburtz and Fuhr proposed a foundation (Stiftung) model for the *Kameradschaft*, which would work "in a supporting role" to the GmbH.[109] Further, they revised their original thoughts on the *Kameradschaft's* autonomy, suggesting "The choice of the *Kameradschaft's* chairman requires the permission of the management of the GmbH," and further, that "the orchestra's General Manager should belong to the executive [of the *Kameradschaft*] and will be active in the latter's budget and accounting."[110] Risky as it was, Diburtz and Fuhr appeared to have strong backing from the musicians who were anxious for the restoration of some degree of self-determination.

At this stage, the Ministry caught wind of the *Kameradschaft* initiative. With the assurances proposed in the revised plans, the official response offered a permission to proceed. While the asset issue would have to be scrutinised carefully, the RMVP bureaucrats saw a careful crafting of the *Kameradschaft* statues as opportunity to "exercise a sufficient influence over the assocation."[111]

The delicacy and intricacy of drafting an acceptable legal framework for the *Kameradschaft* took many months. In October, 1937, a projected charter of the *Kameradschaft der Berliner Philharmoniker* was circulated, wherein the RMVP insisted on stricter terms.[112] The RMVP bureaucrats were relying heavily on their administration appointees to ensure the *Kameradschaft* did not grow into a threat. To underscore the point, in the official constitution of the *Kameradschaft*, it was spelled out: "The appointment of the association's chairman will be made by the RMVP with the recommendation of the association's members." Further, the Ministry reserved veto over the naming of Honorary Members, permission for clause changes to the *Kameradschaft* constitution, and the right to determine the dispatching of the *Kameradschaft's* holdings, should the entity be dissolved.[113]

Finally, in the spring of 1938, it appeared the long struggle to establish the *Kameradschaft* had resolved. The first meeting was set for June 15th, at the Alte Fischerhütte restaurant on the Schlachtensee.[114] Invitations went out, officially celebrating "[that] despite major difficulties and thanks to the support of the Minister [Goebbels], the *der Kameradschaft der Berliner Philharmoniker* can finally be established."[115] An meeting agenda was drawn up. The *Vertrauensrat* approved the candidacy of cellist Friedrich (Fritz) Mayer as first *Kameraschaftsführer*.[116] The precise role Goebbels played in facilitating the *Kameradschaft's* formation is not clear, but it appeared the Ministry's fears, through legal stringency and perhaps superior interjection, had been allayed.

As a precaution vis a vis Mayer's appointment, Hans von Benda requested the orchestra musicians "To provide possible objections or concerns about the appointment of Herr Mayer as the leader of the *Kameradschaft*."[117] This curious phrase could be understood as a charitable final check on orchestra opinion, or a more pernicious solicitation for denunciation. Mayer however, had already passed the Nazi-dominated *Vertrauensrat* and so appeared a unanimous choice. But, on June 11th, four days before the planned *Kameradschaft* inauguration, an urgent internal RMVP message fell like a bombshell: "Mayer, the musician designated as leader of the *Kameradschaft*, is not a Party member!"[118]

The Ministry scrutinised every aspect of the *Kameradschaft* plan, and fashioned its tenets politically air-tight.[119] It reasons unimaginable the bureaucrats would have overlooked a background review of Herr Fritz Mayer. And yet, they were shocked to discover Party records showed no "proof of political standing" for Mayer at all.[120] Whether some bureaucrat fell asleep at the switch on Mayer's nomination, or the *Geschäftsführer* deliberately withheld information, hoping to slip Mayer through in the last moment, or if Mayer was denounced by a colleague, the first *Kameradschaft* meeting in June was promptly scuttled, postponed indefinitely until completion of a proper investigation into Fritz Mayer.

On June 24th an NSDAP report was filed with the Berlin Philharmonic, giving Mayer a clean political record.[121] Though not a Nazi, Mayer was permitted to accede to his post.[122] A new inaugural *Kameradschaft* meeting was set for the 15th of September. The memo to members of the orchestra announcing the September founding assembly stated:

> Now that the extraordinarily great difficulties that stood in the way of founding the *Kameradschaft* have been overcome we hereby express our wish that the lofty goals of the *Kameradschaft* should contribute to strengthening and deepening the solidarity within our orchestra and to remind us that we, each in his place, are all in the service of the National Socialist people's community, ready at any time to serve the Führer, Volk, and Reich.[123]

The message was clear. Several high-ranking representatives of the RMVP were in attendance that night to watch Fritz Mayer officially installed as *Kameradschaftsführer*.[124] When Mayer resigned five years later, he was succeeded by Karl Rammelt.

In spite of a range of precautions, not all was consistently passive and harmonious within the Berlin Philharmonic. On occasion, tempers flared. In 1942, during a recording session, several principal wind players protested for better honoraria.[125] The group presented the radical proposal of the "The production of gramophone recording within the orchestra's *Kameradschaft*." This degree of independence was precisely what the Ministry had feared sanctioning the *Kameradschaft* might lead, though it is not clear the extent of the support for the initiative among the orchestra as a whole. Von Westerman's response was quick and harsh: "The fact that a small group in the orchestra does not have the appropriate appreciation for the nature of the community and collaboration of the orchestra [...] is more than regrettable."[126] The subservient status of the *Kameradschaft* was upheld.

The communal culture of the Berlin Philharmonic was at once unified and fractious. The orchestra represented a group of men bound together by common musical cause, a sense of tradition, and a unique organisational culture. Aside from issues of race and politics, however, there were other areas in which social cleavages divided the Philharmonic community. To begin, though revered as the paragon of German music, not every member of the Berlin Philharmonic was in fact German. *Konzertmeister* Johannes Bastiaan's father was Dutch; Solo-cellist Tibor de Macula was Hungarian; cellist Hans Bottermund was part Danish; percussionist Geronimos Avgerinos was born to Greek parents in Alexandria, Egypt; flautist Karl Achatz had Swedish ancestors, trumpeter Paul Spörri was Swiss.

In addition, the orchestra comprised men from a number of generations. Though retirement age was nominally sixty-five in 1943, there were still musicians in the orchestra who had played under Brahms. The youngest members of the orchestra, meanwhile, did not even have memories of hyperinflation in the 1920s. The tensions between men like Lorenz Höber, Richard Wolff and Otto Müller and their politically-ambitious Nazi colleagues to a great extent reflected this generational divide. Kleber, Schuldes, Fritz Schröder and most other NSDAP member orchestra colleagues were born around the turn of the Twentieth Century, and reflected the Nazi movement as a politics of relative youth. They had not known the Philharmonic in its days of self-governing success. This contrasted with the experience of men such as Otto Müller who was first elected orchestra *Vorstand* in 1895, and represented the Berlin Philharmonic for the next thirty-five years, or even Lorenz Höber, who joined the orchestra in 1916, when Anton Schuldes was still a teenager. The two sides, reflecting very different experiences and visions of the orchestra, did not often overtly clash, but, as common with significant generation gaps, a level of mistrust was always present.

In 1939, a memo was circulated to orchestra members, further underlining the generational and ideological divide:

> As you all know, our Third Reich places extraordinary value on each individual's athletic training, health permitting [...] to our chagrin, we are forced to note that a large number of the younger members of our orchestra, although they are physically capable, refrain from athletic activity [...] We reiterate it is the obligation of each member to maintain the health of himself, his family, and thereby his entire people through regular athletic engagement.[127]

When Erich Hartmann joined the Philharmonic in 1943 after

having been wounded as a soldier on the Eastern Front, he reported being astonished how the Nazi colleagues in the orchestra befriended and admired him, though he himself was no Pg.[128] On account of his service to the "Fatherland", for them, he was a hero. Men such as Georg Diburtz, Karl Leuschner, Lorenz's brother Wilhelm Höber and Richard Wolff, meanwhile, were veterans of the Great War, and though no less courteous to their new arrival, were less prone to trumpeting empty rhetoric. Through initiatives such as the *Kameradschaft* and use of the *Hilfsfonds* (see Chapter 3), the senior generation made consistent attempts to achieve some extent of autonomy for the orchestra, and interpose a degree of distance between the Berlin Philharmonic and the Nazi Reich.

Despite the at times more subtle, occasionally highly explicit political pressures from Party and government on the musicians of the Berlin Philharmonic, the fact remains the orchestra had much to be thankful for. In 1933, the Nazi Reich saved the Berlin Philharmonic from bankruptcy.[129] Though the musicians lost the bulk of their right to self-determination in the process, as a *Reichsorchester*, they were not only financially secured (see Chapter 3), but celebrated, elevated, praised and esteemed like no time before. After the struggle of past times, the Berlin Philharmonic was made to feel important, recognised in equal measure to its own sense of worth. All the regime asked was for the orchestra to remain obedient, and play music gloriously. And this they did, under Furtwängler and others, for larger and more diverse audiences than ever (see Chapter 4), touring more intensively (see Chapter 7), cheered, paraded, and embraced. As Werner Buchholz wrote on behalf of his colleagues:

> [...] with its artistic discipline and his nationally conditioned tone quality and specific way of making music [...] one sees the Berlin Philharmonic performing its lofty purpose for the Fatherland as an emissary of German art and for the German Volk.[130]

In exchange for these services the musicians of the Berlin Philharmonic were treated to numerous instances of Nazi benevolence. Goebbels' brilliance was in realising the institution was composed of individuals, and established a system of favours and largesse binding each musician to the institution, which, in turn, was bound to his agenda.

Hitler's *Treudienst-Ehrenzeichen* (badge of honour for loyal service)[131] was but one ornamental example of this twisted system of mutual exploitation. The orchestra members were made to feel like family: at the funeral of hornist Gustav Kern, one of the original *Philharmonikers*, Goebbels sent his representative, Dr. Drewes, to present a wreath.[132] The musicians were invited to mingle in Goebbels' personal circle.[133] In December, 1938, the RMVP extended to the orchestra a rare treat, "to offer another, special little Christmas joy on the first Christmas in the new Greater Germany (following the annexation of Austria)"—a Christmas bonus.[134] Seven months later, on the same memo announcing the orchestra's program for the *Reichsparteitag* in Nürnberg, the orchestra received another small raise, a result of a readjustment in salary deductions.[135]

The Reich stepped in to ensure the Philharmonic could always attract the best German musicians into its ranks, and keep them there. When Hornist Martin Ziller received a lucrative offer to cross over to the *Berliner Staatsoper* (State Opera), Stegmann appealed to the RMVP to sweeten Ziller's Philharmonic conditions,[136] which they did.[137] The RMVP also provided an infrastructure of convenience for the Berlin Philharmonic. In 1939, the orchestra engaged a new principal horn player. Adolf Handke came to Berlin from Bremen, and required accommodation in the capital. On Handke's behalf, Stegmann wrote to the RMVP: "We have learned of a number of apartments in newly contstructed buildings have been appropriated for civil servants of the Reich,"[138] recommending the musician be considered for a place. Being in the public service certainly had its advantages.

Of a more sinister nature, the RMVP also maintained an infrastructure for the procurement of musical instruments. Hitler himself apparently bemoaned that "The musicians of the Vienna Philharmonic apparently have many old violins, whereas the Berliners have only very few."[139] The RMVP operations, overseen by *Generalintendant* Dr. Drewes, contracted agents to find and acquire instruments for the Reich collection.[140] Some instruments were bought, others, presumably, stolen.[141] The fruits of these pillaging operations were made available, often to choose from a wide selection, to musicians of the Berlin Philharmonic. This process was also effectuated through agents, obscuring both the instruments' origins and the identity of the loaning benefactor. Only after the musicians chose their instruments, would the Reich's magnanimousness be revealed in the press.

In this manner Erich Röhn received a Peter Guarnerius of 1750,[142] Solo-Cellist Tibor de Machula an instrument ""from the school of Guarnerius"[143] and *Konzertmeister* Johannes Bastiaan a valuable Guadagnini.[144] The RMVP was also pro-active in sealing the musicians' fidelity, in 1942 seeking a genuine Stradivari for new *Philharmoniker* concertmaster, Gerhard Taschner[145] For such valuable gifts, signing a brief contract pledging "May this instrument resound to the honour of German art" or "May this instrument bring the music of German masters to your fellow countrymen with pride and honour"[146] would have seemed small chore.

Small chore it was, and indeed, and but a token compared to the regime's greatest gift to the Berlin Philharmonic: *Unabkömmlich* or *Uk-Stellung* (indispensable) status. Under this status, Berlin Philharmonic musicians were deemed indispensable, and exempted from military service. The first steps were taken within weeks of the outbreak of war: "From this point on, a deferment from military service status will be obtainable at conscription offices for all persons continuing in service [with the orchestra]."[147] It may have been Furtwängler who first suggested it, but in his capacity as the orchestra's patron, it was Goebbels who realised the necessity in excusing the Philharmonic from compulsory military obligations to facilitate his objectives. To maintain the group's musical coherence and promote its collective mobility, service training and, when the time came, combat duty, were waived. The Philharmonic was bestowed not only *Uk-Stellung*, but *doppelte Uk-Stellung* (doubled deferment).[148] In this respect, the Berlin Philharmonic was in exclusive company reserved within RMVP jurisdiction only for certain essential branches of the *Reichs-Rundfunk-Gesellschaft* (The Reich's broadcasting authority).[149]

The principle of *Uk-Stellung* for the orchestra was much simpler to declare than the practice of its administration. In Nazi Germany, all men were required to register with local *Wehr-bezirkskommandos* (WBK) or *meldeamts*. The WBKs were the responsible offices for military drafting and/or authorising exemptions. WBK officers' decisions could be entirely discretionary. It was apparently known among orchestra musicians that certain WBKs "had a special understanding for artistic concerns," and colleagues were encouraged to live in those Berlin neighbourhoods.[150] Occasionally, a musician would be called to service, despite Goebbels' official decree. This required an official appeal from the Berlin Philharmonic administration to the RMVP to overrule the WBK summons.[151]

Though Philharmonic musicians were in theory guaranteed immunity from military duty, the reality of war made official assurance of their privilege acute. Status as a 'Philharmoniker' was not enough. "It is completely and urgently necessary," continued Karl Stegmann after the pronouncement, "for each individual who receives any summons to the Wehrmacht, inform this office immediately and without exception."[152]

It took an extended time for each musician's case to be examined, and their *Uk*-status approved or denial appealed as necessary, before the orchestra in its entirety was exonerated from the threat of Wehrmacht draft. As the war dragged on, *Uk-Stellung* acquired an exponential significance, but also bred more red-tape. *Wehrpäße* (Military ID cards) were required of the musicians,[153] the younger of whom grew increasingly conspicuous in Berlin as their contemporaries were called to the front. All musicians were required to notify their WBKs of any changes in address, and to obtain rubber stamp authorisation from their *Wehrmeldeamt* to leave Germany for concert travel.[154] In July 1942, members of the Philharmonic were issued personal letters from Goebbels for use in attestation to the WBKs. These official documents, "at the behest of our ministry"[155], served at the same time to remind the musicians of the extreme privilege such favour accorded:

> You have been given *U.k.-Stellung* by me, by authority of the Führer, for the realisation of important propagandistic and cultural assignments. In your official capacity, your way of life, and your general behaviour, you are expected to manifest a commensurate awareness of personal and

business obligations. You must be continually mindful
of the hardships and dangers that the soldiers on the
battle field must endure, which even the hardest and
most dutiful labour in the homeland cannot equal. Dr.
Goebbels.[156]

The members of the Berlin Philharmonic knew precisely how
fortunate they were. At the start of the war, musicians were informed
about the need for economy: "The war necessitates sacrifices from
every individual. As an organisation of the Reich, we must submit to these measures of austerity."[157] As the war encroached, three
Berlin Philharmonic musicians perished in bombing raids;[158] Paul
Spörri chose to return to the relative safety of his native Switzerland
in 1943; Curt Christkautz, a violist, was schlepped away at intermission of a Philharmonie concert by a vicious mob of the Nazi
Volkssturm, but the orchestra remained active and coherent. Indeed,
the Philharmonic increasingly received treatment like an elite
military division. In May 1944, orchestra musicians were issued
Bunkerausweise (Bunker ID cards), undersigned by the RMVP. The
directives read: "Because the entirety of the Berlin Philharmonic
Orchestra must always be ready for action in its high, artistic special
missions, at home and abroad, members of the orchestra and their
families may take refuge in the nearest bunker during air raids."[159]

In September 1944, with the declaration of 'total war' (*totalen
Kriegseinsatzes*) all German State theatres and orchestras were disbanded, save the Bayreuth Festival, a symbolic case, since it only
operated one season of the year, and the Berlin Philharmonic.[160]
Again, Furtwängler may have approached Goebbels to save 'his' orchestra, but at this stage, the vetting paradigm of political interest
had shifted dramatically. Germany was losing its epic war. Under
such dire circumstances, the request, even ultimatum of one celebrity
artist would have been vastly insufficient to sway a savvy politician.
To Goebbels, the Berlin Philharmonic represented one of his most
powerful tools of propaganda. The worse things got for Germany,
the more Goebbels needed the Philharmonic. "The Herr Minister",
Furtwängler wrote to von Westerman in Summer, 1944, "would like
to see the Berlin music life continue in its principal activities as it
was before."[161] And so, the orchestra played on.

The most striking example of the Berlin Philharmonic as conservatory of Germany's musical future was the case of Gerhard Taschner. Taschner was a violin prodigy born in the Sudetenland. After studying with famous pedagogues in Budapest and later in America, Taschner became concertmaster of the orchestra in Brünn in 1938, at the age of seventeen.[162] Though a relative musical backwater, in 1941, the noted conductor Hermann Abendroth gave a concert in Brünn, where he heard the remarkable young virtuoso. In 1941, the war was peaking, and German men were being called into service by the thousands. Abendroth was concerned Taschner would be among them, and feared the loss of such an extraordinary German musical talent. He spoke to Furtwängler, who arranged for Taschner an audition in Berlin. The audition was successful, and at the age of nineteen, Gerhard Taschner became a concertmaster of the Berlin Philharmonic. The bureaucratic process in securing Taschner's *Uk-Stellung* was pedantic,[163] the procedure required both tact and dilligence—qualities not necessarily part of the musician's natural comportment—and called upon all the high offices at Furtwängler's and the Philharmonic's disposal to secure.[164] But Taschner's investiture in the orchestra may well have saved his life. He left the Philharmonic immediately after war's end in 1945 to pursue a solo career.

The Berlin Philharmonic was more than a bastion of privilege though. During the war, the orchestra also mobilised in its own ways to protect its resources. In September 1939, within a week of the invasion of Poland, the orchestra announced its participation in *Luftschutzdienst* (air raid watch duty) for the Philharmonie.[165] In this episode, all the strands of Philharmonic internal politics and culture came together. Though air raid surveillance was a professional activity overseen by police prefects, "It is the honorable duty of our orchestra to take part in the air raid defence network," read the circular announcing the initiative. "We acknowledge that all the gentlemen of the orchestra assume this duty joyfully and willingly, as it also protects their own place of activity."[166] The plan called for a nightly rotation of musicians to sleep in the Philharmonie and integrate with police-run fire fighting and emergency rescue operations. Orchestra *Obmann* and NSDAP loyalist Wolfram Kleber assumed responsibility for the orchestra's *Luftschutzdienst* duty assignments, in coordination with Lorenz Höber to ensure "...that it can be brought into harmony with the musicians' orchestra duties." Though an entirely superfluous initiative, the initial memo firmly iterates: "We hereby declare that participation in the air raid network is, for all members of the orchestra, D U T Y !!"

Even as Kleber was nominally chief of *Luftschutzdienst* activities, and likely one of the architects behind its institution, it fell to Höber, the competent organiser, to oversee harmonisation of the musicians' Pflicht with the professional police services.[167] Every night, up to four Philharmonic musicians were required to bring their own pillows to sleep in the Philharmonie. In the event of an alarm, the musicians were to don a *Luftschutzuniform*, including steel helmet and gas-mask, and rendezvous with the on-duty police supervisor for further instructions. "The gentlemen will not be deployed on evenings when they have rehearsal on the following day,"[168] it was assured.

Despite the bravado of a call to honour and duty, it seems not all members of the Berlin Philharmonic were enthusiastic about the imposition of Philharmonie defence activities which were, essentially, the orchestra's voluntary commitment. When the orchestra went on tour, or during summer holidays, no one was left behind to attend to air raid duty anyhow. In October 1942, a package of reforms was introduced, in conjunction with the *Kameradschaft der Berliner Philharmoniker*, to combat apathy and instil a degree of professionalism and consistency in *Luftschutzdienst* obligations. In 1942, air raids were becoming more threatening Berlin occurrences. A full night's sleep was getting rare. No longer a safe, altruistic exercise in institutional servitude, *Luftschutzdienst* was incurring increasing pressure on musicians untrained in fire fighting or rescue operations, and who by day were working long hours too. The plan called for the *Kameradschaft* to collect RM 2 per month from each musician "for the duration of the war."[169] This money would be used to hire Luftschutz cover during orchestra tours, holidays, and weeks when the orchestra had particularly heavy programmes. Even though "in principle every individual is obligated to serve in the air raid defence network,"[170] it was acknowledged some did not participate. The scheme however, rewarded those who stuck to their duties, offering RM 2 per person per service from the government (paid via the GmbH), plus an additional RM 1 per person per service rebate from the *Kameradschaft*. An orchestra player who fulfilled one *Luftschutzdienst* night every fortnight would make back their *Kameradschaft* dues and in fact turn a RM 4 profit; those who performed no service would forfeit RM 2 a month.[171]

On the night of January 29, 1944, the Philharmonie was bombed by British warplanes. Erich Hartmann was on *Luftschutzdienst* that night, and described the trauma this event represented for the orchestra.[172] The increasing difficulties they had experienced travelling in foreign countries were now coming home. In addition to the priceless concert hall itself, the orchestra lost many valuable instruments, the bulk of its institutional archive, and a portion of its music library that night. Though concerts were rescheduled for other Berlin venues, such as the Staatsoper and the Titania-Palast in short order, arrangements were quietly made to transport all secondary instruments and unnecessary archival materials out of the city. In cooperation with an assortment of Reich ministries and private organisations, the Philharmonic's treasury was stashed in a bunker in Plassenburg bei Coburg, Bavaria.[173] After the war, this hideaway was found pillaged and looted.

As the war drew to its conclusion matters got indelibly worse. The Philharmonic's glass bubble fortification suffered a major rupture with the destruction of the Philharmonie. In addition to instruments and music, the orchestra's families were moved out of the city. As Gerhard von Westerman wrote to Furtwängler who had already early in 1945 taken refuge in Switzerland:

> Every day brings new surprises and it is obvious that the majority of the orchestra will be drafted into the *Volkssturm* in spite of all safeguards. I am happy for every day that the our protection continues [...] What the next weeks bring us is unavoidable. Currently we are suffering cutbacks to public transport. S-Bahn, U-Bahn and trams will soon be accessible only to those with special passes. Our regulated occupation is jeapordised by sentry duties in the *Volkssturm*, entrenchment assignements, etc. But, as I said, for the moment everything is still all right. Please remain assured that we will do everything to remain together as an orchestra. But will that be possible?[174]

Erich Hartmann recalls the mood of panic among his colleagues at the dawn of 1945.[175] Unlike him, the vast majority of the Philharmonic's musicians had never experienced war, and even those veterans of the Great War knew this was something very different. The government propaganda about the advancing Red Army terrified many men. In the war's final months, with the realisation of the inevitable end, three members of the Berlin Philharmonic committed suicide. Bassoon player Heinrich Lieberum, violinist Bernhard Alt, and bassist Alfred Krüger independently took their own lives out of fear for what would become of them and their families if they fell into the clutches of the Soviets.[176] Krüger was a Party member, his two colleagues had no political affiliations; in reality, all three had little, or at least no more to fear than anyone else. Lieberum, Alt and Krüger were simply victims, and as such tragic exemplifications, of the awesome power of Nazi propaganda—a terrifying machinery in which they themselves had played a part.

Furtwängler had fled Germany via Vienna and Prague in January 1945 for Switzerland, where he remained until the end of the war.[177] Yet even with the departure of their guardian, the musicians of the Berlin Philharmonic retained their extraordinary Uk-status. In March 1945, with the Red Army crushing Berlin's suburbs, the RMVP again over-ruled an attempt to draft orchestra members into military action, declaring "that the members of the of the Berlin Philharmonic Orchestra shall remain free of any military deployment or, to be precise, *Volkssturm* service so as to continue the exercise of their orchestral duties, which are important to the war effort."[178] On the 14th of April, 1945, three weeks before the Third Reich's ultimate capitulation, as *Volkssturm* thugs were shoving rifles into the hands of children in futile defence of the capital, the *Reichsverteigigungskommissar für den Reichsverteidigungsbezirk Berlin* (Reich's defence kommisariat for the defence of the Berlin) issued a further iteration of the Philharmonic's *doppelte Uk-Stellung* status: "[The musicians of the Berlin Philharmonic Orchestra] will be needed in their workplaces in the interest of the defence of the Reich, even in the event of imminent enemy threat."[179] The music must go on.

It seems von Westerman spoke to *Rüstungsminister* and music lover, Albert Speer, to secure this final act of favour for the orchestra. Goebbels, it is rumoured, was prepared to sacrifice the Berlin Philharmonic during the war's last weeks. The significance, however, was neither Speer's deference towards great art, nor the fact it was he, not Goebbels who apparently spared the Philharmonic musicians from decimation. Why did the members of the Berlin Philharmonic deserve clemency while innocents all around them were being sent out to slaughter? Playing Beethoven better than anyone else could be no justification. At a certain point, Speer's thoughts must have turned to after, and the importance of preserving something of that remarkable musical culture for the future.

Here, it is notable to reflect upon the remarkable success of Goebbels' strategy. The Berlin Philharmonic was always famous, but during the Third Reich, under Goebbels' custodianship, it became indispensable; the orchestra went from a proud local band to German cultural ambassador to the world. It became unbearable for Speer to think of a future Germany without this jewel of his country's cultural heritage. In this respect, therefore, despite some terrible losses, Goebbels did in fact save the Berlin Philharmonic.

Chapter 3

Finances and Balances

> With its strong dedication to the arts, the Third Reich immediately recognised that our orchestra and its hitherto existing activities in cultural propaganda would constitute an effective and valuable instrument of the Reich and, consequently, in 1934 it took the orchestra into its care and brought its financial troubles to an end with the acquisition of all its shares and a promise of subsidies to balance missing capital.[1]

THE BERLIN PHILHARMONIC'S FINANCIAL STRUGGLES in the late 1920s and early '30s are often cited as the key to understanding its subdued 'take-over' by Goebbels and the Nazi Reich. The truth is somewhat more complex. The orchestra's superlative quality alone could not guarantee its survival, but indeed might rather be seen as one of its damning flaws: the Philharmonic had been running an untenable business model for decades, and longed for public subsidy for years prior to 1933. Only with a share of fortuitous and significantly, opportunistic reciprocity could the institution's future be ensured. The Berlin Philharmonic's pact with the regime was resultant of the orchestra's dire financial situation from the mid-1920s onward, combined with a certain hubris on the part of the orchestra-collective, balanced by Goebbels' vision of cultural propaganda. This dance played itself out in a wild pattern of benefit and regulation.

Keeping the Philharmonic solvent had always been a delicate matter. Operating as an independent, non-State organisation, the orchestra's revenue sources were limited, while its overall expenditures, including salaries, pensions, supplemental services, insurance, and touring costs expanded exponentially. The hyperinflation that hit Germany after the First World War overwhelmed the orchestra's record of keeping costs in line with revenues. Within six months, between December 1922 and June 1923, musicians' monthly wages, indexed to inflation, rose from 50 000 Marks per month to over 2 000 000 Marks.[2] In November, 1923, a single concert program cost 200 billion Marks.[3] The introduction of the Rentemark in December 1923, chopping figures by about 10 000%, restored some sense of proportion to gages and prices, but the fragile balance of the Berlin Philharmonic's finances had been thoroughly smashed. By 1926, the Philharmonic was running an accumulated budget deficit of at least 90 000 RM.[4]

The orchestra's largest single expense category was wages. In this respect, the orchestra was competing at disadvantage against its state-supported cousins. State orchestras, such as opera orchestras, had larger budgets from which to offer salaries, pensions and benefits. The Berlin Philharmonic, meanwhile, had to rely overwhelmingly on touring and concert box-office returns to generate revenue. Problematically, Philharmonic musicians demanded remuneration comparable to their colleagues in other orchestras, not scaled to orchestra revenues.[5] The argument was based on the Philharmonic's superior musical quality, and the necessity of attracting and maintaining high-calibre players. The result, however, was a significant and ever-widening budgetary deficit.

Furthermore, the Berlin Philharmonic resisted downsizing its membership. Comprising shareholding *Aktiv-Miglieder* (active members) and a rotation of contracted *Saison-Mitglieder* (seasonal members), at roughly one hundred musicians, the orchestra was larger than most of its symphonic peers, though smaller than state opera orchestras. Philharmonic subscribers, it was argued, were accustomed to big repertoire performed in full *Besetzung* (instrumentation), and Furtwängler would accept nothing less. *Aktiv-Mitglieder* were on average 20% better paid than their seasonal colleagues. Despite the crippling effects of hyperinflation, and the exponential financial burden, in 1924, the orchestra expanded from 54 to 58 *Aktive-Mitglieder*, and five years later, to 66.[6]

To offset its escalating financial obligations, the Berlin Philharmonic toured. The orchestra relied heavily on income from foreign touring. In the 1920s, performances at Scheveningen and London represented a financial boon. Though travel, transportation, and accommodation expenses were high, as late as 1930-31, the Berlin Philharmonic still turned an annual RM 160 000 profit on its international appearances.[7] The Philharmonic's argument then, as *Vertreter seines Vaterlands* ("representatives of the Fatherland"), framing their touring activities *den Kulturellen Interessen des Deutschen Reiches zu dienen* ("to serve the cultural interests of the German Reich")[8], was entirely specious. Much as touring might have represented an aspect of national pride or musical prestige, the orchestra's extensive performance schedule outside Berlin was essential to its financial needs—to the orchestra's very survival. That such appearances also bore political currency was entirely coincidental.

By the mid-1920s, revenues from touring and Berlin ticket sales were insufficient. Patrons groups and individual donors, contributed some financial help, but not nearly enough to meet operating costs.[9] To cover the revenue-to-expenditure gap, the Berlin Philharmonic sought government subsidies. Though the earliest forms were small contributions of encouragement from the City of Berlin, over time intermittent requests for *Beihilfe* (governmental aid) grew to a matter of dependency. In order to continue touring, operating at its enlarged size, with wages comparable to their colleagues in the Staatsoper, the Philharmonic required a steady flow of public funding. The amounts requested corresponded directly to projected annual budgetary shortfalls.

From RM 90 000 in 1926 to May 1929, the Berlin Philharmonic's projected deficit totalled RM 400 000, by December the figure had escalated to RM 480 000. This figure was far in excess of what any one level of government could shoulder. The *Arbeitsgemeinschaft* of that year represented at once a partnership between levels of government pooling the resources necessary for covering the orchestra's substantial shortfall, while at the same time proposed entering into the GmbH's legal structure in an attempt to control orchestra expenses. RM 480 000 was set as an absolute cap for public investment, and the orchestra was instructed to operate within these constraints.[10] Though the plan eventually crumbled, the Philharmonic's financial needs did not abate, and through the 1929-30 season, the

City of Berlin and the German Reich poured almost exactly the same foreseen amounts formalised in the *Arbeitsgemeinschaft* plan into the orchestra on an ad hoc basis simply to keep the institution afloat.[11]

While municipal funding remained steady from 1929 through 1933, political wrangling besieged the State government. In 1930 the Reich subsidy dropped from almost RM 120 000 to just RM 8 000.[12] This slowly climbed back to RM 65 000 in 1932. Though a far cry from the orchestra's actual needs, this figure still represented just over 20% of the *Reichministerium des Innern's* (Reich's Ministry of the Interior) entire budget for scientific and artistic purposes.[13] With this dramatic decline in state subsidy, the Berlin Philharmonic began posting significant debts.

In 1931, from an overall budget of a little over RM 1 350 000, the Philharmonic posted an accumulated debt of RM 56 445,90, leading accountants to express concern that "the Philharmonic Orchestra is suffering particularly from the current, extraordinarily disadvantageous economic situation, and an improvement of these conditions cannot be expected in the forseeable future. [14] Through that season, the orchestra slashed musicians' wages by 6%, then a further 12%.[15] Simultaneously, political discussions were underway to finalise the Philharmonic-Sinfonie-Orchester fusion. In 1932, the Philharmonic's earned revenues covered less than 40% of orchestra expenses.[16] Even the possibility of stable funding could not guarantee a balanced budget.

In 1932-33, Philharmonic expenses totalled over RM 1 000 000, marginally less than the previous year due to a reduced touring schedule. Despite the City of Berlin exceeding its allotted budget by over RM 90 000,[17] the orchestra continued racking up debts. In 1931-32, the Berlin Philharmonic posted accumulated annual debts, in excess of short-term deficits, totalling RM 83 000, in 1932-33, RM 143 000, in 1933-34, RM 167 000.[18] Furtwängler, the Philharmonie, Wolff and Sachs concert agency, music rental companies, instrument transportation companies, insurance companies, tax collectors, 45 orchestra pensioners, and the 105 active orchestra musicians themselves, were all owed large sums.[19] A later audit remarked that "Based on the accumulated debts and deficits from the fiscal year 1930-30, the managing directors should have [...] already filed for bankruptcy or or initiated legal dissolution proceedings ."[20] This desperate situation did not change with the Nazis coming to power in 1933.

By spring of that year, the orchestra was posting monthly shortfalls of RM 40 000 to RM 50 000.[21] The orchestra's subsidy needs rose another 20%. Under intense pressure from creditors, in May, the Berlin Philharmonic standing "unmittelbar vor dem Bankerott", begged the RMVP for RM 30 000 "within three days." [22] In response, the Ministry offered RM 15 000 and a request for access to the orchestra's accounting books.[23] Two months later, the orchestra again wrote to the RMVP, requesting a *Beihilfe* of RM 70 000 "as it is urgently necessary to settle all outstanding debts for the purposes of orderly management."[24] Thus began the gradual financial coupling of the Berlin Philharmonic with the RMVP.

Though the plan of integrating the Reich, by way of the RMVP, into the GmbH emerged already in May 1933,[25] it was by no means apparent at that time, that the RMVP would shoulder the orchestra's entire financial burden. For one, the RMVP did not as yet have its own budget;[26] secondly, negotiations continued for many months with the *Reichsrundfunkgesellschaft* (Reich's Broadcasting Authority) and the *Preussische Finanzministerium* (Prussian Ministry of Finance) seeking additional partners, suggesting a coalition approach to subsidising the Philharmonic was still the principal agenda;[27] thirdly, though the City of Berlin was keen to divest itself of responsibility for the Philharmonic, its financial infusions remained essential to the orchestra until the declaration of the *Reichsorchester* in October, 1933.[28] Up to that time, the hectic patchwork system of financial management brought on by arduous economic times, political instability, and the orchestra's obstinacy towards measures of austerity, unremittingly applied.

Ultimately, however, to fulfil the orchestra's needs while conforming to Goebbels' and the Reich's Machiavellian interests, only the exclusive arrangement of a *Reichsorchester* would suffice. This seems to have become clear to both sides over the summer of 1933. Through the following months, the financial, legal, and political means were mobilised to realise this conversion.

In 1932, in conjunction with the Berliner Sinfonie-Orchester merger, the *Berliner Philharmonische Orchester GmbH* recapitalised from RM 48 000 to a base capital value of RM 66 000. This figure expanded the share base from 66 to 105 shares at RM 600 each, distributed one for each member of the enlarged orchestra formation, plus a RM 3 000 share held by the City of Berlin.[29] On January 15th, 1934, the German Reich, represented by the RMVP, bought out 90 musician shareholders for the full value of their shares. This was reported to the *Reichsfinanzministerium* in February, 1934.[30] In December, 1934, the outstanding fifteen shares owned by the dismissed former Sinfonie-Orchester musicians, along with the City of Berlin's orchestra holdings, were transferred to the proprietorship of the Reich.[31]

With these transactions, Goebbels and the Nazi Reich acquired the Berlin Philharmonic Orchestra GmbH as legal property. The musicians became public servants, and the GmbH, though formally retained, was reformed as a so-called 'Ein Mann' GmbH. The Reich owned the Philharmonic, and could use it for its purposes. In exchange, the Reich would provide a steady flow of cash to finance the orchestra's—and by extension the Reich's own—activities.

In 1934, Furtwängler wrote a blistering response to the report of the government-appointed *Reichssparkommissar*, who was contracted to review the Philharmonic's books and organisation, and make suggestions for reform. Irritated with bureaucrats making ignorant recommendations for savings and cutbacks in his domain, Furtwängler asserted that "from an economic point of view, an orchestra, just like an opera house, is and will remain a subsidised undertaking."[32] He insisted that though the orchestra had once enjoyed financial self-sufficiency, "yet such a state of independent profitability cannot be considered or hoped for as a foundation for the future."[33] These statements, though fact, were not necessarily obvious in the case of an organisation formed out of active rebellion against a system of patronage, which had long and vehemently clung to its autonomy, even unto its own fiscal detriment. The plea here, however, was not just for subsidy in general, but a statement that for the orchestra to perform at its best, it could not be expected to function under fiscal constraints.

This was a concession the Reich was, at least in theory, prepared to make. In contrast to the *Arbeitsgemeinschaft* principle of cost control, the RMVP's agenda in assuming a controlling interest in the Berlin Philharmonic in 1933-34 was rather an expansion of the orchestra's activities. The Berlin Philharmonic was only of use as an asset when its visibility, mobility, accessibility and quality could be maximised. Its independent revenue sources exhausted, such a plan required an actual increase in the orchestra's subsidy level to facilitate increased concertising and travel. With the Philharmonic's integration into the RMVP as an asset of the Reich, the orchestra represented a sort of Ministry satellite or sub-department. The orchestra's financial needs could be fully underwritten by the government because the Philharmonic was, in essence, a component of it, with Goebbels personally overseeing the taps. In this way, Furtwängler's intention, and the orchestra's appetite could be indulged. Subsidising the Berlin Philharmonic was less a matter of granting money to a third party, than simply transferring funds between pockets of the Reich.

In 1933-34, with the ad hoc assistance of the Reich Interior and Propaganda ministries supplementing the City's substantial contributions, the Berlin Philharmonic's income through subsidy totalled RM 469 000.[34] When the Reich took sole control in 1934-35, the subsidy increased to RM 517 463,66.[35] To wrest this amount from the *Reichsfinanzministerium* required some finesse and the employ of political leverage:

> As the Herr *Reichsfinanzminister* will have surely recognised, our company is receiving substantial subsidies from the Reich's financial resources enabling its first rate concert events, which are of paramount importance for Germany's cultural life.[36]

Initially, the financing system was extremely inefficient. Karl Stegmann, *Kaufmännische Geschäftsführer* of the Philharmonic, would, on an ongoing basis, submit funding requests to the RMVP calculated upon immediate needs and short-term projected expenses. Subsidy funds were not allocated to specific budgetary areas, but rather served as a majority supplement (the orchestra's regular earned revenue—touring aside—rarely accounted for over one quarter of its financial needs) servicing everything from salaries to office supplies to concert posters and programmes. Monthly requests ranged from RM 5 000 to RM 50 000.[37] These invoices would then be forwarded to the *Reichsfinanzministerium* for approval and/or modification.[38]

The advantage of this system was its responsiveness to the orchestra's evolving financial needs. In January 1935, for instance, after Furtwängler's resignation, the Philharmonic was obliged to repay hundreds of cancelled subscriptions. This expense was simply factored into the monthly statements, and the *Reichsfinanzministerium* authorised an additional RM 30 000.[39] The same applied to the RM 5 700 pay-off to the former Sinfonie-Orchester musicians.[40] By this quick-fix infusion method, the orchestra closed 1934-35 with an officially—if artificially—balanced budget.[41] The fact was, however, the Berlin Philharmonic was effectively a subsidiary of the RMVP, and the RMVP relied on appropriations from the *Reichfinanzministerium*. Orchestra financing, therefore, was an internal government matter, and as such, the orchestra's books would always be skewed in favour of political, as opposed to economic considerations.

Though flexible, the early, improvised funding process generated innumerable accounting headaches. While increasing expenditures thanks to its new-found source of credit, the Philharmonic still maintained debts from before the GmbH buy-out in excess of RM 40 000 as late as 1938-39.[42] Meanwhile, the *Reichfinanzministerium* was being used as an unlimited charge account. But in 1934, managing an orchestra was a new experience for all involved, from Karl Stegmann to the *Finanzministerium* bureaucrats to Goebbels himself; it took time to establish budgetary parameters and a stable funding formula.

To alleviate the bureaucratic hassle of an endless stream of invoices, beginning in 1937, the Philharmonic *Geschäftsführung* (management) presented annual budget projections upon which the *Finanzministerium* could calculate a yearly subsidies.[43] These projections, however, were invariably underestimated. In 1939-40, for example, the Philharmonic's earned revenue exceeded expectations by almost 140%.[44] This despite the outbreak of the war. The unexpectedly large return, however, though did not indicate the orchestra turned a profit, or lead to a reduction in subsidy. Even as earned revenues increased by up to 65% from 1935 to 1940, expenditures over the same period grew at an almost identical rate.[45] Indeed, in 1940, despite overshooting projections, the Philharmonic still posted a RM 33 353 loss, a gap filled de facto out of reserve funds.[46] In 1942, a decent year for earned revenues, the orchestra relied on Reich money for over 60% of its funding,[47] of a budget which, by 1943, had climbed to over RM 2 000 000 per year.[48]

The engine of the Berlin Philharmonic's earned revenue was subscription concerts, of which Furtwängler's ten *Philharmonische Konzerte* were the prestigious focal point. The Alte Philharmonie had a capacity of approximately 2000 seats. The subscription rate for the *Philharmonische Konzerte* series was about 50%.[49] Subscriptions in 1936-37, for example, cost RM 20 to RM 75 for the ten main concerts. Due to high demand, subscriptions were also available for preview or so-called *Voraufführungen* at RM 20 to RM 45. Individual concert tickets cost from RM 2 to RM 9 and RM 2 to RM 5 respectively.[50] For the period between 1934 and 1944, those twenty concerts alone represented almost 40% of the Philharmonic's Berlin earnings.[51] Beginning in 1938, "due to the extraordinary demand for concerts conducted by Furtwängler," a number of *Philharmonischen Konzerte* were also repeated in an additional, non-subscription concert,[52] generating a windfall in the order of RM 10 000 per concert.[53]

In addition to the *Philharmonische Konzerte*, the Philharmonic offered subscription series for choral concerts in conjunction with the Bruno Kittel Chor, and continued the tradition of four-to-five concert package under the directorship of other distinguished conductors.[54] Non-subscription *Sonder-konzerte* of various incarnations bore a similar admission cost to these series, ranging from RM 1 to RM 6 per concert. These concerts were never repeated, nor were the popular Sunday and Tuesday night concerts, which up to 40 times per year could open the Philharmonie to patrons for less than RM 1.[55]

Though politically attractive, the discounted popular concerts accounted for major losses. Not always sold out, they offered an average return of less than RM 1 000 per concert.[56] In 1937, Hans von Benda divided the *Sontags-und Dienstags Konzerte* "because on the one hand they no longer met with great public interest and on the other hand no longer matched the artistic reputation of the orchestra,"[57] into a subscription series of Symphonic Concerts which generated more profitable returns,[58] and a series of *klassischen Abenden*, ("classical evenings," predominantly involving Beethoven's works).[59] The result renewed public interest in the short term, but by the later half of 1938-39, the cheaper seats for the new series were, according to Stegmann, sold only 1/4 to 1/3 of the seats.[60]

With the security of the Reich's treasury on their side, however, the purpose of such reforms was rather to minimise the Philharmonic's losses than necessarily to post gains. As reported Stegmann, "For some years now, the affordable concerts have attracted increasingly smaller audiences. [...] It thus seems practical for our orchestra to put on only first-rate concerts in the future." [61] Under the reshaped concert programme, the new *ersten Rang* (first rate) concert series could bring in up to RM 3 500 per concert even if not sold out.[62] These reforms accounted for a rise in Philharmonic concert revenues while the actual number of Berlin performances declined.[63]

Meanwhile, the orchestra's civic duties formerly offered in the inexpensive *Sontags- und Dienstags-Konzerte*, were channelled through an annual number of fixed-price student and outdoor Schlüterhof concerts, and a series of low-priced concerts in cooperation with the *Deutsche Arbeitsfront NS-Gemeinschaft "Kraft durch Freude"* (German Worker's Front NS-organization, "Strength through joy").[64] The alliance with this latter organisation, proved especially beneficial.

In 1938, *"Kraft durch Freude"* swallowed the municipal *Berliner Konzertgemeinde*, thereby integrating a local music patrons' association capable "of filling concert halls through their countless opportunities for advertising." [65] The plan of supplementing Philharmonic concert attendance with blocks of discounted tickets apparently did not work, as *"Kraft durch Freude"* undercut the Philharmonic with even cheaper concerts of its own presentation.[66] *"Kraft durch Freude"* developed its own Philharmonic series, for which, even as late as 1943, the organisation was able to offer up to RM 5 000 per concert.[67] The relationship between the Berlin Philharmonic and *"Kraft durch Freude"*, another instance of the regime's machinery shifting assets between itself, is discussed in more detail in Chapter 4.

In 1939, the Berlin Philharmonic made RM 457 000 from 83 concerts in Berlin. In addition, the orchestra earned another RM 45 000 from radio and broadcast performances. [68] Broadcasts and recordings represented the other localised means of generating revenue. Already in 1934-35, the State Radio contributed RM 72 000 to the Philharmonic coffers.[69] Over the following years, four to six radio performances per year, plus recordings and further broadcasts consistently netted the Philharmonic a minimum RM 35 000, peaking at RM 70 000 with the beginning of the war in 1940, and again at RM 75 000 as the end drew near in 1944.[70] As well as reflecting the use of radio and the profile of the orchestra under the political climate, this pattern also responded to von Westerman's appointment as *künstlerische Leiter* (artistic director) of the Berlin Philharmonic, and his advantageous connections with the *Reichsrundfunksender* (Reich's broadcast authorities).

Long before the advent of the Third Reich, touring was an important part of the Berlin Philharmonic's musical profile, and of its financial underpinning. In 1929, the orchestra's income from touring equalled that of its Berlin box-office.[71] Though the costs incurred from travel were far greater, the orchestra's subscription series in Hamburg and Leipzig, as well as its international appearances, were substantially more lucrative than its local Berlin activities. The traditional Hamburg concerts, for example, raised roughly RM 10 000 per concert, four to seven times a year.[72] In the benchmark year 1940, ten Philharmonic concerts within Germany returned over RM 111 000. The 30 foreign appearances of the Berlin Philharmonic the same year averaged RM 5 700 per concert.[73] By comparison, in 1934-35, the orchestra gave only eight performances abroad, four in Hamburg, another fifteen across Germany.[74]

The enormous advantage of the arrangement post-1934, however, was the alleviation of travel costs from the Philharmonic books. Whereas in earlier times, a large part of their tour earnings was swallowed by travel costs such transportation and accommodation, tours during the Third Reich were undersigned, "Im Auftrage des Reichsministeriums für Volksaufklärung und Propaganda." (By order of the Reich's Minstry for the People's Enlightenment and Propaganda).[75] In this way, while the orchestra distributed salaries and per diems, the State assumed responsibility for transportation and accommodation.

Over the ten years from 1935 to 1945, the Philharmonic's budgetary parameters remained fairly steady, consistently running deficits of 50% to 60%, while the gross numbers increased. Over the five year span from 1935 to 1940, Reich subsidies doubled.[76] During the same period, the orchestra's actual number of performances, both at home and abroad, remained consistent between 178 and 191.[77] The difference in expenditures derived partly from an escalation in Reich-ordained concert tours (requiring per diems etc.), partly out of the State's generosity, and partly due to the increasing of the Philharmonic's own appetite in proportion to the means available. As long as Goebbels and the RMVP could maintain political leverage with the *Reichfinanzministerium* to secure financing, the Philharmonic could continue expanding its budget with impunity. The trick was keeping the accountants of the *Finanzministerium* bureaucrats at bay.

As an integrated appendage of the State, the Philharmonic was subject to both the regime's benevolence and intra-governmental bureaucratic scorn. In the former case, Goebbels scored a coup on behalf of his acquisition in 1936 of a special *Reisekostenzuschuss*. This, he proudly proclaimed, "The Führer and Reich's Chancellor has henceforth decreed [...] and that the artistic achievements and the outstanding relevance of my orchestra in cultural politics justifies the distinction of its members."[78] The *Reisekostenzulage* (travel cost bonus), intended as a windfall additional to regular travel costs, represented a sort of RM 170 000 bonus for the orchestra's service as "the most demanding of all of the orchestras of Germany, with regards not only to time, but also physical and mental aspects." [79] The *Reisekostenzuschuss* was the first example of targeted funding in the Reich-Philharmonic relationship, paid out on the basis of touring days per individual musician to a maximum of 56 travel days and RM 170 000, in recognition of the elevated expenses incurred through Reich-sanctioned travel.

Immediately this plan presented problems. Did touring mean all concerts outside Berlin or only foreign tours? Answer: all concerts. [80] Should State or Party-sponsored appearances be calculated within the 56 days? No.[81] Was the bonus an equal payment to all musicians or progressively assessed? Progressive, incumbent upon years of service. [82] While an open check-book financing policy was problematic, targeted funding opened the door for even more equivocation. The accountants and bureaucrats had a field day.

Already annoyed by political meddling and its irresponsible business practices, the *Reichfinanzministerium* and the *Reichsrechnungshof* scrutinised every item of Philharmonic expenditure intently. When the orchestra negotiated *Instrumenten-, Saiten-, Rohr- und Blattgelder* supplements from the RMVP, the *Rechnungshof* (Court of Auditors) imposed an explicit RM 5,50 per month cap on all musicians, irrespective of instrument group.[83] When the Philharmonic submitted a receipt for RM 340,15 for shoe repairs following a tour to England, the Finance Ministry authorised only RM 144,15 in reimbursement.[84] In 1939, the *Reichsminister der Finanzen* turned down the revised *Philharmonic Dienstordnung*, for, among other reasons that "I cannot agree to the increase of the previous clothing allowance of RM 10,63 to RM 12."[85] The question of *Tagesgelder* for both domestic and international tours, in addition to the *Reisekostenzuschuss*, became a topic of endless pedantry.

In addition to its sources of earned revenue, the Berlin Philharmonic GmbH also owned or controlled a small number of assets. The status of these assets required several years to fully clarify after the absorption of the orchestra into the Reich, but demonstrated both the limits of the orchestra musicians' collective initiative, and the frontier of State prerogative.

One such case, the *Hilfsfonds des Berliner Philharmonischen Orchesters*, concerned the estate left by the late director of the Philharmonie, Herr Peter S. Landecker. On the occasion of its 50th anniversary, Landecker gifted the orchestra RM 25 000. Landecker, a long time friend and patron of the Philharmonic, in his final testament, he donated another large sum in cash and *Hypothek* to the Berlin Philharmonic to remain "for any reason at any time" in possession of the orchestra's musicians.[86]

Both donations were accepted by the GmbH as *eine juristische Person* (a legal entity) on behalf of the orchestra musicians, and invested in two funds: a *Hilfsfond* (aid fund) and the *Pensions- oder*

Witwen- und Waisenkasse (retirement, bereavement, or orphan's fund). While the *Pensionskasse*, established in 1893, had been heavily invested in stocks and was predominantly wiped out by the hyperinflation of the 1920s, the *Hilfsfond*, with a total value of RM 100 000 in 1933,[87] was prudently converted from equities to property in 1931.[88] The two interest-bearing resources were operated by the *Geschäftsführung* as funds to be drawn upon for assistance, either in the form of non-State pension support for retired Philharmonic musicians and their families, or contingency resources for the orchestra community or individual members in need.[89] In the frantic period between 1930 and 1933, Höber used his prerogative on a number of occasions to loan the Philharmonic substantial amounts from the Hilfsfonds account to keep the orchestra solvent.[90] As of 1934 also, at least seven musicians held personal loans from the Hilfsfonds for reasons ranging from moving costs to mortgage financing to medical expenses.[91] In 1937, long after the financial needs of the orchestra and its musicians had been stabilised, Lorenz Höber and Otto Müller, on account of the explicit nature of Landecker's donation and its private use to the orchestra members, wrote to the RMVP requesting "the aid fund be allocated to the musicians for a special fund."[92]

This was not the first time Landecker's estate had been brought to the Reich's attention. In 1934, the Berlin Philharmonic GmbH was assessed a bill for RM 13 500 in inheritance tax on the *Hilfsfond* investment.[93] Since the *Hilfsfond* proprietor, the GmbH, had been purchased by the Reich, Stegmann claimed the orchestra had no money to pay the bill. Rather, he suggested "We must demand this contribution from the Reich separately so that we can return it to the Reich in the form of estate tax."[94] Stegmann found himself in the precarious position of essentially telling the *Reichfinanzministerium* to pay itself. The situation was more complicated, however, because a 1935 audit confirmed that the the Hilfsfonds assets "der Gesellschaft nicht zusteht" ("do not legally belong to the company").[95]

Alerted to the presence of Philharmonic property outside its shares, the RMVP shortly thereafter imposed an amendment clause to the *Berliner Philharmonisches Orchester GmbH Gesellschaftsvertrag* stipulating all outstanding GmbH assets beyond its base capital, "is allocated to the German Reich for the purpose of charitable care and preservation of the arts. The RMVP will decide the appropriation of these funds in accordance with the Reich's Minister of Finance."[96] Höber and Müller's 1937 letter was a challenge to this assumption all properties formerly belonging to the GmbH were now properties of the Reich.

The *Kameradschaft* episode had shown the risks involved for the RMVP in allowing the orchestra members control over independent means. The bureaucrats were wary. No immediate response to Höber and Müller's request was forthcoming until in May 1939, the RMVP announced, on recommendation of the *Reichsrechnungshof*, the dissolution of the Hilfsfonds.[97] This was met with dismay by members of the orchestra. Immediate action was delayed while Stegmann attempted to negotiate with all interested parties. In 1940, Stegmann reached a compromise agreement wherein the RMVP lost no authority, a number of outstanding financial issues were resolved, the musicians had several material concerns addressed, and the Hilfsfond property was liquidated, eliminating further debate.

Under the plan, the Hilfsfonds account would be spent repaying a long outstanding debt to the City of Berlin and re-equilibrating the *Gesellschaftskapital* which had been incomplete since the 1934 GmbH share purchase. The musicians were concerned about disparities between themselves and their colleagues in other orchestras.[98] They therefore proposed dispensing of the remaining Hilfsfonds on accumulating a substantial musical instrument collection, developing a proper institutional archive, establishing a recording collection— "this would be of exceptional significance, as it would offer the opportunity to compare and control, respectively, the performances of the orchestra in individual years and decades"[99]—and, in view of the Berlin Philharmonic's 60th anniversary in 1942, commissioning a "notable author of musical matters to write the history of our orchestra from the beginning of its exsistence in an easily understood form, in order to demonstrate to the general public the development and present importance of the orchestra in the context of Germany's musical life."[100]

It was clearly beyond hope that the Ministry would allow the musicians of the Berlin Philharmonic to administrate over their own budget as they once had done. Yet with these steps to expand and diversify the orchestra's institutional base, the musicians did exercise a degree of independent initiative essential to their communal spirit, and proved, as in the case of the *Kameradschaft*, that though a dictatorship, the State could be negotiated with.

The same conditions applied to the issue of pensions for orchestra musicians. Before 1934, Philharmonic players were self-employed shareholders in a private cooperative. As such, they had no recourse to institutional pensions beyond what the orchestra could provide. The *Pensionskasse* was established to supplement musicians after retirement, raising funds through dues, private donations and a annual benefit concert. Pensions were paid out of dividends from the *Pensionskasse* capital invested in the stock market. For a time, this worked well, but with the decimation of the German economy following the First World War, the value of the *Pensionskasse* too plummeted. In 1924, the fund had a value of just RM 5 873—hardly enough to generate sustenance for the Philharmonic's accumulating number of retirees.[101] These men and their families suffered like tens of thousands of other unemployed musicians during the German Depression of the 1920s.

When the Reich purchased the shares of the *Berliner Philharmonisches Orchester GmbH*, it was unresolved who would be responsible for the orchestra's pension liabilities. "Pension liability is not included in the company's balance sheet" recognised the auditors in 1935.[102] Here again, the orchestra possessed assets not part of the GmbH, but owned and operated by it. The Reich bought the GmbH's assets as well as its liabilities, but could not practically or legally run a mutual fund. The musicians who had sold their shares became public servants, meanwhile, could be covered by protocols governing public service pensions, but these men had also over many years paid into a fund which was no longer under their control.

The solution was only pieced together over a number of years. New members of the orchestra, it was agreed, would be pensioned under general public service terms in conjunction with the *Reichsmusikkammer* via the Bavarian health insurance company. The 79 former GmbH shareholders meanwhile, were guaranteed by the Propaganda Ministry, a continuation of their previous autonomy and flexibility."[103] This meant maintaining the *Pensionskasse*, administered by the *Orchestervorstand*, as a mutual fund, supplemented by a small yearly State transfer subsidy. Practically, the Philharmonic's investments, buoyed by Germany's slowly rising economy, could offer musicians competitive pension rates in the RM 500 per month range, or roughly 60% of their average salaries. In 1938, administration of the *Pensionskasse* was transferred to the *Kammeradschaft*.

In truth, Herr Landecker's generous donations to the Philharmonic musicians in the early 1930s were not altogether magnanimous gestures. The Berlin Philharmonic never owned its own concert facility. Rather, rental of Landecker's Philharmonie was a major tax on the orchestra. In 1933, the Philharmonic paid RM 30 000 for use of his facility.[104] Indeed, concert hall rental overall formed an important element in orchestra expenditures.

In 1937, the Berlin Philharmonic signed an exclusive contract with the Philharmonie precluding use of the concert hall by any other symphony orchestra formation.[105] The contract called for an annual rental charge of RM 67 500. Though guaranteeing the Philharmonic a permanent home, this amount was inflated by approximately 35% over the actual rental fees as levied on a per performance basis.[106] At year's end between 1937 and 1940, the orchestra was required to shell out a supplemental sum, typically in excess of RM 20 000, to make up the difference.[107] When the contract came up for renewal, it was thought, particularly at Furtwängler's insistence, the Philharmonie monopoly worth the excess expenditure.[108] So long as there was no enforced index between costs and revenues, the matter of a few thousand Reichmarks did not seem to matter.

From 1935 onward, the Philharmonie line item was integrated into a general accounting category titled *Konzertbetriebskosten* (concert operating costs). Beyond hall rental, within this field, the Philharmonic also calculated ushers, staff, box office, and use of the Philharmonie's various other rooms. Small things, such as an additional dressing room, could run an additional RM 4 000 annually—roughly the equivalent of the orchestra stage manager's yearly income.[109] The annual budget for *Konzertbetriebskosten* rose by a factor of ten between 1935 and 1943.[110]

The Berlin Philharmonic's single largest expense was wages. These consisted of administration salaries, conductor and soloist honoraria, and orchestra musicians' salaries. In all areas, the *Reichfinanzministerium* and Reichrechnungshof repeatedly called for rollbacks, yet each column rose every year from 1935 on.

While standardisation was a feature of public service employment under the Third Reich, the Philharmonic operated just on the cusp of the Nazi bureaucracy. The musicians were civil servants, governed by a *Dienstordnung* and an RMVP-probated *Anstellungs- und Besoldungsordnung* (Employment and Salary Charter) *der Berliner Philharmonischen Orchester G.m.b.H.*[111] As such, the musicians had their own collective, if imposed, contractual relationship with the Reich. The orchestra's managers, however, though political appointments to the Philharmonic, were technically not subject to the orchestra's codes, but rather listed as 'directors in the ministries.'[112] From a certain bureaucratic angle, the Berlin Philharmonic was a department of the RMVP.

When Karl Stegmann became *kaufmännischen Geschäftsführer* of the Berlin Philharmonic in 1934, he was offered a monthly salary of RM 700.[113] In relative terms, this brutto amount roughly matched the wage of an orchestra concertmaster,[114] exceeded the average rank player by over 30%.[115] After completion of his one year probationary contract, Stegmann was renewed from October 1st, 1935 at a salary of RM 800 per month.[116] This was more than the head of any other *Reichspropaganda-amt.*[117] Nevertheless, in 1938, Stegmann petitioned the RMVP to switch public service employment categories, from the Compensation Class XIII (department heads in government ministries) to salary level 'A' for employees in the civil service,'[118] capturing a short cut to a significant raise in the process.

Unfortunately, this petition coincided with the renunciation of Stegmann's NSDAP membership following an accusation he had once belonged to a *Druidenloge*. Though Stegmann was rehabilitated through a *Gnadenakt des Führers* ("Act of Grace of the Führer")[119], this smear offered petty government officials an excuse to deny his claim: "I do not believe that Stegmann's position at the Philharmonic Orchestra is so difficult or demanding," wrote a bureaucrat in the same office where once Stegmann had been entrusted with the complete *Gleichschaltung* project of the Reich's premier musical ambassador. "Also the current moment does not appear especially appropriate with his Party membership having been narrowly rehabilitated."[120]

Stegmann, of course, did not agree. "I take notice," he wrote in defence, "that my occupation has become more comprehensive and responsible since I was hired. The financial revenue, which in 1934 was still around 1 million Marks, has risen to 1,5 million Marks this year; thus my responsibility for collecting and disbursing those funds has also grown by about 50%."[121] Responding to pettiness with like, he complained that Lorenz Höber, who had no official representative capacity outside the orchestra, received a higher salary, and that over the previous five years the *2. Geschäftsführer*'s salary has remained unchanged while the *Orchesterwart* (orchestra stage manager) "had received a noteworthy increase in salary in the meantime."[122] (In 1941, Franz Jastrau, the Philharmonic's *Orchesterwart* made RM 4 330[123]). The plea appeared to work. By 1943, Stegmann was receiving RM 1 000 per month[124], RM 500 less than Intendant von Westerman, but once again on par with the Philharmonic's concertmasters.[125]

Despite Stegmann's feeling of importance and responsibility, the distinction between first and second *Geschäftsführer* was marked from the outset. In his first and only contract with the Philharmonic in 1934, Rudolf von Schmidtseck received a monthly salary of RM 1 000, commended to RM 13 200 per year after the first six months.[126] It is not known what terms von Schmidtseck's successor, Hermann Stange, managed to negotiate, but Hans von Benda's 1938 salary totalled RM 1 100 per month, including supplemental allowance for a family of four children.[127] Von Westerman's conditions before taking the position of *1. Geschäftsführer* of the Berlin Philharmonic included a RM 1 200 monthly salary, plus a RM 300 per month expense allowance. Both stipulations were granted unconditionally. Von Westerman was the only administrator to have a contract directly with the orchestra, and as such, his RM 18 000 annual salary was the only administrative wage appearing on the Philharmonic books.[128]

This was true except for two years, 1940-42, when Friedrich Herzfeld found his way onto the Philharmonic payroll. Herzfeld was ostensibly hired by the Philharmonic to write the history of the orchestra proposed in the earlier Hilfsfonds dissolution discussion. A confirmed Nazi, his highly politicised 1941 biography of Furtwängler was never authorised by the conductor.[129] Nonetheless, he managed to get himself hired at RM 600 per month as orchestra program editor.[130] Under questioning from Reich auditors, Stegmann let it leak that Herzfeld was "in keiner Weise voll beschäftigt" (by no means completely busy).[131] In this instance, RMVP and Reich accountants were in full agreement, and the Philharmonic's resident historian was off the job by Spring, 1942.

At RM 12 000 to RM 18 000 annually, the salaries of the Philharmonic 1. and 2. *Geschäftsführer* were high compared to other ministry officials, and compared to the musicians they managed. At the same time, they paled in comparison to the amounts commanded by the orchestra's conductors and visiting soloists. In 1933-34, the Philharmonic paid conductors aside from Furtwängler RM 12 200 for Berlin concerts and another RM 22 150 for its leaders on tour. Divided by the number of concerts, this did not represent an exorbitant number. This is due to a number of factors. First, the cancellation of concerts by high-profile Jewish conductors such as Bruno Walter and Otto Klemperer reaped a savings for the orchestra. Second, income from most non-*Philharmonische Konzerte* in Berlin was insufficient to justify large honoraria for conductors or soloists. Furthermore, it could not be permissible either personally or from an optical point of view to offer a guest artist in excess of Furtwängler's per-concert fee.

In 1934, with the Philharmonic's reorganisation under his leadership, Furtwängler proposed a fee structure of RM 1 000 per appearance to a maximum of 22 contracted appearances per season.[132] "I am prepared, " he magnanimously declared, "to assume the organisational tasks associated with being the leader of the Philharmonic Orchestra and thereby of Berlin's entire concert scene, on a voluntary basis. I ask only to be paid for my artistic achievements according to my merit."[133] The financial arrangement was agreed and codified in Furtwängler's contract designating him *Dirigenten des Berliner Philharmonischen Orchesters* later that year.[134] Furtwängler also had the benefit of writing off travel and communications expenses to the Philharmonic.[135] In relative terms RM 1 000 per concert was a bargain. In 1929, Furtwängler had received RM 50 000 a year, plus a RM 15 000 *Aufwansentschädigung* (expense allowance).[136] In 1932-33, Furtwängler was on a RM 2 500 monthly stipend.[137] Meanwhile, in 1934-35, the Philharmonic could make as much as RM 10 000 on a Furtwängler-led *Philharmonische Konzert*.[138]

When Furtwängler resigned from the Philharmonic in December 1934, his contracts were dissolved by mutual consent. When he returned to conducting thereafter, the former terms no longer applied. From 1935 to 1938, the conductor's fee as a guest artist was RM 2 000 per concert.[139] In 1938, Furtwängler submitted a formal demand to double his fee again, to RM 4 000 per concert for upwards of twenty-five concerts per season.[140] Once again, the money was not the Philharmonic's, so they were amenable. Taking up the case, Stegmann argued:

> At that time he was very modest with his fees because the Berlin Philharmonic Orchestra was depending on its own means, and he worked to secure its very existence. Now that our financial foundation is secured, it appears only fair for to him to demand the appropriate payment for a conductor of his caliber.[141]

Stegmann compared Furtwängler to a film star "who also commands extraordinarily high fees." [142] Whatever the justification, from the orchestra's point of view, they had no choice. Even bureaucrats recognised that "Furtwängler's persona is so intimitely linked to the Philharmonic. In particular, the orchestra's financial revenues are almost entirely dependent on Furtwängler's conducting."[143] This, of course, was not entirely true. Furtwängler's concerts were the orchestra's most important source of earned revenue, but the Philharmonic's largest single source of income was the government.

RM 100 000 to RM 120 000 was the initial prediction for Furtwängler's yearly income from the Philharmonic after the raise.[144] In fact, the Philharmonic paid the conductor RM 171 350 in 1938, 210 000 in 1939, and 184 000 in 1940.[145] In 1940, alarmed auditors set a ceiling at 1939 levels[146]—the revenues from Fürtwängler's concerts were being almost completely consumed by the conductor's own fee demands. Film star or not, to keep in perspective, in 1940 a Berlin Philharmonic concertmaster was making roughly RM 1 000 per month,[147] and the orchestra *Geschäftsführung* a combined RM 40 000 per year. Meanwhile, Furtwängler could take home up to RM 20 000 per month.[148] In 1938, he even got the Berlin Philharmonic to pay his RM 4 000 fee for a Wiener Philharmoniker concert in Berlin.[149]

On one level, this could be seen as a simple matter of restitution, as Stegmann suggested, Furtwängler seeking compensation for his years of modest demands while the Philharmonic was struggling. It could otherwise be understood as a cynical taking advantage by Furtwängler of the orchestra's dependence upon him, exploiting the Philharmonic's weakness and fear of losing him. Finally, the financial ploy could be read as a further step in the dance of mutual exploitation between regime and conductor, using the Philharmonic as both financial vehicle and beautiful reward in system, crudely put, of bribery. Goebbels was happy to funnel Germany's greatest living conductor all the money he wanted through the Philharmonic in order to keep him cooperative; meanwhile, Furtwängler used his leverage with the Berlin Philharmonic as a bargaining tool to prove his strength and independence vis a vis the regime.

Soloists' fees also rose exponentially over the years, from a little over RM 20 000 in 1934[150] to RM 40 000 in 1937 to a height of RM 60 000 in 1940.[151] Pianists Gieseking and Kempff, as well as violinists like Georg Kuhlenkampff could command as much as RM 1 000 per concert,[152] as much as a Berlin Philharmonic concertmaster would make in one month.[153] Another highly-paid soloist was Edwin Fischer who could collect up to RM 1 500 per concert. Remarkably, in 1939, Furtwängler offered Fischer a rebate to perform the conductor's own piano concerto together with the Philharmonic, sharing the RM 4 000 honorarium 50/50 over a five concert German tour.[154] At a Philharmonic-produced Sonata Abend in 1940, Furtwängler played chamber music with Kuhlenkampff, from which both performers walked away with RM 1 400, and the orchestra nothing.[155]

By comparison to those of conductors or soloists, orchestra players' wages were a fraction the amounts, but multiplied over one hundred musicians, were no less contentious or competitive. Salaries were assessed monthly based upon a base wage commensurate to years service, then augmented with bonuses such as *Wohnungsgeld*, *Leistungszulage*, *Keidergeld*, *Kinderzulage*, and the *Reiseaufwand*.[156] Wages in 1942 ranged from about RM 600 for an unmarried musician of less than three years experience, up to over RM 1 000 for a concertmaster or principal cellist. Lorenz Höber also received a premium salary.[157] Though attempts had been made by Nazi agitators early on to index remuneration with political allegiance,[158] there was no correlation between salary and Party membership. Most musicians were tenured for life after passing their probation year.[159] The initial wage formulae were complicated, dating back to the time when musicians were also shareholders, paying themselves according to the financial means of their cooperative. The new *Dienstordnung* brought in by the Reich after the declaration of the *Reichsorchester* codified some salary terms, but still left room for quibble and negotiation.

Concertmasters, for example, were not subject to standardised contracts, rather holding private contracts with the GmbH. When Hugo Kolberg joined the Philharmonic in 1935, he was lured away from a good position in Frankfurt with a five year contract at RM 1 000 per month.[160] At the time, the other Philharmonic concertmaster Siegfried Borries, was only making RM 675 monthly. Borries appealed for a raise to RM 900, but received RM 800 in negotiations with Stegmann, acting both on behalf of the orchestra and the RMVP.[161] Meanwhile, 2. solo-cellist Hans Bottermund was making RM 821,90 while the younger 1. solo-cellist Arthur Troester received only RM 800. When he received an offer of a professorship in Hamburg, Troester used the opportunity to petition for a raise to RM 1 000 (all figures Brutto).[162] The moment Troster's raise came through, Tibor de Machula, the Philharmonic's other 1. solo-cellist, claimed to have an offer from America for a $1 250 a month position. He too was bumped up from RM 800 to RM 1 000 to keep him happy. Then Siegfried Borries returned with another request to be put on equal footing with his fellow section leaders—RM 1 000.[163] The third concertmaster, Erich Röhn, who was considerably younger, was stuck at RM 800 until Borries left the orchestra in 1940; thereafter he was promoted to RM 1 250, and in 1943, offered a structured five-year contract ranging up to RM 1 500[164] for a musician "who in recent years has worked his way up to become one of the leading violinists on Germany's musical scene."[165] Of this long-term scaled approach, it was stated, "a measure that is, in terms of cultural politics, easily justifiable for the Berlin Philharmonic Orchestra, given the expected strong demand for first-class concertmasters following the war."[166] The end of the war came, but long before Röhn reached the RM 1 500 monthly threshold.

As part of the broader practice of *Gleichschaltung* in areas of public expenditure, and in order to try to control such games of one-upmanship and discretionary pay-scales, discussions began in 1935 for a standardised regulation for conditions of payment in all major cultural orchestras.[167] In early spring 1936, the RMVP and *Reichsfinanzministerium* reached an agreement in principle in this regard in an attempt to regulate musicians' widely variable salaries.[168] The plan called for all German state-supported orchestras to be categorised into ranks by quality, and assessed a commensurate wage structure. Concertmasters and soloists were to be included in the formula too. Significantly, the ordering criteria was primarily a matter of quality. Though Nazism espoused such radical, pernicious ideological rhetoric, ultimately, quality, a facet of artistic integrity and accomplishment, as opposed to percentage of Nazi Party members, for example, or strategic geographical significance, was what counted in relation to the level of state support.

News of the plan reached the Berlin Philharmonic via *Aufsichtsrat* chairman Walter Funk, who assured the orchestra *Geschäftsführung* the Philharmonic would occupy the new *Tarifordnung*'s highest category. Meaningfully, this distinction, the Philharmonic would have to share with the Berlin Staatsoper-Orchester.[169] The ensuing episode of the *Tarifordnung für deutschen Kulturorchester* exemplifies the case of a bureaucratic problem being subsumed into the political sphere, and epitomises the inherent conflicts between bureaucratic order, institutional entitlement, ideological persuasion, and personal power fostered by the Nazi system.

With the stipulation of sharing supreme orchestra status, the Berlin Philharmonic *Geschäftsführung* immediately smelled a rat. The Staatsoper-*Orchester* stood under the patronage of Hermann Göring, Hitler's protégé, *Ministerpresident* of Prussia, the Prussian Minister of the Interior, and Goebbels' arch rival. This personal rivalry was fought on numerous battlefields, including the cultural plain. The new *Tarifordnung* presented an opportunity for Göring to put his orchestra on equal footing with Goebbels' *Reichsorchester*.

On behalf of their patron, and in defence of their orchestra's interest, von Benda and Stegmann launched a concerted campaign protesting the plan. Not only would an equalisation of the two orchestras in political terms jeopardise the Philharmonic's unique, elite status, the suggestion that both orchestras should "be on equal terms, materially speaking, in the future,"[170] in their opinion, completely misrepresented the operational realities of the two ensembles.

Their argument was based upon two pillars: the Philharmonic's taxing work load, and its extraordinary material necessities. Von Benda and Stegmann went into great depth elaborating the Philharmonic's arduous schedule of concertising and touring, comparing the thirty average monthly services per musician in the Berliner Staatsoper-Orchester to their orchestra's ca. fifty.[171] Not just in quantity, but on ideological merit, "from all sides—*Kraft durch Freude, NS Kultur-Gemeinde*, culturally political concerts etc.[...] demand far more engagement from each member as in any other orchestra."[172] Concerning material needs, the argument remained similar. Compared to an invisible opera orchestra, "the members are considered to be representatives of German artistry and must therefore be particularly well dressed both during concerts and otherwise."[173]

Von Benda and Stegmann knew well in making these points the matter was not simply bureaucratic or political, but personal. They also knew, however, that theirs was the objectively stronger hand, and after asserting their arguments, went for the crux: "The Philharmonic is and must remain the leading and best orchestra of not only Germany but of Europe." The *Geschäftsführung* therefore requested "a special, one-time performance bonus."[174] The request was couched in terms of compensation for additional Furtwängler concerts across Germany after a planned tour to France was cancelled, but the challenge was clear and deliberate: the Berlin Philharmonic's accomplishments should set it apart.

Goebbels assented to the *Leistungszulage* notion, and authorised it unilaterally.[175] This represented a humiliating incitement to Göring who required the Prussian Finance Ministry to match Goebbels' bonus for "the Staatskapelle of equal artistic value."[176] Göring's voice at the *Preussische Finanzministerium* returned fire, warning Goebbels his engineering of the new *Tarifordnung* to the singular advantage of his Philharmonic would leave him open to public charges of prejudice and conflict of interest.[177] Hot on the heels of this confrontation, Tietjen, Göring confidante and Intendant of the Staatsoper, suggested the whole matter should be rethought, and that rather than a codification of orchestra standards, a certain *bewegungsfreiheit* (freedom of movement) would be more useful.[178]

In October 1936, Goebbels scored an advantage try for his domain with the *Reisekostenzuschuss*, spelling out emphatically:

> ...that the performances of the Berlin Philharmonic Orchestra are obviously comparable with—and superior to—those of a mere opera orchestra. The musician of the Reich's leading, representative concert orchestra has a different task than a member of an orchestra designed for the opera, a task that embodies individual performance to a much greater extent.[179]

This cash injection for the Philharmonic trumped anything Göring's ministries could provide, but did not address the fundamental problem of streamlining the pay structure for State-supported orchestras. For Goebbels and the Philharmonic, the battle was won, but the war still raged.

To address the larger matter, a *Sondertreuhänder* was appointed to establish a sensible hierarchy of orchestras and interests.[180] This man was Hans Hinkel. After months of study, he recommended the creation of a *Sonderklasse* rank, to which the Philharmonic would, naturally, belong. The new *Tarifordnung für die deutschen Kulturorchester* (Tarifordnung for the German cultural orchestras) was instituted on May 15, 1938 consisting of five Vergütungsklassen and one *Sonderklasse*, placing the Berlin Philharmonic firmly at its summit.[181] The Staatsoper Berlin shared *Klasse I* with the orchestra of the Deutsche Oper Berlin, the Bayerische Staatsoper, Hamburger Staatsoper, the Dresdener Staatskapelle, and the Gewandhausorchester of Leipzig at a base wage structure roughly 10% below.[182] But while the Philharmonic's status was guaranteed, the issue remained whether the orchestra would eventually share the *Sonderklasse* pedestal.[183]

The decision was significant first purely as a matter of money. The new *Tarifordnung* abolished Goebbels' make-shift RM 170 000 *Reisekostenzuschuss*. In the intervening two years, Philharmonic musicians had grown accustomed to the benefits of the grant "that guaranteed the entire orchestra an income as they had never known before," [184] and would not stand for a reduction, even if still the best-paid orchestra under the scheme. They were discontent with the progressive scaling of the new salary structure, ranging from a base salary of RM 383.83 per month for musicians with less than two years of service up to RM 602.30 for those with over ten, and the new standardised travel supplements now assessed on a monthly basis.[185] In real terms the musicians' monthly salaries rose, but depending on their age and seniority, the revised bonus system could result in a slightly reduced yearly income.

That said, more significant than the actual wage level, was the optical and material rapport to other German Kultur-Orchester. As Stegmann argued:

> It is not so important whether the income of the Berliner Philharmonic Orchestra members be raised yet again or not. It is, rather, important that we maintain the material advantage that we have received over all other orchestras through the travel bonus.[186]

For this reason, von Benda and Stegmann lobbied to retain the *Reisekostenzulage* or some other form of subsidy advantage, clearly delineating the Berlin Philharmonic orchestra from all others.[187] So significant was this principle, the Philharmonic *Geschäftsführung* prepared a concession "in response to the publicly repeated wishes of the Herr Reich's Ministor of Finance, to save on personnel costs."[188] The proposal called for limiting the orchestra's size at 105 musicians, though plans were in place to expand to 110.[189] The savings of RM 30 000, it was argued, would offset a partial restoration of the former travel subsidy in the form of a *Reiseaufand*.[190] This *Aufwandsentschädigung* (compensation for expenses) would be applied in equal instalments of RM 60 per month to all musicians.[191]

Meanwhile, through his connections to the Reich and Prussian Finance Ministries, Göring had managed to negotiate his Staatskapelle into the *Sonderklasse* alongside the Philharmonic, one on history—"a leading concert orchestra of worldwide repute", the other on potential—"in future the nation's leading opera orchestra"[192] In his independent proclamation, Göring reiterated that f the Philharmonic Orchestra in Berlin were to receive a bonus over the general pay scale, his *Preussischen Finanzministerium* would match it for the Staatskapelle.[193] Goebbels, as NSDAP *Gauleiter* of Berlin, fought back suggesting the Deutsche Oper orchestra, an institution also under his patronage, would be equally entitled to the *führende Opernorchester* (leading opera orchestra) mantel. If the Staatskapelle were to accede to the *Sonderklasse*, the Deutche Oper should too.

Naturally, these assertions rippled up and down the hallways of the RMVP, the *Reichsfinanzministerium* and the Berlin Philharmonic. "All of these orchestras would absorbed into the special class ," remarked one bureaucrat on the escalating ridiculousness of the situation, "which would make the original purpose of the special class would be rendered illusory."[194]

At this stage, the Philharmonic's *Aufwandsentschädigung* proposal took political prevalence, further augmenting the farce. With Göring standing firm on the Staatskapelle's ascendance to the *Sonderklasse*, the *Reichsfinanzministerium* accepted the notion of an equal formal status for both orchestras, but proposed to give the Philharmonic Orchestra a special bonus in addition to the normal earnings of the special class. This would comprise the fixed RM 60 monthly bonus proposed by von Benda and Stegmann, and essentially create a *Sonderklasse* to the *Sonderklasse*—a *Sonderklasse Plus*.[195]

Despite some bickering from former GmbH shareholder musicians complaining about wage inconsistencies under the new rules compared to the old,[196] Berlin Philharmonic members by and large profited from the *Tarifordung Sonderklasse* Plus arrangement.[197] The plan likewise appealed to the *Reichsfinanzministerium* because though it called for an immediate increase in overall salaries, the 5% escalation was manageable under the *Tarifordnung*'s assurance of long-term stability.[198]

This, however, was just the beginning. The provisions of the Tarifordunung did indeed take Tietjen's notion of *Bewegungsfreiheit* into account by issuing orchestras a *Leistungszulage* (performance bonus). Responsiveness not being a common property of bureaucracy, this was another example of struggling inconsistencies within an ideology which at once esteemed art and was obsessed with order. The *Leistungszulage* represented an attempted compromise between the necessary bureaucratic rigours of a responsible budgetary scale and the acknowledged qualitative criteria of that scale. Orchestras were free to independently offer a 15% *Leistungszulage* bonus[199] to individual musicians either in recognition of service, or as an attractive contractual incentive, to up to 40% of the orchestra's musicians.[200] The Berlin Philharmonic offered two levels of *Leistungszulage*, one of RM 75 per month for sixteen primary players, plus eight secondary musicians at RM 37.50.[201]

Problems abounded in this scheme, however, regarding its application and accounting. Should the prescribed supplementary amounts, sized to *Vergütungsklasse* be issued up front, or applied for on an individual basis? (Included in the State subsidy transfer.) Was it necessary for an orchestra to completely fill its 40% quota? (No.) Did granting the *Leistungszulage* imply obligatory auxiliary services? (Perhaps.)[202]

The Leistungszulage also bred a climate of competition between orchestras. This was precisely what Tietjen and Göring had had in mind by Bewegungsfreiheit. Rivalries had always existed, but the bad blood between the Berlin Philharmonic and the Berlin Staatsoper Orchester, for example, now had an objective fiscal scale, both in terms of overall rank and in individual musicians' contract conditions. Games of musician poaching emerged.

Just prior to the ratification of the new *Tarifordnung*, the

Staatsoper Orchester made overtures to hornist Martin Ziller, who had joined the Berlin Philharmonic in 1935. With assurance of standing on the same *Sonderklasse* pay scale as the Philharmonic, the *Staatsoper* offered Ziller a pensionable solo horn position where he was allegedly presented the highest level of salary, whereas with the Philharmonic he was still in level IV based on seniority. [203] Despite the Philharmonic's *Reisekostenzulage* or supplemental RM 60 Aufwand, the *Leistungszulage* principle allowed Tietjen to help Ziller jump the seniority cue, and put him in the top pay category, with fewer services, immediately. [204] Of course Goebbels and the RMVP would not stand for such devious, if altogether legal behaviour, and the move was rebuffed.

Matters became more complicated shortly thereafter, with the *Anschluss* (annexation of Austria) and the necessity of integrating the orchestras of Austria into the *Tarifordnung* scheme. The placement of the Wiener Philharmoniker was crucial, but on account of tradition and all qualitative criteria, no rank below *Sonderklasse* could legitimately be justified. While the other Austrian orchestras slotted neatly in between third and fifth tiers, [205] the addition of the Wiener Philharmoniker alongside the Berlin Philharmonic and Staatskapelle in a now not so exclusive *Sonderklasse* stoked further debate. If three, why not more? The emphasis on Berlin and Vienna misrepresented the weight of the German musical scene, which also had a strong capital in Munich.

Sure enough, within one year of the Wiener Philharmoniker's accession to the *Sonderklasse*, Hitler himself entered the fray with the wish the that Bayerische Staatsoper orchestra should be promoted to the others' elite company. [206] The Müncheners arrival, however, came with a stern warning that by decree of the Führer, "any move by the orchestras or opera houses of Berlin to hire away musicians of the Munich State Opera to Berlin, are strictly forbidden." [207]

With a *Sonderklasse* of four, at least two of which appointed by personal favour rather than any form of exceptional merit or due process, the *Tarifordnung* experiment crumbled. The *Sondertreuhänder*, Hinkel, was reduced to a rubber stamp on the whimsical decisions of the Reich's most powerful personalities for the system's upper ranks, while "for reasons of cultural politics," namely budgetary restraint from the *Reichfinanzministerium*, the orchestras of the lower categories were granted freedom to define themselves.[208] Goebbels' Deutsche Oper once again knocked at the *Sonderklasse* door, with domino repercussions: "If the Deutsche Oper were to enter the special class, there would be no objections to promoting the [Berlin] *Volksoper* to Class I; however, if the Deutsche Oper remained in Class I it would be difficult to account for bringing the *Volksoper* into Class I as well."[209]

It was an exasperating personal, practical, administrative and symbolic mess only an executive decision could clear. And the ultimate dilettante authority in Germany was Hitler himself: "The special custodian should execute the Führer's decision with respect to the composition of the special class so that this question which has caused so much trouble can be resolved once and for all."[210]

Hinkel's appeal to Hitler fascinatingly illustrated the intricacy of Nazi discourse:

My Führer!

When we came into power the affairs of the cultural orchestras were in utter disarray and the musicians without social support. Therefore it was necesssary, for social and for cultural-political reasons, to gather the supporting organisations into a large-scale system and secure the economic basis for the musicians. That is why the *Tarifordnung* was created for the cultural orchestras. […] Therein the orchestras have been divided into five classes, above which a special class remains. Originally, this was only the Berlin Philharmonic, because it, as an especially representative orchestra, should have the top position and because its travel activities make extraordinary demands on the musicians. Later, in addition, the Prussian Staatskapelle, the Vienna Philharmonic and, by your special request, my Führer, the Bavarian Staatskapelle all joined. […] The Saxon Staatskapelle and the Leipzig Gewandhaus have been seeking membership in the special class for some time now, which they justify based on their great artistic tradition and capabilities. Other orchestras which cannot compete, such as Weimar and Linz, also want to be

accepted into the special class. This ambition to be at the
top, in itself delightful, is a sign of the strong cultural will
that has awakened in all parts, as well as an economic
boom. [...] I therefore ask for a decision whether, in light
of these trains of thought, the established composition
of the special class should remain or if an expansion
should take place, whereby the very basis for a special
class would become admittedly, very broad.[211]

This letter was the first of several nervous drafts, and revealed
much of situation. First, the Berlin Philharmonic's claim to special
status was undisputed. Their *Sonderklasse* classification, however, had
become redundant as politics over-took a bureaucratic and partly
normative assessment process. These politics were personal and ideological, directed by power, greed, and dilettantish behaviour, and
mitigated any sense of procedural balance.

Beyond Goebbels and Göring's pathetic proxy war, and Hitler's
own whimsical inclinations, the orchestra in Weimar, for example
had only just been promoted based on an explicit decision of the
Führer to *Klasse I* the year before. The orchestra in Linz, whose claim
was based exclusively on the coincidence of Hitler's place of birth,
was meanwhile in the *Klasse IV* by quality assessment.[212] These orchestras' sense of entitlement was political in the same way the Berlin
Philharmonic regarded its symbolic value as justification for running
a completely unrealistic business model. So long as regime benevolence was available, there were always parties, in this case orchestras, ready to take advantage. Indeed, Weimar and Linz expressed
their intentions "to hire for themselves the best orchestra members
from the Dresdener Staatsoper, the Leipzig Gewandhausorchester,
the Hamburg State Opera etc."[213] Dresden and Leipzig were great
orchestras, but posed no competition to the Berlin Philharmonic in
terms of exceptional service to the Reich. Putting Weimar and Linz
above them in rank, however, would mean almost certain ruin for
the Saxon orchestras, as the sharks awaited their chance to tear away
their best players.

Still, adjudication—fairness was beyond contemplation—in this
affair, depended on a matter of values. The presentation to Hitler was
couched in extremely cautious terms regarding the overall state of
musical culture in the Reich, painting juvenile shenanigans in terms

of healthy ambition. The matter by this point had long since departed the sphere of fiscal management. The issue at stake was a dispute between functionality and ideology—if Hitler himself would chose some semblance of effective management over rewarding subjective persuasions.

He did not. On June 1st, 1943, the *Sonderklasse* of the deutschen Kulturorchester welcomed five new members: the Leipziger Gewandhausorchester, the orchestra of the Deutsche Oper Berlin, the Hamburger Staatsoperorchester, the Dresdener Staatskapelle, and the newly minted Bruckner-Orchester Linz.[214] The Thüringische Staatskapelle Weimar, meanwhile, found its way into the evermore crowded Klasse I.[215] What began as a process to discern fiscal transparency and accountability ended in a sad, mangled, meaningless mess.

Once the *Tarifordnung* proceedings lost any sense of order, the Berlin Philharmonic withdrew from the game. Goebbels assured the Philharmonic musicians collectively, then the *Geschäftsführung* in a private meeting "that in addition to the new pay scale, the travel expense bonus would guarantee the material security of the orchestra."[216] The orchestra had its *materielle Vorsprung* in the Reiseaufwand, while the forces influencing other orchestra rankings were beyond its control.

Still, skirmishes persisted. Stegmann and successive Philharmonic Intendants continued using the *Staatsoper* as foil in to wrest more money from the RMVP, while Göring scored a few stinging points for his Staatskapelle in unregulated areas such as tour *Tagesgelder*, often securing for his orchestra unreasonably high per diems, much to the Philharmonic's dismay.[217]

The Philharmonic, however, got the last sardonic laugh when, in September 1944, the *Staatsoper* was dissolved, its employees and ensemble disbursed to service the losing war effort. When the Berlin Philharmonic had lost its own home, the Philharmonie, in January 1944, *Staatsoper Intendant* Tietjen was not above playing politics to squeeze the rival orchestra for exceedingly high rental fees for his hall. There was little remorse then, from the Philharmonic's point of view, in seeing the Tietjen's ensemble's demise:

After the State Opera closed down its opera operations, we initiated negotiations to perform all of our large concerts this winter in the *Staatsoper* building. The previous lease demand of the *Staatsoper* was RM 12 000 for one day, because the general management calculated the loss of revenues for an opera performance. After the closure of opera activities, such a high rent should be out of the question. We have therefore applied to the general management for a reduction of this implausibly high lease."[218]

Money matters almost by definition breed pettiness. During the Third Reich, finances became embroiled in a toxic mix of greed, self-interest, intrigue and entitlement. The Nazis came to power full of promises. Their robust economic performance yielded windfalls, particularly in areas of ideological importance—the military, sports, and culture. The Berlin Philharmonic benefited immensely from the regime's realigned spending priorities, but competition, even under National Socialism, was stiff. The system was a strangely perverted form of crony capitalism whereby orchestras and artists could inflate budgets by all means of claim: personal, political, qualitative, ideological, geographical, symbolic. Each of these were qualities for which the regime, under certain circumstances, would pay. The Berlin Philharmonic embodied all these qualities, and more, and was therefore invested with wide-ranging fiscal privilege with only limited accountability.

The Philharmonic's experience was ultimately one of tenuous privilege. Musicians were not the best paid in Germany, nor were its administrators on par with the artists they engaged. The orchestra's inflated budgets, however, allowed for the flexibility to keep the musicians happy with contract terms and bonuses, kept Furtwängler firmly on board by meeting his exorbitant fees, and assured the long-term financial security of the orchestra, with the State picking up the tab. All this, as the Philharmonic tenaciously defended its exclusive status within a highly politicised musical marketplace.

Chapter 4

Philharmonikers at Work

THE CONVERSION FROM bourgeois musical institution into a holding of the State altered the range and nature of the Berlin Philharmonic's performance appearances. While the Nazi Party counted numerous musical groups within its membership, and many state, provincial and city orchestras across Germany could have been considered more sympathetic to the Nazi cause, by virtue of its singular musical quality, the regime identified the Berlin Philharmonic as its musical ambassador. By ensuring the orchestra's financial stability, the regime essentially procured Germany's finest orchestra to fulfil its needs.

The Nazi regime embraced artistic culture, entrenching music as a fundamental social value. These purposes walked the fine line between education and propaganda: through subscription concerts, radio broadcasts, popular concerts, recordings and command performances, the Berlin Philharmonic was celebrated as one of the jewels of German artistic achievement, performing great German music for bigger and wider audiences than ever before. This was both a matter of personal persuasion among the Nazi leadership and the crude yet pervasive cultural critique at the heart of Nazi ideological. The Berlin Philharmonic was beneficiary in both senses, enjoying the privilege of admiration by Party elite and prospering from the exposure provided by Nazi infrastructure. This, combined with Germany's improving economic situation, allowed the orchestra to achieve a remarkable balance: during the Third Reich, under Nazi patronage, the Berlin Philharmonic managed to refine its elite image, in political, programming, and professional terms while expanding and diversifying its audiences to unprecedented levels.

Though a certain degree of hyperbole was invoked in the controlled press, the basic principle of popular access to great art could not be deemed malevolent. On other occasions, however, the orchestra was commissioned to perform at specific events which merited no constructive pretext. This chapter will analyse the range of musical activities of the Berlin Philharmonic, where concerts were given, for whom, highlighting the musicians' manifold functions, and their distinct ethical problematic: artists, entertainers, ambassadors, of the Berlin Philharmonic and of the Third Reich.

Berlin Philharmonic musicians' service loads during the Third Reich were intensive. The orchestra had always maintained a busy schedule of rehearsing, performing and touring, but in the years following 1933, the orchestra's activities multiplied. Alongside its traditional concert series in Berlin and elsewhere in Germany, the Philharmonic's additional duties involved an escalated touring schedule and an increased number of *Honorar Konzerte*, and government command performances. At over 100 musicians, a degree of player rotation permitted *Philharmonikers* some respite during certain weeks, but aside from concertmasters, who were afforded leave for extra-orchestra performances,[1] the one free day per week promised in musicians' service contracts often failed to materialise.[2]

The Berlin Philharmonic season typically ran from the third week in August to the first week of July. During the season, the orchestra would rehearse and perform a new programme on average every two days. In 1934-35, musicians rehearsed 331 times and gave 178 performances, totalling 509 services for the season.[3] In 1936-37, the orchestra performed 205 times in Germany, plus another 365 rehearsal duties and international appearances, for 570 services.[4] In 1938-39, the orchestra performed 191 times with 257 rehearsals, totalling 448 services.[5] The reduction in rehearsals between 1937 and 1938 was partly attributable to an increase in the number of tour appearances, which repeated previously-rehearsed programmes.[6] Minus the orchestra's six week summer vacation, orchestra services averaged over 1,5 per day from 1934-35 onwards.

While entering a plea for special status under the new *Tarifordnung der deutschen Kultur-Orchester* (*Tarifordnung* of German cultural orchestras), the Philharmonic management submitted the following portrait of the orchestra's hectic life:

On the evening of May 8, the Orchestra played in Munich after having to travel the same day from Zurich to Munich, following 16 concerts in 17 days. The end of the concert followed the return journey to Berlin. On the 9th of May, the day of arrival in Berlin, the orchestras has rehearsals in the Philharmonic and in the evening a big Beethoven concert, conducted by Dr. Furtwängler. Already on Sunday, the 10th of May, begin rehearsals for the Missa solemnis. During these rehearsals and performances of the Missa solemnis there are about 7-8 rehearsals under Prof. Abendroth in preparation for the Balkan trip. After only two days' break, the Balkan trip begins, which lasts until the morning of May 30, with railway journeys often lasting 15-24 hours.[7]

Despite the increased playing demands, it was imperative the orchestra's musical standards not diminish. This was not only a matter of artistic integrity, but also of political necessity. For the Berlin Philharmonic to be most effective as an instrument of propaganda, it needed to be most effective as a musical instrument too. This meant rehearsals could not be sacrificed, the orchestra's musical spirit had to be strengthened, not undermined, and every musician should feel compelled "to put all of his energy into the service of the orchestra."[8] Good salaries, praise, and the lending of instruments from the RMVP could help maintain a degree of private content, but such benefits could not themselves guarantee collective artistic excellence. The orchestra needed to maintain its commitment to quality work, each musician stretching his mental and physical limits without breaking. Balancing the rigors of serious music making with expectations from within the orchestra community, the government's demands, and the interests of the Philharmonic's diverse audiences was complex and taxing.

"The musician," acknowledged Furtwängler, "can only carry out a certain number of services before his health and artistic performance capacity are impaired."[9] Indeed, exigencies of the Philharmonic's schedule and demands reportedly took their toll. The Berlin Philharmonic's musical culture, inheritance of its self-governing founding principles, lived on a spirit of proud *Mitarbeit*, but also proud discipline. "The strain on the nerves and the mental concentration" of the orchestra, it was remarked, "are coompletely extraordinary." [10] The orchestra's singular quality was not simply a matter of talent, but the result of an ethic. This created glorious music, yet also an air of tension: "This collaboration is tied to the orchestra's spirit of self-criticism, whereby, while working together colleagially, when necessary, musicians' criticism can lead to a serious confrontations."[11]

Despite fame, prestige and a heavy workload, the Philharmonic would still rehearse a minimum three to five times prior to a Furtwängler *Philharmonische Konzerte,*[12] at four hours per service, except on performance days when morning rehearsals ran from ten o'clock in the morning until one in the afternoon.[13] These sessions were serious and intense. Occasionally, the strain was overwhelming:

> Service in our orchestra is the most exacting in Germany, not only in terms of time, but physically and mentally," [14] wrote Karl Stegmann to the RMVP on the matter of the orchestra's extreme demands. "It causes terrible strain on the nerves!" he insisted, citing an unnamed hornist who suffered a stroke apparently due to stress, a flautist who sought a plethora of unusual cures for his nerves, and an insomniac violinist who could not handle the stress, and had to be pensioned prematurely.[15] Musicians were so engaged with their Philharmonic commitments, it was argued, between performing, rehearsing and touring, they rarely had occasion for additional work in guest appearances or teaching, activities common amongst colleagues in other orchestras.[6]

Depending on the conductor, venue of concert and series, the orchestra would rehearse anywhere from once to six times in preparation for a concert.[17] With its more frequent conductors, the Philharmonic developed close relationships, often recapitulating repertoire over several seasons. Such was the case with Furtwängler. He remained the orchestra's dominating musical figure, continued to exercise considerable influence over programming, and consistently received the most rehearsal time of any Philharmonic conductor. Beyond scheduled rehearsals for concerts, Furtwängler also enjoyed the luxury of having the orchestra at his disposal for readings of his own compositions. When he completed his *Second Symphony* in 1942, for example, Furtwängler scheduled a full dozen extra readings and sectional rehearsals prior to the premiere.[18]

Beyond the typical rigors of practice, travel, and performance, together with the stringent expectations within the orchestra, working with Furtwängler, and his combination of perfectionism and volatile temperament, also generated a particular stress level among the musicians. "The most easy going director isn't the best for the orchestra," wrote Lorenz Höber. "Case in point: Furtwängler, who more than any other conductor, makes great demands on the capacity of each individual."[19] As Furtwängler was the orchestra's most frequent collaborator too, these pressures were both acute and regular. The strain made it occasionally difficult for the musicians to bear, but played a decisive role in fostering the orchestra's musical accomplishment.

When Hitler expressed an interest in hearing Furtwängler conduct Bruckner at the Deutsches Museum in Munich (a highly explicit, if altogether whimsical request),[20] it was noted that "It would of course be most convenient if the Berlin Philharmonic could come with Furtwängler to Munich. It would be inconvenient for Furtwängler to conduct the Munich Philharmonic because he would have to go through a series of rehearsals before every major concert to establish the crucial inner connection with the players."[21] This observation revealed much. First, it expressed anticipation of the conductor's uncompromising commitment to rehearsal preparation, even for a capricious command performance. Second, it conveyed the presupposition of an *innere Verbindung* (inner connection) between composer, conductor and orchestra, as well as a palpable reverence for great music and musicians. Hitler did not just like the megalomania of having an orchestra play at his command, but on a certain level, respected the art itself. Third, by this time, the Philharmonic's close relationship with Furtwängler dated back over twenty years; the comment did not indicate a performance by the Berliners would not require rehearsal at all, but rather assumed rehearsal could take place on a much higher level, given the intimate, mature familiarity between the conductor and orchestra.

Hitler's 1943 Munich request also typified the tenor of the relationship between the Berlin Philharmonic and the State, of which it was an asset. During the Third Reich, the Philharmonie became a playground for symbolic political posturing, with the Philharmonic its principal toy. When Furtwängler returned to conduct the Philharmonic in 1935 following his spat with the regime, the April 25th concert was hailed as a monumental public and critical success. More significantly, the event took place with most of the Nazi elite, including Hitler, Goebbels and Göring, as well as *eine Reihe von Botschaftern und Gestanden der ausländischen Staaten* (a gathering of ambassadors and foreign state officials) in attendance.[22] Writing to *Staatssekretär* (State Secretary) Funk at the RMVP, inquiring if he too would be attending the musical and political event of the Spring, Karl Stegmann remarked: "Of course we hardly need to point out that the orchestra would appreciate the great honour of a visit from the Führer, since he unfortunately still hasn't found the time to attend one of our concerts this winter."[23]

This degree of decorous familiarity between regime officials and the orchestra was typical. The orchestra enjoyed the attention of the elites, and elites enjoyed making use of a superlative jukebox. This is not to suggest the Nazi leaders had no respect for great music. On the contrary, it was the orchestra's very greatness that allowed it to transcend purely musical fascination, to assume a symbolic role. Hitler attended Philharmonic concerts with some regularity.[24] Goebbels enjoyed playing games comparing other orchestras with *his* Philharmonic.[25] Decisive was the orchestra's quality.

At the 1933 convening of the Party faithful in Nürnberg, the musical entertainment featured the *Nationalsozialistische-Reichs-Sinfonieorchester* (NSRSO) under Nazi stalwart, Franz Adam. According to Goebbels, the performance was atrocious.[26] "Here belongs only first class," he wrote despondently.[27] On account of the poor artistic showing the previous year, for the 1934 Nuremberg *Reichsparteitage*, there was no doubt whom to call: the Berliner Philharmoniker. In 1934, however, there were problems. First, the Philharmonic still contained two Jewish musicians, Nicolai Graudan and Gilbert Back. The two presented the Nazi leadership, not to mention the musicians themselves, with a profound ethical dilemma. On one hand, the pragmatist Goebbels, in concession to Furtwängler, authorised the orchestra to appear under all circumstances as *eine Einheit* (as a single entity), despite non-Aryan presences.[28] Ideologues such as Alfred Rosenberg, meanwhile, maintained, "that the two still present Jews could on no account play in Nuremburg."[29]

The second problem was artistic. Hitler expressly wished for Furtwängler to conduct at the Nuremberg festivities. Communicating through von Schmidtseck, the conductor agreed to entertain the possibility of doing so, but categorically refused to accept Party suggestions on programming.[30] This period coincided with rising tensions in the Hindemith debate, when Furtwängler was extremely sensitive to political interference on his territory. Again, the Party was faced with a dilemma of priorities: to hear what they wanted or hear who they wanted? In the end, Adam's NSRSO was reprised for another season.[31]

In 1935, the Party leaders managed to convince Furtwängler to appear in Nürnberg to conduct Wagner's *Meistersinger* on September 10, the evening prior to the official opening of the Party congress.[32] The conductor did indeed appear, but with a local orchestra. The *Leipziger Gewandhausorchester* was that year's *Reichsparteitage* elite orchestra in residence.[33] Finally, in 1936, doubtless much to Goebbels' relief, the Berlin Philharmonic made its first appearance in Nürnberg, noticeably without Furtwängler. The significance and seriousness of the event was not lost on the musicians. As an anonymous Philharmonic musician, presumably violist Werner Buchholz, recalled:

> The train could only have been bound for Nuremberg: most of the passengers were SS and SA officers; [...] For the Philharmonic musicians, there is much to experience on the road, but there is at least as much work too. We would have liked to take a stroll through the gloriously busy and adorned city, but for us first and foremost came rehearsal. By 4pm we were already seated at our music stands. It lasted until 6:30. We hardly had an hour to rest before the cultural programme began [...] At 7:45pm, changed into our formal attire, the orchestra was ready to go. The house was packed, full of the excitement that major events herald. In the first row was the government

of the Reich. Suddenly the excitement died down and the audience rose in unison—the Führer entered—the festival began. What happened next was experienced by the world through radio and press. As the last notes of *Prometheus* by Hugo Wolf, sung by Bockelmann, faded away, Rosenburg gave a grand speech. Beethoven's *Pastorale* followed, led by Peter Raabe. The Führer stepped up to the podium. He greeted us with a fascinating warmth radiating from his persona. We sensed the magnitude of the moment we are experiencing and in which we had been blessed to participate.[34]

In 1937, the Philharmonic and Furtwängler were invited to return to Nürnberg once more, to frame a speech of the *Führer*. A Beethoven programme was strongly recommended.[35] Fortunately for Furtwängler and the Philharmonic, they were double-booked. The 1937 *Reichsparteitage* coincided with another regime-commanded engagement—the international World's Exhibition in Paris. The Philharmonic's role representing the Third Reich abroad was far more important than providing musical gilding for an annual Nazi festival. In Paris, the Philharmonic played a series of four concerts, representing Germany with repertoire ranging from the infamous *Horst Wessel-Lied*, conducted by Hans von Benda, to a crowning performance of Beethoven's *Ninth Symphony* with the Bruno Kittel Chor under Furtwängler.

In 1938, however, it was made sure there were no scheduling conflicts. The Berlin Philharmonic performed at the *Reichsparteitag* (*Kulturtagung*) decorating speeches by Hitler and Goebbels. Hans Weisbach, principal conductor of the Leipziger Sinfonie-Orchester and frequent guest conductor with the NSRSO, led the Philharmonic in Bruckner's *Seventh Symphony*. Furtwängler appeared with the Wiener Philharmoniker.

"We hereby inform you," read the last Philharmonic Rundschreiben before the orchestra's 1939 summer holidays, "that Herr Dr. Furtwängler will conduct our orchestra at this year's Nuremburg Rally. It is our great pleasure to inform you of this and we will give you details about the necessary rehearsals as soon as they have been determined."[36] More significant than the *grösste Freude* (great pleasure) of the announcement, or the at least provisional prospect of Furtwängler leading the orchestra, was the confirmation that for such overtly political appearances, the orchestra would nevertheless rehearse conscientiously. As Hans von Benda wrote to the RMVP of the orchestra's spirit: "the Reich's Orchestra must be available for all of Germany's official occasions, which is also the burning desire of the orchestra itself."[37]

For such appearances, neither the orchestra nor its members were paid a fee, travel and accommodation were spartan;[38] despite these considerable drawbacks, playing at Nürnberg, as well as other such overtly political functions was always taken seriously. Though individual Philharmonic musicians may have disagreed with the political convictions on display at the Nürnberg rallies, collectively, the orchestra felt itself in appropriate company among the honoured representatives of the Reich, and not only tolerated ordeals up to and including personal distaste for Nazi politics in order to maintain this elevated status, but also took an extremely professional attitude even to the most contrived of appearances.

In 1936, for example, the Berlin Philharmonic featured prominently at the Olympic Games. At the opening ceremonies, the orchestra gave the world premiere of one of Richard Strauss' most underwhelming opuses, the *Olympischen Hymne*. Though commissioned on short notice, the work was still rehearsed thoroughly by the Philharmonic, under the composer's own direction. As early as June, a full two months before the opening of the Games, Strauss was already working with the orchestra on the piece.[39]

The Philharmonic was further front and centre during the Olympic festivities participating in the Reich-sponsored International Olympiad for composers. As orchestra-in-residence for the contest, the Berlin Philharmonic performed the world premieres of works by Lino Livabella ("Der Sieger"), Kurt Thomas ("Olympische Kantate"), Paul Höffer ("Olympischer Schwur"), Renzo Massarani (Italy), Kosaku Yamada and Ito-Novol (Japan); Hans Luckasch, Norbert Sprongl and Karl Pilss (Österreich); Robert L. Sanders, Roy Harris and Quincy Porter (USA); A. A. Langeweg and Marius Monnikendam (Holland); and Marc-Cesar Scotto (Monaco), among others. The winner, acclaimed by the 'international' jury consisting of eight Germans and two foreigners, was Werner Egk for his titanic *Olympisches Festmusik* scored for symphony orchestra, triple choir, women's chorus, children's chorus and wind band.[40]

For other celebrations too, the Berlin Philharmonic was on call. The orchestra played concerts in honour of Hitler's birthday, either for the Führer live or on radio, each year from 1937 on,[41] under conductors ranging from Helmuth Thierfelder to Hans Knappertsbusch, Karl Böhm, and infamously, Furtwängler himself in 1942. Not every concert was an 'official' birthday tribute on the Philharmonic's calendar, but all were invariably so framed in the press. Confirming intentions, three days before Furtwängler conducted Bach and Beethoven with the Berlin Philharmonic at a special *Feierstunde* of the NSDAP celebrating Hitler's birthday in 1942, a RMVP memo was circulated iterating, "In planning future trips abroad, the Berlin Philharmonic must ensure that the orchestra is, on principle, in Berlin for the Führer's birthday (18th to 21st of April) and available for any possible celebrations."[42] In 1943 and 1944, it was Knappertsbusch's turn to lead the Philharmonic's *Führer Geschenke* (Gift to the Führer).

The orchestra also appeared every November at annual celebrations for the founding of the *Reichsmusikkammer*, embellishing speeches by Goebbels, Hinkel and others with Wagner's *Meistersinger Vorspiel*, as well as the *Tage der Deutschen Kunst* (German Art Days) in Munich, a yearly event where Hitler himself would deliver speeches on the eternal struggle between 'German' and 'degenerate' art. There again, the cost to the orchestra and its members was high: "Accomodation is to be paid by each gentleman himself [...] the demand for individual rooms cannot be guaranteed in any way. Complaining to us is futile."[43] Individual members complained,[44] yet the orchestra as a whole rehearsed appropriately and performed obediently. Identification with the best of German culture and praise from the elites of German society fed the orchestra's sense of self-worth and by extension, determination for quality.

Every season, the Berlin Philharmonic gave a number of additional command performances *Im Auftrage des Reichsministeriums für Volksaufklärung und Propaganda* (By order of the RMVP), at the behest of the government, or in service to the Party:

- In 1938-39, at the Reichsmusiktage in Düsseldorf, and "Auf Veranlassung der Reichsjugendführung" (For the occasion of the Reich's Youth Leadership), a special concert for the Hitler Jugend with Furtwängler.[45]

- The *Reichsmusiktage* (Reich's Music Days) again in 1939-40, along with another appearance for the *Hitlerjugend* (Hitler Youth), this time under Abendroth.[46]

With the start of the war, many mass exhibitions and conventions such as the Nürnberg rallies and the *Kultur-und-Musik Tage* were necessarily abandoned, yet

- In 1940/41, the Berlin Philharmonic played at a celebratory hour of the *Höheren fliegertechnischen Schule* Berlin-Adlerhorst in the course of work with the *Wehrmacht*.[47], and offered a Furtwängler-led concert at the opening of the German Theater in Prague.[48]

- The following year saw a *Sonder-Chorveranstaltung* of Pfitzner's nationalist cantata, *Von deutscher Seele*, presented for the Party elite in Berlin, and a concert for the *Reichspropagandaleitung* der NSDAP again under Abendroth.[49]

- This latter event was repeated in 1942-43, along with *Sonderkonzerte* (special concerts) for the Hitler Youth and the S.S.[50]

- In 1943-44, the Philharmonic played a Beethoven concert in the Mosaic Hall of the Reich's Chancellery, and gave a private concert with Jochum for the *Reichspropagandaamt* (Reich's Office of Propaganda).[51]

- Later in 1944, the orchestra again performed for the Hitler

Youth, and offered a special concert for invited guests of the ministry in the *Berliner Dom* (Cathedral).[52]

Less significant than the orchestra's volition to participate in events like these, however, was the desire of the Nazi elites to employ it. Though other orchestras played at the Nuremberg rallies, the Olympic stage was full of acts other than the Berlin Philharmonic, and birthday tributes to Hitler came from far and wide, it was the Berlin Philharmonic, rather than some Nazi Party musical organ, or group more obviously ideologically affiliated with the Führer,[53] which the Nazi elites most coveted. By projecting it abroad, presenting it to young Party members, and using it for their private purposes, the Nazi elites employed and deployed the orchestra as an 'educational indulgence', basking in the glow of a national treasure. Reciprocally, while utterly compromising itself through participation in blatantly propagandistic exercises, by virtue of its artistic diligence, the Berlin Philharmonic represented a kind of qualitative seal of legitimacy for the regime.

The Bruckner performance in Munich in 1943 was just another example of the quasi-private employ of the Philharmonic by Hitler, Goebbels, Göring and others. The leaders truly admired the Berlin Philharmonic, and as such were not above objectifying it as a tool for politics, conciliation, and things yet more disingenuous. The Berlin Philharmonic embraced its supreme status of *Reichsorchester*, not necessarily on the level of its individual members, but collectively, as the celebrated symbol of the highest standard in German music.

On a number of occasions, the orchestra was also used as a laboratory for obscure musical experiments "by order of the Reich's Ministry," as when "at the wish of Herr Reich's Minister Dr. Goebbels, a choral piece in collaboration with the Bruno Kittel Choir will take place on the 7th of June at 5pm in the Philharmonic in the presence of Herr Reich's Minister Dr. Goebbels."[54] The unidentified piece was very likely a new composition by Bruno Rentsch entitled "Der ewige Ruf" ("The Eternal Call"), which was performed at a *Feierstunde der Reichsmusikkamer* at the Theater des Volkes (the giant Deco-style Circus Theatre next door to the famous Theater am Schiffbauerdamm) in November 1939. This work, of suspect musical merit, was presented between speeches by Goebbels and Robert Ley.[55] "It is the duty," orchestra members were reminded, "of all musicians—also principal players—to participate in the festivities."[56] Among other luxurious calls to curious duty (privileged was the ambitious composer, and presumably his benefactor, to rehearse a work-in-progress with the Berlin Philharmonic), the orchestra was summoned to another special rehearsal the day before New Year's Eve 1941 to read through the *Japanische Festmusik* by Richard Strauss; running time, about one hour.[57]

Though Strauss' *Japanische Festmusik* remains another of the composers more negligible works, Japanese music and conductors featured prominently with the Berlin Philharmonic under the guise of what was termed *'Kulturaustausch'* (cultural exchange). For propagandistic, but also ideological purposes not entirely anathema to contemporary ideas about the universality of music and the value of cultural exchange, the orchestra participated in a number of concerts in the spirit of 'friendship between nations', not only with Axis partners. In 1934, the orchestra gave *Deutsch-Schwedisch* and *Deutsch-Dänische* concerts, performing contemporary music from both countries, concerts which were also broadcast on radio. In the Olympic year of 1936, a Viscount Hidemaro Konoye of Japan first lead the orchestra in a programme of German music.[58] Later that season, Franciso Mignone presented a programme of South American composers, and another Japanese composer-conductor, Kazuo Yamada, conducted a radio broadcast of contemporary Japanese highlights. In 1937, Leo Borchard lead a series of *Sonderkonzerte* "mit Werken von Ausländern" (with works by foreigners): an *Englischer Abend* (English evening), a *Französischer Abend* (French evening) and an *Italienisch-Ungarischer Abend* (Italian-Hungarian Evening). These programmes ran parallel to three *Sonderkonzerte* with foreign conductors coupled with German soloists.[59]

Naturally, beyond esoteric interest, the message of these programmes also manifested a racial dimension. Rather than encouraging a discourse between cultures, the agenda was in fact to cement the prejudice of racial segregation and the pseudo-scientific ethnography upon which Nazi ideology was founded. "It is one of the most superficial statements," offered the Philharmonic's press by way of introduction to the international musical exchange scheme,

> that art is international. Certainly in theory it may be like
> so many other abstract designations. Maybe those who
> speak this wisdom think that the 'international' is only
> accessible in the musical scores. Nevertheless, artwork—
> its presentation and its execution—are rooted deeply
> in individual nationalities. One need only think of the
> masters and masterpieces of the peoples most involved
> in the development of music: Germans—Italians—the
> French to recognize this immediately. But that is not the
> purpose here. This recognition is so simple and clear that
> volumes could be filled with it, which has indeed already
> happened. It is our justified and undeniable pride that we
> Germans have such great and powerful works that, when
> placed into the weighing dish, launch all other musical
> expressions steeply skyward.[60]

As if to prove the point, the RMVP commissioned the Berlin Philharmonic to specifically programme works of foreign composers under foreign conductors with the intention of showing that even if they did not create it, Germans could do it better. In 1938, the Philharmonic played a *Deutsch-Griechisches Austauchkonzert* under Piloktetes Economides and Petro Petridis

Evanghelatos, with music by Riadis, Kalmiris, Petridis, Skalkotas, as well as the *Zweites Internationales Austauchkonzert Italien-Deutschland* (Second International Exchange Concert Italy-Germany) with a programme including Calabrini, Parodi, Cherubini, Porrini, Pizzetti, Lualdi ("Africa, Rhapsodie Coloniale"). Three weeks after the start of the war in 1939, the Philharmonic performed a *Konzert des Ibero-Amerikanischen Institutes und der Deutsch-Spanischen Gesellschaft* (concert of the Ibero-American Institute and the German-Spanish Society) in cooperation with the Reich short-wave broadcaster. The orchestra played works by Albeniz, Gomes, Caturla, Fabini, Buchardo, Klatovsky, Soro, then crowned the evening with Wagner's *Meistersinger Vorspiel*. Viscount Konoye returned to the Philharmonic in 1940-41 as part of a government-ordered series of concerts with *ausländischen Gastdirigenten* (foreign guest conductors) from Axis-partners Spain, Italy, Japan and Croatia.[61] The following season, another Japanese conductor and composer named Otaka led the Philharmonic in a programme of contemporary Japanese music (including a piece by Konoye), sandwiching a Bach suite.[62]

From the *Reichsparteitag* to concerts for the Hitler Youth to performances of *Ashiya Otome* for large orchestra and percussion by Otaka, the propagandistic agenda to Berlin Philharmonic concertising was plain; and yet, no other orchestra gave such concerts, or were promoted in a comparable way. Its command performances and mandated service to the Reich in fact represented a form of recognition. Beneath overt political function, the orchestra was respected as something unique and exceptional. Expressed conversely, it was the Berlin Philharmonic's musical superiority that lent its performances propagandistic value. The pressure and excitement of such privilege motivated the orchestra, while Party and government could share in and trumpet the virtues of quality.

Despite their prominence, however, special rehearsals and command performances represented only a small part of the Berlin Philharmonic's overall activities. The vast majority of the orchestra's performances remained its concerts for local Berlin audiences. These concerts were not merely entertainment by comparison to the orchestra's political commissions, but were vital to the orchestra's musical, financial and institutional health. Furthermore, the regime required the continued legitimation of the Philharmonic's extraordinariness through earned musical success.

Historically, the Berlin Philharmonic did not produce its own concerts. The orchestra was a self-governing musical association, but had neither professional administrative infrastructure, nor a permanent home. Rather, the orchestra worked with a number of producing partners to arrange concert programmes, sell tickets, and distribute publicity. This allowed the orchestra flexibility in its programming and autonomy in its governance, but also restricted its ability to operate without assistance from impresarios, agents and other specialised production companies. The City of Berlin sponsored *Volkstümliche* concerts at popular prices in the Philharmonie and at various venues around the city. The Backhaus concert agency coordinated the discounted *Sonntags-und Dienstags* concert series. Otherwise, the Berlin Philharmonic was essentially available for rental to firms or individuals willing to pay.[63]

The most important of the orchestra's producing relationships was the partnership with Konzertagentur Wolff & Sachs. Hermann Wolff had been a supporter of the Philharmonic from its very beginning in 1882, and was instrumental in securing the services of distinguished musicians such as Hans von Bülow, Joseph Joachim, and Richard Strauss to work with the orchestra during its early years.

The Philharmonic's premiere subscription series, the *Philharmonischen Konzerte*, was organised by Wolff & Sachs. The ten concert series formed the core of the orchestra's season both musically and financially. The agency engaged successively Hans von Bülow, Arthur Nikisch and Wilhelm Furtwängler as principal conductors of the series. These men were not contracted to the Berlin Philharmonic, but to the Konzertagentur Wolff & Sachs to lead the orchestra's signature series. Only by virtue of the *Philharmonischen Konzerte*'s dominating profile in the orchestra's season, were consecutively von Bülow, Nikisch and, from 1922, Furtwängler, considered de facto music directors of "das erste Konzertinstitut Deutschlands" ("Germany's foremost concert institution").[64]

The visionary qualities of Hermann Wolff, and upon his death, his widow Louise, in elevating the Berlin Philharmonic through its collaborations with the greatest conductors and soloists of the age, were recognised as instrumental to the orchestra's artistic development. Financially, however, the orchestra was somewhat handicapped by this relationship.[65] The Wolff & Sachs agency took a 20% share of *Philharmonischen Konzerte* box-office receipts, as well as so-called *Vermittlerrabatts* (broker's fee) for concerts produced and artists engaged for the Philharmonic.[66] The firma Bote & Bock, used by the Philharmonic and Wolff & Sachs as a ticket-distribution agency also claimed a 5% to 6% commission on its services.[67]

Financially disadvantageous contacts such as these were tolerable in times of economic prosperity, but by 1930, the model was untenable. In April 1930, the Berlin Philharmonic attempted for the first time to produce a *Philharmonische Konzert* under its own auspices, so that all expenditures (conductor, soloists, hall rental, presale costs, etc.) should be under the control of the orchestra management.[68] This resulted in a distinctly improved financial return.[69] Based upon the experience of self-producing, the orchestra renegotiated its arrangement with Wolff & Sachs. Under the deal, the orchestra's terms were improved, but the *Philharmonischen Konzerte* remained presented under the concert agency's patronage. This agreement was criticised as highly *"ungünstig"* (inconvenient) by the new orchestra management after 1933.[70]

With the advent of the Nazi regime's involvement in Berlin Philharmonic affairs, the question of the orchestra's relationship to external producers was scrutinised on many levels. It was found that the tangled web of contractual and personal producing relations handicapped the orchestra, and proved financially detrimental. The practice of 'hiring' the orchestra was also anathema to a *Reichsorchester* service.[71] For the orchestra to function effectively to its prescribed propagandistic ends, at least on the domestic front, presentation of Philharmonic activities needed to be streamlined, and re-contextualised. Specifically, it was recommended the Philharmonic should acquire its own producing infrastructure, including artistic direction, which would be accountable to the RMVP. The *Reichssparkommissar* responsible for assessing the orchestra's needs in relation to *Gleichschaltung* practices, went so far as to suggest all co-producing and/or external producer relationships were completely eliminated.[72] The RMVP, therefore, would act as sole sponsor, the Philharmonic itself as sole producer.

As conductor of the *Philharmonischen Konzerte*, and self-appointed "Führer" of the Philharmonic Orchestra, Furtwängler was key to any reformation of the programming structure. In principle, he was supportive of the notion "that all concerts of the orchestra be in future organised by [the orchestra's] own management."[73] This arrangement would consolidate his prerogative to shape the orchestra's overall programming after his own taste, while the regime's financial support, moving away from dependency on commercial producers, would perhaps offer greater flexibility in the range of artistic choices.

Furtwängler was concerned, however, about the capacity of the orchestra's infrastructure to handle the production demands of a series such as the *Philharmonischen Konzerte*. "Personally, I am not necessarily for the elimination of private initiatives," he responded to the *Reichssparkommissar*, "whether they originate from a concert agency or from the orchestra itself as offers on a case by case basis."[74] He recommended maintaining the relationship with Wolff & Sachs, supplemental to the orchestra's expanding producing capacities. This Furtwängler offered out of at least two additional concerns: first, loyalty to the Wolff family, which had chosen him over Richard Strauss as heir to Nikisch as leader of the *Philharmonischen Konzerte* in 1922.[75] Second, out of concern for the Wolffs' future, for they were Jewish. Though the agreement between the Philharmonic and the Wolff & Sachs agency was categorically incompatible with the regime's intentions for the orchestra, the fact the Philharmonic's primary impresario, Louise Wolff, was half-Jewish (her mother was Christian),[76] expedited the need to dissolve this dependency.

As the 1934-35 season began, Wolff & Sachs, along with all other Berlin producing companies, were eliminated from Philharmonic season programming. By April 1935, the Wolff & Sachs had their license revoked by the *Reichsmusikkammer*, and the firm was disbanded. Upon hearing the news, the famous violinist and pedagogue, Carl Flesch, wrote to Louise Wolff from exile in London:

> My honored friend, the simultaneous news of your 80th birthday and of the liquidation of the concert management has partly gladdened and partly shaken us […] In any case you can liquidate your enterprise satisfied in the knowledge that you have done limitless good for the German music scene. The Hermann Wolff agency was no ordinary concert manager—it furthered and fertilized the German music scene and therefore takes a place of honor not only in its own field but in the history of the last 40 years of music.[77]

Heartbroken after losing the institution her husband had built and in which she had invested so much of her life, Louise Wolff died within months.

The Berlin Philharmonic, up to 1934, was essentially a bourgeois musical institution. Though it performed an array of 'popular' programmes, and gave concerts for students, even divorced from direct aristocratic patrons, the orchestra was ever-dependent on patronage, from impresarios like the Wolffs, or wealthy supporters such as Herr Landecker, owner of the Philharmonie concert hall. The assistance of such benefactors kept the orchestra proudly independent, but the Philharmonic essentially depended on a specific class of concert-goer, one responding to quality, and willing to pay substantial prices for it.

The *Philharmonischen Konzerte* series represented the orchestra's artistic signature; they were expensive and prestigious events. Their audience comprised primarily of an educated middle-class. Tickets were on average double the price of other orchestra concerts, and revenue from the twenty evenings annually exceeded the box office income from all the orchestra's other Berlin appearances combined.[78]

The success of the orchestra among the local Berlin and wider European bourgeois intelligentsia was important to the Nazi leadership too. The notion in reforming the Philharmonic into a *Reichsorchester* was not fundamentally to transform the way the orchestra made music, what it played, when and for whom, but rather to amplify those qualities that had brought the orchestra fame and praise in the past, while extending access to more diverse audiences. The regime required the legitimation of the bourgeois class, to which most of the Nazi leadership belonged, not only in general political terms, but also to preserve the Berlin Philharmonic's image and institutional pride. Only with health in the orchestra's musical culture, in achievement and perception, could it be useful for propagandist purposes. For this reason, even without Wolff & Sachs' guidance, maintaining the Philharmonic's musical traditions, in terms of programming and scheduling, remained a priority.

Despite the deep reforms the orchestra underwent through the 1932-33 and 1933-34 seasons, the foundation of the Philharmonic's musical activities remained the *Philharmonischen Konzerte*. The orchestra came to produce these Monday night Furtwängler-led concerts successfully, bankrolled by the RMVP. Furtwängler, by far the biggest draw in German classical music at the time, was initially contracted to conduct all ten programmes.[79] After his resignation and reconciliation in 1934-35, he continued to lead the majority of the prominent concerts, but as an artist with no fixed relationship to the orchestra, no longer conducted the entire series. With his name-association to the *Philharmonischen Konzerte* however, the orchestra counted over 1000 subscribers to the main series, plus several hundred more for the public *Vor-Konzerte* (pre-concerts).[80]

Philharmonischen Konzerte typically took place on Monday evenings at 19:30, once a fortnight from October to March.[81] The *Vor-Konzerte* were public dress rehearsals, held either Sunday morning at 11:30 or the morning of the concert itself, depending upon other schedules. All *Philharmonischen Konzerte* were given in the Philharmonie. Tickets for these concerts were relatively expensive, but the array of conductors, soloists and repertoire was almost always first rank. With this continuity, the orchestra retained its elite identity, bourgeois following, and image of musical integrity.

Though these many continuities were conscientiously enforced, the Nazi era also brought some departures from the orchestra's traditions. Anti-Semitism affected not only the orchestra, its musicians, its programming, and its business partners, but also changed the make-up of the Philharmonic's audience. It cannot be accurately ascertained what percentage of the Berlin Philharmonic's patrons or subscribers prior to 1933 were Jewish, but the city's assimilated Jewish community typified the orchestra's core audience.

From 1935 on, the entrances to the Philharmonie bore a warning: "Nichtariern ist der Zutritt nicht gestattet" (Entry for non-Aryans forbidden).[82] But, as Bertha Geissmar observed as early as April 1933, the Nazis transformed the concert-going public even without taking direct legal measures: "The Jews stay away from the concerts. They were intimidated, and their pride forbade them what the law would still allow. Nazis, meanwhile, did not often attend because the orchestra had not yet been 'brought into line'."[83] The struggles of Jewish wives of Philharmonic musicians to attend concerts, a product of the intense suspicion in German society transferred to the concert hall, accentuated the stringency, and effectiveness, of Nazi ideology.[84]

A some point between 1933 and 1935, Jewish Philharmonic patrons had their subscriptions revoked. Nevertheless, despite the loss, demand for Philharmonic tickets rose steadily through the 1930s. This fact may be attributable to a number of factors: Germany's improving economic situation; the new availability of tickets with the liquidation of Jewish subscriptions; the reach of State promotion of the orchestra; the successes of culture instruction as part of education/propaganda; or even the spiritual solace of music in increasingly arduous times. Whatever the causes, just as demand and attendance climbed, so too did ticket prices, even during the war.[85]

From 1938-39, the *Philharmonischen Konzerte* were broadcast live on the Deutschlandsender radio, "so that from now on the famous concerts of the Philharmonic could be made accessible to the whole world."[86] The outbreak of the war, though detrimentally impacting a number of other concert series, did not diminish enthusiasm for the *Philharmonischen Konzerte*. Indeed, in 1939/40, it was decided "because the concerts under the conductorship of Dr. Furtwängler are subject to such an extraordinarily high demand and the concerts, including the previews, were completely sold out long before the season's begin," to repeat the concert programs again on Tuesday nights.[87] In 1942-43, Furtwängler's concerts were offered up to four times "because even after with additional repeat concerts, the demand was just as strong as before."[88]

Popular demand for Furtwängler concerts was so great, the Philharmonic needed to put a cap on subscriptions, and resolved to abolish the automatic renewal rights of subscribers from season to season. This surprising initiative was justified in the ideological spirit of the times: "We wanted to offer all friends of music the chance to obtain a subscription, in particular since long-time subscribers were seen by many of the less fortunate as representatives of a social privilege that no longer corresponded to the spirit of our time."[89]

Though drawing tremendous accolades and astronomical fees, Furtwängler was not altogether pleased with the degree of his success. According to Hans von Benda, the conductor on a number of occasions expressed a desire to diminish his appearances with the Philharmonic.[90] In 1936, Furtwängler appealed to Hitler personally for release from the majority of his conducting duties over the coming year, claiming a desire to devote himself to *"ungelegte Eier"* (unhatched eggs).[91] As a result, for the first time in fifty years, the 1936-37 *Philharmonischen Konzerte* series did not boast a principal conductor.[92]

In 1939-40, Furtwängler again expressed "that he would perhaps never conduct again—or only in to a much reduced extent." [93] Whether due to feelings of political discomfort, a persistent interest in composing, or purely characteristic expression of his unpredictable temperament, Furtwängler consistently wished to curtail his commitments to the Berlin Philharmonic. He never conducted the complete *Philharmonischen Konzerte* series after 1933-34, and later called for the number of concerts to be reduced from ten to eight. [94] This was rejected, maliciously denounced by von Benda: "The 10 Philharmonic concerts (*Philharmonische Konzerte*) are significant to the whole world, and a reduction of the number of these concerts for purely egotistical reasons would mean a shock to the entire concert program of the Philharmonic." [95] Von Benda's melodramatics aside, this episode illustrated the significance of the concert series for the orchestra and in the public perception, and Furtwängler's own sense of entitlement to sculpt the orchestra's programming after his interests.

By 1944, as the war was closing in on Berlin, Furtwängler and von Benda's successor, Gerhard von Westerman, once more discussed the possibility of reducing the number of *Philharmonischen Konzerte* from ten to eight. Goebbels, however, was against such a reduction, again on symbolic terms. Under Goebbels' stewardship, the Berlin Philharmonic had been turned into an icon of the Reich, with the *Philharmonischen Konzerte*, under Furtwängler's direction, as its centrepiece activities. An *Abbau* of the institution of the concert series would have amounted to an unmistakable statement of the regime's weakness. This was not only unacceptable to Goebbels, but a point Furtwängler understood too. "I was," the conductor wrote to von Westerman, "not delighted by the Herr Minister's decision that all ten concerts should be continued. But in the end it is his expressed wish and the necessities of war—because that is what we're dealing with—are not something which I want to oppose." [96] With the letter, Furtwängler submitted his six programmes (the other four concerts to be led by Clemens Krauss, Ernest Ansermet and Karl Ellmendorf) for the coming season. [97] The Third Reich's demise cut the 1944-45 *Philharmonische Konzerte* season drastically short.

In the years prior to 1933, distinguished conductors such as Bruno Walter and Otto Klemperer were offered their own Wolff & Sachs-produced subscription series with the Philharmonic along side Furtwängler's primary series. Walter and Klemperer were both Jewish. When their appearances were effectively prohibited in 1933, Walter was replaced by Erich Kleiber, Kapellmeister at the *Staatsoper* for a six-concert series, while Carl Schuricht took over direction of the Philharmonischer Chor. When Furtwängler resigned in December 1934, hundreds of subscribers to the *Philharmonischen Konzerte* cancelled their subscriptions. Within several weeks, a provisional schedule was drafted to fill the outstanding dates. Curiously, Furtwängler himself appeared to have no qualms offering recommendations on who should replace him: Knappertsbusch, Abendroth, Jochum, Pfitzner, and Böhm.[98] All were closely associated with the NSDAP. Still more peculiar, Furtwängler seemed to have been under the impression Kleiber was a member of the NSDAP too (which he was not).[99] Abendroth and Jochum were engaged, but subsequent concerts fell to Carl Schuricht, Hermann Stange, and Peter Raabe.[100]

As compensation to disgruntled patrons, novice impresarios Karl Stegmann and the new *1. Geschäftsführer* Stange made a blunder by offering all *Philharmonischen Konzerte* patrons "As a certain compensation for the fact that other conductors will be leading the *Philharmonische Konzerte* in place of Herr Dr. Furtwängler, we are prepared to offer you a visit to one of the last concerts of Kleiber gratis."[101]

Though Erich Kleiber had resigned from the *Staatsoper* in solidarity with Furtwängler, this slight to his stature, 'cheapening' Kleiber's Philharmonic series, was taken as an offence. A lawyer promptly replied to the Philharmonic on Kleiber's behalf, noting the proposed free attendance at concerts was offered "without the consent of my client represents not only the abuse of my [sic] name, but also damages the prestige and appeal of any concerts that he conducts."[102] The lawyer obtained an injunction, barring the Philharmonic from giving away Kleiber concert tickets. Kleiber cancelled his remaining two appearances with the Philharmonic. In retaliation, the orchestra inquired with the RMVP if they had grounds for a countersuit based upon breach of contract.[103] Shortly thereafter, Kleiber left Germany, rendering moot the debate. The following concert in the Kleiber series was led by the Nazi veteran, Leopold Reichwein.

Furtwängler's resignation not only triggered a realignment of the *Philharmonischen Konzerte*, with indirect impact on Kleiber's series, but also laid the foundation for a number of organisational partnerships important to the Berlin Philharmonic in subsequent years. In 1934, the Berlin Philharmonic was new to producing its own concerts, and required help. In the aftermath of the 'Hindemith Affair', the orchestra was coupled with the State-established *Reichsmusikkammer* to assist in steering the orchestra through the crisis, supplementing the Philharmonic *Geschäftsführung* with organisation, infrastructure and advice. In the *Reichsmusikkammer*, Nazi-affiliated composers and conductors had a powerful lobby group. Stange and Reichwein were but two of a number of beneficiaries who used connections in the *Reichsmusikkammer* for access to the Philharmonic.

Further to programming, fearing a stark drop in audience either as an expression of solidarity with Furtwängler or as a result of public disinterest without the orchestra's major drawing card,[104] a number of plans were discussed in early 1935 to supplement Philharmonic concert attendance. These initiatives included a partnership with the newly-formed *Berliner Konzertgemeinde*. Founded by the City of Berlin as a sort of patrons' society, the Berliner *Konzertgemeinde* bought blocks of tickets for concerts at substantial discounts and distributed them to families, clubs, and workers' groups across the city.[105] Over time, the *Konzertgemeinde* began producing its own concerts at smaller Berlin venues, and was eventually absorbed into the Philharmonic's other important patrons' organisation, the NS-Gemeinschaft "Kraft durch Freude" ("Strength through Joy").[106]

As the name suggested, the *NS-Gemeinschaft* "Kraft durch Freude" was both a cultural and a political organisation. Founded by Robert Ley, *Reichsorganisationsleiter* der NSDAP, the organisation was a branch of the *Deutsche Arbeitsfront*, and operated in tandem with the *Reichskulturkammer* and Alfred Rosenberg's *Kulturgemeinschaft* to support "die Einheit zwischen Künstler und Volk" (unity between artist and the people).[107] Funded in large part by the *Reichskulturkammer* under Goebbels' direction,[108] "Kraft durch Freude" represented an extension of Nazi cultural politics into events programming. In Nazi Germany, politicisation and culturalisation marched hand in hand, and the Party formed "Kraft durch Freude" as a means of bringing Germans workers in contact with German culture and German art: "Die Kultur dem ganzen Volke und das Volk lebt in der Kunst" (Culture for all people, and the people live in art).[109] The organisation staged programmes, sponsored events, and, like the Berliner *Konzertgemeinde*, bought blocks of tickets to concerts and theatre performances, which it in turn made available to schools, workers, community groups and Party organisations, at highly subsidised prices.

"Kraft durch Freude" expressed a 'popular' mandate, advocating accessibility in accordance with Nazi precepts, both social and aesthetic. Though the organisation also promoted overtly Nazi artists such as Elly Ney, and the NS-Sinfonieorchester under ideological stalwart Gustav Havemann, as one of Germany's internationally recognised cultural treasures, introducing broader audiences to performances of the Berlin Philharmonic, as qualitative demonstration of the nation's musical prowess, was a major coup. Unlike the *Konzertgemeinde* which supplemented the orchestra's traditional Philharmonie concerts, "Kraft durch Freude" developed an arrangement with the Berlin Philharmonic creating its own series within the orchestra's season. For a fixed fee, "Kraft durch Freude" would essentially hire the Philharmonic for concerts in the Philharmonie, but also at a variety of venues such as sport halls and parks. As it was funded by the Party and the *Reichskulturkammer*, the organisation could offer thousands of tickets at less than one Mark a piece.[110]

The plan was highly successful. By removing the Philharmonic from its Philharmonie home, the orchestra was temporarily shed of its bourgeois image, suggesting greater accessibility for other classes. The larger venues also often created a popular event aura around the concerts. The orchestra generated solid revenues through up-front honoraria, and great music was made available to new audiences for a fraction the cost of the Philharmonic's main concerts. By producing concerts under its own *Regie*, "Kraft durch Freude" could also, as part of its 'educational' agenda, stipulate programming, putting heavy emphasis on the German classics such as Wagner, Richard Strauss, Weber, Brahms, Bruckner, and Beethoven.

Cooperation with the Berliner Konzertgemeinde and "Kraft durch Freude" allowed the Berlin Philharmonic to perform for larger and more diverse audiences than ever before. Eventually, the Berliner Konzertgemeinde was integrated as a subsidiary of the national NS-Gemeinde (KdF). Though both groups prized the Berlin Philharmonic for its musical excellence, as business propositions, they posed the orchestra problems. The *Konzertgemeinde* (Community Concert) was expected to buoy ticket sales for main Philharmonic programmes other than the *Philharmonischen Konzerte*. Tickets for subscription concerts with Jochum, Böhm, Schuricht, Knappertsbusch, and others, were made available to the Konzertgemeinde for an average of RM 2. But while the Berlin organisation promoted the concerts, it could not guarantee sales. Meanwhile, the *Konzertgemeinde* itself was producing concerts with similar soloists, in various local venues around Berlin with ticket prices less than one Reichsmark: "[the Berlin *Konzertgemeinde*] has, doubtless due to the great number of its events that are especially cheap, had the effect that a portion of our audience has drifted over to them, because they can see the concerts from the *Konzertgemeinde* for cheaper than ours." [111]

At the same time, "Kraft durch Freude" concerts were undermining the Philharmonic's own 'popular' concerts too. Though priced in the RM 0.70 to RM 2.00 range,[112] by 1937, these so-called *Sonntags-und Dienstags* (Sunday and Tuesday) Philharmonie concerts, of which the orchestra once offered more than fifty per year, were were not even half full. According to Stegmann's analysis, "This shows that the audience is limited and naturally goes where it can see the concerts it wants for cheapest."[113] "Kraft durch Freude," through its community and Party connections, could mobilise more people, and produce a better show for less than the Philharmonic on its own. From 1938-39 on, the Philharmonic withdrew completely from the business of 'popular' concerts, submitting "that in the coming season, the cheap concerts will be entirely dropped as there is no need for them. In return, we will put on concerts of special works in cooperation with KdF." [114]

Curiously, the decline in Philharmonic attendance for popular concerts in the late 1930s, coincided with the expansion of the *Philharmonischen Konzerte* series from two to three to four performances per programme. This suggested even if the overall concert-going audience of Berlin was limited, there was not one audience, but rather several distinct groups of patrons and potential patrons. "Kraft durch Freude" events were cheap and accessible, but also pompous affairs, accompanied by Nazi paraphernalia, fanfare and hyperbole. Awash in swastikas, "*Es spielt das* verstärkte *Berliner Philharmonisches Orchester*" (the *enhanced* Berlin Philharmonic Orchestra)[115] read their posters bombastically, and conductors (Erich Orthmann, Olav Kielland et. al.) were not always of the highest standard. Nevertheless, these concerts seem to have been well attended, and, together with the Berlin Konzertgemeinde's own concerts (rarely full symphony concerts, but often featuring major soloists like Edwin Fischer and Georg Kulenkampff for less than 10% what tickets would cost at the Philharmonic)[116], likely did steal a number of the Philharmonic's more casual patrons.

The Philharmonic's trademark concerts, meanwhile, became the refuge of an economically resurgent middle class. If this was a consequence of rising economic prosperity invested in the trappings of bourgeois culture, a reflection of blossoming Furtwängler adulation in the age of the *Führer*, or as an example of resistance to the politicisation of culture, can only remain speculative. The result, however was an increasing liberalisation or *bourgeoisation* of the Berlin Philharmonic rather than a reform of its elite image.

In addition to the *Philharmonischen Konzerte*, the Philharmonic's Berlin season broadly included:

- A number of smaller three to six concert series led exclusively by a single distinguished conductor other than Furtwängler.

- Eight to ten further individual concerts with both established and lesser-known conductors, a random gathering later grouped into a 'Sinfonie-Konzerte' subscription series, little brother to the *Philharmonischen Konzerte*.

- A series of several dozen popular concerts—dubbed *Sontags und Dienstags Konzerte*.

- Three choral concerts with the Bruno Kittel Chor.

- A row of concerts with the historic Berliner Sing-Akademie.

- One to three concerts with the Philharmonischen Chor.

- Several modern music concerts in collaboration with the Preussischen Akademie der Künste.

- Up to six so-called 'Schlüterhof' summer concerts (precursors to the Waldbühne concerts).

- A variety of *Sonder-, Benefiz- and Honorar-Konzerte* (special, benefit, and honorarium concerts).

Most years, the orchestra also gave popular and cultural-politically successful Beethoven cycles under a mixed bag of conductors. These models were reformed and refined by successive *künstlerische Leiter* (artistic directors) as the Philharmonic transitioned from its former freely associative form to a stable, regulated institution.[117]

In 1937-38, Hans von Benda offered a major overhaul of the Philharmonic programme. His first proposal was to reduce the Philharmonic's load of so-called *Honorar-Konzerte*, holdovers from the time the Berlin Philharmonic could be rented or hired for a fee by groups or individual. The row of annual Sing-Akademie concerts was one of the better, high-profile, examples of this policy, where the venerable choir group's popular concerts accompanied by the Philharmonic grew into a Berlin tradition. Still, the Sing-Akademie had no official affiliation to either the orchestra, the Philharmonie, or the Reich. The Berlin Philharmonic was paid a fee for its services within the activities of another organisation. This was precisely the sort of engagement von Benda was looking to minimise. Though Sing-Akademie concerts never disappeared from Philharmonic plans completely, the orchestra's association with the venerable choral group diminished over the following seasons to the level of sporadic large-scale events.[118]

The Philharmonic's own 'popular' concerts under a mixed-bag of batons, were also no longer commercially viable (see Chapter 3).

top: The *Vorstand* of the orchestra, Lorenz Höber in conversation with Furtwängler at the Philharmonie circa 1935.

bottom: Karl Stegmann in conversation with a colleague at the Philharmonie circa 1939.

top left: Hans von Benda (left) and Furtwängler, Bayreuth, 1937.

top right: Gerhart von Westerman, 1940.

bottom: The cello section, 1939. First stand: Tibor de Machula and Hans Bottermund; second stand: Wolfram Kleber and Friederich Mayer; third stand: Fritz Lesse and Karl Rammelt; fourth stand: Ernst Fuhr and Felix Tschirn; fifth stand: Max Paulus and Walter Gerke.

top: The Berlin Philharmonic chamber music ensemble, circa 1940. From right to left: Erich Röhn, Carl Höfer, Werner Buchholz, Wolfram Kleber, Alfred Krüger, Martin Ziller, Oskar Rothensteiner, Alfred Bürkner.

bottom: The Philharmonic family: orchestra and guests at a garden party hosted by Furtwängler at Potsdam, 1935. Furtwängler is in the middle of the front row and Hermann Stange is fifth from the left.

top: Leo Borchard, Philharmonie, circa 1940; the three trombonists in the background are Friedrich Quante, Willy Walther and Ernst Heidrich.

bottom: Inauguration of the *Reichskulturkammer* in the old Philharmonie, November 15 1933; at the lectern, is Minister of Propaganda, Joseph Goebbels.

The old Philharmonie, February 1944. Photo by violinist Alfred Hornoff. A caption on the back reads, "Photo taken at the peril of my life (death penalty)."

Top left © Scherl / Berlin Philharmonic Archives. Bottom: P.K. Wisch / Berlin Philharmonic Archives.

top: A post-concert reception in Berlin for the touring London Philharmonic, November 1936. From left to right: Carl Schuricht, an unknown guest, Peter Raabe, Sir Thomas Beecham, Wilhelm Furtwängler, Hans von Benda.

bottom: A reception in Paris, 1941. From left to right: Gerhard Taschner, Ernst Heidrich, Erich Röhn, two unknown officials, Arthur Troester.

top: Trip to England, 1937. The five horn players of the Berlin Philharmonic Orchestra, from left to right: Willi Koch, Martin Ziller, Otto Hass, Leonard Tiersch, Gustav Otto.

bottom: Trip to Scandinavia, 1942. Franz Jastrau with the double basses at the airport.

The Berlin Philharmonic with Furtwängler in Copenhagen, 1942.

Moreover, poor attendance had a "devastating effect on the orchestra" where the players felt depressed, when after "tremendous efforts—up to 580 performances per season, they were still frequently faced with sparse attendance. In those circumstances it was impossible to avoid such a workload having a negative effect on the performances themselves."[119] As a remedy, von Benda proposed doing away with the 'popular' concert series entirely, instituting in their place four pre-Christmas "klassichen" Konzerte with "erschwinglicher Eintrittspreise" (affordable ticket prices)[120], while repeating main Philharmonic series concerts at discounted prices through associations such as "Kraft durch Freude" and the Berliner Konzertgemeinde "so that in the future every fellow German could partake of the performances."[121]

Further, von Benda contracted the 1938 Beethoven cycle to a single conductor, Carl Schuricht. The Beethoven cycle, presenting all the symphonies together with the major concerti in eight to ten concerts over about two months, was one of the Philharmonic's most successful enterprises. Though the tradition predated the 1933 rise of the Nazis, Beethoven's primacy in the cannon of German composers framed the series in a new musical-political light. The allocation of conductors to the concerts was political, and not terribly distinguished (names like Heinz Bongartz, Hermann Stange, Bruno Vondenhoff, Gustav Havemann, Walter Meyer-Giesow). Benda's proposal brought a new dimension of artistic integrity to the proceedings: "The intention of generally improving the attendance of the concerts should be realised with a more relaxed programming policy incorporating more [popular] composers, like Mozart.[122]

From a programming cornerstone in the mid-1930s, the Beethoven Cycle over the following seasons was gradually rendered obsolete, eventually supplanted through von Westerman's programme restructuring by independent, three-concert Abendroth, Böhm, Jochum, Knappertsbusch, and Schuricht subscription packages. This initiative further liberalised Philharmonic concert-going, partly restoring the old Wolff & Sachs conductor-based programming model, while refocusing emphasis on middle-class audiences paying full prices for the fulfilment of their partisan musical tastes (Böhm fans, Jochum fans, Furtwängler fans etc.).

Hans von Benda's 1938 programme reforms, together with von Westerman's restructuring plans in the 1940s, further emphasised the orchestra's focus on quality and away from 'popular' commitments. The orchestra gave no more than three non-subscription concerts of 'modern' music per season (see Chapter 5), in conjunction with the Preussischen Akademie der Künste,[123] while by 1940, the Berlin Philharmonic's under-rehearsed, under-attended 'popular' concertising was limited to just three concerts in cooperation with the Berliner Konzertgemeinde under the umbrella of a Philharmonic series called "Beschwingte Musik"(Lively Music), and five "Kraft durch Freude" programmes which usually repeated programmes from other series.[124]

The diversity of audiences for which the Berlin Philharmonic performed meanwhile, was greater than ever. This was reflected in season programming, where repertoire would recur with astonishing frequently, but for the benefit of distinct audiences. In little over one year, from April, 1937 to May, 1938, the orchestra performed Beethoven's 9th Symphony on no fewer than six separate occasions:

- on April 2nd at the conclusion of the 1937 Beethoven cycle under Karl Elmendorf;

- in a Furtwängler *Sonderkonzert* on April 18th/19th, 1937;

- again under Furtwängler on September 6th, 1937 at the *Weltausstellung* (World's Fair) in Paris;

- at the Philharmonic's traditional *Volksbühne* New Year's Eve concert with Arthur Rother;

- under Schuricht in April, 1938 as part of the 1938 Beethoven Cycle;

- and at the *Reichsmusiktage* on May 19th, 1938 under Hermann Abendroth;

The ideological significance of *Die Neunte* (The Ninth) aside, each performance addressed itself to a different public with little overlap: the Beethoven cycle was a minor subscription package offering those popular symphonic works to families and the Berliner *Konzertgemeinde* at discounted prices; Furtwängler's *Sonderkonzert* was an exclusive, expensive non-subscription event, attended by a row of Nazi elite and broadcast on radio as a *Vorfeier* for Hitler's birthday; the Philharmonic was sent to Paris upon commission of the government as Germany's musical ambassador to the World's Fair, where it played for an international audience of tourists, journalists and diplomats; the New Year's Eve concerts were formal gala occasions in the traditional aristocratic mould, beginning at 11PM, timed to ring in the New Year with champagne and the "Ode to Joy" at midnight; while the *Reichsmusiktag* in Düsseldorf was an overtly ideological event open to Party members, students, and interested public for purposes of education and cultural enrichment.

In 1942, the Philharmonic again reprised Beethoven's *Ninth Symphony* under Furtwängler three times in one month—as part of the *Philharmonischen Konzerte* (21.3.42) with the Bruno Kittel Chor, at a "Kraft durch Freude" event the following day (22.3.42), and on April 19th at a *Feierstunde der NSDAP zu Hitlers Geburtstag* (birthday), preceded with a rousing speech by Goebbels.

The initial goal of setting the Berlin Philharmonic on its feet as sole producer of its own concerts, shutting out 'lecherous' intermediaries such as Wolff & Sachs and the Backhaus agency, did not last either. Through its relations to its proprietors in the Reich leadership, the *Reichsmusikkammer*, the Berliner Konzertgemeinde, the NS-Gemeinschaft "*Kraft durch Freude*", the RMVP, and various other subsidiaries of the State and Party apparatus, the Berlin Philharmonic was chained perhaps even more so than before to the demands of impresarios and benefactors. While the *Philharmonischen Konzerte* essentially ran themselves, much of the rest of the season was filled with forms of obliged performances, command performances, or concerts which blurred the lines between political and musical experience. Such activities also included a range of benefit, school, factory and Wehrmacht concerts.

The 'social' dimension to Philharmonic programming foreseen in the Berliner Sinfonie-Orchester merger plan of 1932, failed to come into force once the city of Berlin lost leverage with the Philharmonic. The prescribed thirty *Volks-Sinfonie Konzerte*[125] were broken down into *Sonntags- und- Dienstags Konzerte*, which eventually gave way to an array of "Kraft durch Freude" and Konzertgemeinde events. Educational student concerts (Jugend Konzerte) [126] were reduced from twelve concerts to just nine by 1938,[127] and ceased to exist completely with the start of the war. The slack in these areas was taken up by special concerts given by the orchestra on a more irregular basis, principally performances for the Hitler Jugend. Concerts given through various Nazi organisations also reached young people in greater numbers than before.

In addition, the orchestra performed benefit concerts for the *Deutschen Roten Kreuz* (German Red Cross), *Winterhilfswerk* (Winter Aid Fund), and *Künstler-Altershilfe* (Retired Artists' Fund), donating their services and the proceeds to these causes. The Philharmonic also gave a limited number of concerts for workers directly in the factories: at Hugo Schneider A.G. (Köpenick); at Stock, the armaments manufacturer in Berlin-Marienfelde; for the employees of Telefunken; and in the factory halls of Siemens and AEG Berlin.[128] These appearances were goodwill concerts, the orchestra appearing gratis, occasionally even making cash donations on top of receipts.[129] Conductors such as Furtwängler, however, though presumably sharing in the spirit of "Pflicht, für die Arbeiter zu spielen (duty of playing for the workers),"[130] collected their usual fees.[131] As hybrid *charity-Dienste*, benefit and workers' factory concerts were often filmed and publicised, registering among the orchestra's propaganda activities too.[132] Finally, the Berlin Philharmonic played for soldiers of the Wehrmacht both abroad (see Chapter 6) and at the Philharmonie in Berlin.[133] Here again, film crews were often on hand to record and broadcast these 'charity' events.

In truth, activities such as performances for workers, soldiers, or fundraisers for public goods were not unique either to the Berlin Philharmonic or in Germany either prior to, or during the war. Orchestras in Great Britain, America and the Soviet Union also participated in benevolent activities. The difference with the Berlin Philharmonic was the degree to which the orchestra was bound to the political machinery of the State. In April 1937, the Philharmonic played a benefit concert for the *Reichsluftschutzbundes* (air raid defence league); later that year, while on tour in Italy, the orchestra gave a fund-raising *Wohlfahrtskonzert* under Carl Schuricht with with gala ticket prices. The concert was billed "unter der Protektion des Reichsministers für Propaganda und Volksaufklärung Dr. Goebbels und des italienischen Botschafters Attolico."[134] In 1944, von Westerman raised the possibility of repeating all Furtwängler concerts "kostenlos für Wehrmachtsangehörige und Rüstungsarbeiter. (free for members of the Wehrmacht and armaments workers),"[135] This was a matter of national pride, goodwill, and political protecting of interests.

The Philharmonic could not simply rest on its normative laurels; beneficiaries of such privilege were morally if not forcibly compelled to contribute to their society and the war effort. The Berlin Philharmonic was concerned with image building. Due to financial constraints under the stretched resources in 1944, the free Furtwängler concert plan could only be partially enacted (partly too because the conductor would not waive his fee).[136] Nevertheless, the orchestra made itself available for a variety of concerts throughout the Third Reich which were in themselves charitable acts, yet contextualised, beg less naïve hindsight. In 1935, the Berlin Philharmonic gave a special performed Bach's *Matthäus-Passion* during a Reichmusikkammer-sponsored Bach-Händel-Schütz-Feier. Though initially promised a fee, the RMVP eventually told the orchestra "would appreciate it if the Philharmonic Orchestra would work without remuneration in support of the celebrations of the Reich."[137] For free then, the Berlin Philharmonic participated in the reactionary musical precursor to the *Reichsmusiktage* in Dusseldorf wherein Goebbels delivered a speech proclaiming, "For the first time, the government has placed itself in support of a musical event of the sort that offers an overview of the musical accomplishments of three masters who [...] established themselves in the fight against foreign domination."[138]

Later the same year, this time for a fee, the Berlin Philharmonic agreed to perform a Liszt, Beethoven and Bruckner programme at the Berliner Sportpalast for the church and social organisation *Katholischen Aktion* (Catholic Action). The event celebrated the

Coronation of the Pope.[139] Given the Pope's close ties to the Hitler regime, this too could not be seen as a purely neutral event. In 1937, the Philharmonic appeared at the XXI Schlessisches Musikfest in the politically-sensitive city of Breslau.

The regime also seemingly recognised the sensitivity of framing Philharmonic appearances. A 1942 memo labelled *Geheim* (secret) described the multiple uses and values of Philharmonic activities: "The press is requested to take note of the following: a) the three guest concerts from Karajan with the Berlin Philharmonic in support of the *WHW* on the December 27th (public, Berlin Philharmonie) on December 28th (for armament workers in Borsigwalde) and on December 29th (for the wounded, in the Philharmonie)."[140] In this instance, benefit, workers' and soldiers' concerts were combined in a single programme.

In September 1939, the Philharmonic was commanded to a series of radio broadcasts. "Herr Reich's Minister Dr. Goebbels has decreed that we will, in the near future, be playing a series of concerts over the radio."[141] The first broadcast was transmitted at 20h, Monday, September 11th, 1939. The programme: Brahms' *First Symphony* and Beethoven's *Leonore III*, conducted by Karl Böhm. A two hour rehearsal was held that afternoon, prior to going on air. Though radio in many ways represented a new means of accessibility for millions of listeners to the glories of the Philharmonic, ten more concerts, two under Furtwängler, were broadcast through September 1939 as the Blitzkrieg crushed Poland.[142] These initial broadcasts formed the basis for the *Unsterbliche Musik* (Immortal Music) series, a row of radio concerts, and cinema trailers celebrating 'immortal' German music with patriotic embellishment.

In general, radio broadcasts constituted another aspect of the Berlin Philharmonic's performing. The *Reichs-Rundfunk-Gesellschaft* (RRG) had been a significant financial supporter of the orchestra pre-dating 1933, and remained an active partner of thereafter, though no longer as a dependent funding source. The RRG broadcast a number of concerts from the Philharmonie, but also scheduled Philharmonic recording sessions in its own studios programmed exclusively for radio broadcast. Radio was one of Goebbels's preferred means of propaganda, and he commissioned a vast amount of cultural programming for the RRG to stoke nationalist sentiment. Naturally, Goebbels' prized musical asset, the Berlin Philharmonic, played a prominent role, projecting national pride and artistic enjoyment to listeners across Germany and on short-wave abroad.

The contract between the RRG and the Berlin Philharmonic called for a four-fold partnership comprising *Senderkonzerte*, broadcasts of *Philharmonischen Konzerte*, broadcasts of other concerts of the Philharmonic, and producing commercial recordings. *Senderkonzerte* were typically commissioned broadcasts, such as those of September 1939,[143] a special short-wave Wagner transmission for North and South America, a *Schwedisch-Norwegischer Abend* (Swedish-Norwegian evening) in 1937, or occasions like the 85th anniversary of Chopin's death. For *Senderkonzerte* (radio broadcast concerts), the Philharmonic provided a reduced *Besetzung* (instrumentation) of 61 musicians, and performed predominantly shorter, popular classics or symphonic excerpts under conductors agreed by mutual consent. Numbering roughly five per season prior to the war, these performances were relatively infrequent because of the expense incurred for transportation of instruments to the *Funkhaus* from the Philharmonie, and the Philharmonic's per-service rate (RM 50 per musician for two rehearsals and a performance).[144] Further, the RRG had its own *Reichssenderorchester* (Reich's Radio Broadcast Orchestra). Finally, it was also thought *Senderkonzerte* might undermine concert ticket sales to the Philharmonic's local audience

By contrast, ticket sales were not a problem for the *Philharmonischen Konzerte*, which from 1938, with Goebbels' blessing, were carried by the RRG live or pre-recorded, nation-wide on Monday evenings.[145] For the broadcast rights, the orchestra received RM 45 000 per season. Therewith, the RRG was transferred rights to primary and secondary broadcast, plus confirmation of a joint understanding that "the dissemination of Philharmonic concerts via foreign radio broadcasters is from the point of view of cultural politics, highly desirable." [146]

Of cultural political significance also, were periodic broadcasts of non-subscription Philharmonic concerts, which were construed under similar terms as the *Philharmonischen Konzerte*, but for a considerably lower fee, could be freely excerpted, and gave the RRG free option to broadcast performances whenever they chose.[147] This was especially useful for strategic programming, such as concert broadcasts as part of the festivities surrounding Hitler's birthday, often when the Philharmonic performances themselves bore no relation to the event.[148]

As for commercial recordings, the Philharmonic made itself available to the RRG, among other recording companies, to record almost anything with anyone, subject to orchestra availability, for a fee. The commercial benefits to record sales were still in their nascent phase at the time, while records were of diminished propagandistic value by comparison to radio broadcast, touring and live performance, all of which meant the Berlin Philharmonic did not make a large number of recordings during the Third Reich. Those it did were under a variety of labels, including Deutsche Grammophon, EMI-Electrola, and Polydor. Even within this still relatively small field, personal, political and commercial battles were waged. In 1938-39, just six months after Furtwängler recorded Tchaikovsky's 6th Symphony for EMI, the Berlin Philharmonic was again hired for a recording of the work, this time on the Polydor label, with the conductor Herbert von Karajan.[149]

The flurry of Philharmonic broadcasts at the start of the war signified the importance the Nazis placed on music as a source of inspiration and patriotism, while placing the orchestra firmly at the forefront of their war-time domestic propaganda campaign. In 1940/41, in addition to the *Philharmonischen Konzerte* broadcasts which moved to Sundays, the *Deutschen Rundfunk* broadcast seven *Senderkonzerte* plus highlights recorded from a plethora of secondary Philharmonie concerts.[150] In 1941/42, the Philharmonic produced four records for the RRG.[151]

The importance of music to the war effort was underscored by the morbidly-named "Unsterbliche Musik deutschen Meister" ("immortal music of German masters"), which began in 1942-43. The initiative was a type of co-production between the *Reichsmusikkammer* and the RRG, both under RMVP control, and was aimed at ideologically binding the struggles of the war with a triumph of German culture. Berlin Philharmonic Intendant, Gerhard von Westerman, with his previous experience working in radio, was put in charge

of programming for the series, which broadcast a full concert programme every week until 1945. The density of the programme
schedule meant material was drawn not only from Philharmonic
performances, but also from concerts by other German orchestras,
archive recordings, and opera performances such as Wagner's *Ring*
from Bayreuth.[152]

Though the aims of the *"Unsterbliche Musik"* broadcasts portrayed the ambivalent mixture of political, ideological, strategic,
educational, and diversionary values characteristic of many of the
Philharmonic's Third Reich activities, discussions surrounding the
series were always couched in qualitative discourse. Jointly lament-
ing the programming dilemmas faced by von Westerman in 1944,
Furtwängler offered "I understand your dilemma with respect to
the 'immortal' music quite well. It really is no small matter to put
together a top-class programme every eight days. My fear is that
without repetitions and other concessions, it will prove entirely impossible to maintain, in the long run. The repertoire—not to mention the artist selection—is simply limited."[153]

The sensitivity of this comment was as revealing as its unique-
ly distorted logic, typifying the artist's construed mentality of the
era. The paradox: Furtwängler and von Westerman shared a genuine commitment to artistic integrity, *"ein höchstwertiges Programm"*
("top-class programme"), not some propagandistic pastiche, even as
the very forum for its presentation embodied the source of unimaginable suffering, of which a limited repertoire was but a token reminder.

Nevertheless, the 1939/40 season stood "under the flag of war"
as Westerman filed in his artistic director's report to the RMVP:

> By decree of the Herr Reichs Minister for Public
> Enlightenment and Propaganda with regards to the
> continuation of cultural events during the war, it was not
> only a possibility but much more an obligation to realise
> all of the concerts planned for this season. At the same
> time it has also become apparent that our initial fears
> that concert attendance would be negatively affected by
> the measures necessitated by the war—blackouts, limited
> public transport service, etc.—were unfounded. On the
> contrary: the war experience brought about an even more

active concern and even larger interest for the offerings
of serious music in the concert going public."[154]

Where difficulties did emerge, such as travelling through Germany
to deliver traditional concerts in Hamburg, the government interceded to ensure the necessary means were made available.[155]

Indeed, the early years of the war were among the most successful for the Berlin Philharmonic, when all the pieces of its musical,
political, commercial, and civic existence harmonised brilliantly. The
war presented the orchestra a heightened sense of purpose, brought
musical experience a new dimension, instilled in audiences a new
urgency, and further blurred the lines between public good and propagandistic service. During the seasons 1939 to 1942, the Berlin
Philharmonic was at an apex, striking a most impressive balance between widespread exposure, popular success, programming consistency, and an acceptable service-load for its musicians.

Eventually, however, the tide of the war turned. Blackouts,
transport restrictions and air raids became dangerous daily realities.
Though interest in serious music did not necessarily waver, access
grew more challenging, for audiences to reach the Philharmonic,
and for the orchestra to fulfil its concert-giving duties. "The principle," wrote von Westerman in his 1942/43 report, "of putting as little
strain as possible on the German Reich's Railway system meant that
we completely abstained from concert tours in the territory of the
German Reich in the fourth winter of the war." [156] The fifty year
tradition of Hamburg subscription concerts was suspended. That
same year, Philharmonic Berlin concerts were rescheduled one to
two hours earlier, commencing at six or six-thirty PM;[157] programmes
were later limited to one and a half hours for patrons to get home
before evening blackouts.[158] Programmes announced "In the event
of an air raid, the entire audience is to proceed to the cloakrooms
and hallways of the ground floor,"[159] and with increasing frequency,
concerts were interrupted by alarm signals, prompting audience and
orchestra to bunker down for hours.

On November 28, 1943, the first Philharmonic concert in
Berlin—a Karl Böhm *Philharmonischen Konzert*—had to be com-
pletely abandoned due to an air raid. The same week, the historic
Berliner Sing-Akademie (today the Maxim Gorky Theatre) was

destroyed by allied bombing.[160] Also the last week of November, the Philharmonic's administrative offices were destroyed. The Philharmonic's tradition New Year's Eve concert, for security reasons, was moved from December 31, to the afternoon of January 1.

Fearing the worst, the Philharmonic did not hesitate to invoke its privilege for precaution, requesting special permission for von Westerman, Stegman, Lorenz Höber, Friedrich Quante, the music librarian, in case of emergency, to be permitted to ride with military or official vehicles in order to reach the Philharmonie as rapidly as possible. [161]

On the evening of January 30, 1944, exactly eleven years after Hitler's proclamation as Chancellor, the Philharmonie was destroyed in a British bombing raid on Berlin.[162] Despite on-duty *Luftschutz* patrol and the rapid response privileges afforded key orchestra functionaries, the Great Hall burned completely, while the adjacent Beethoven Hall was heavily damaged, but remained functional. Countless instruments, music scores, and Philharmonic documents were lost in the blaze. The material damages were high, the psychological shock to the orchestra immeasurable, but the administrative and bureaucratic reflexes were quick to respond. The Philharmonic rented the *Staatsoper* auditorium for its next *Philharmonischen Konzerte* on the 7th and 8th of Feburary, repeating the Furtwängler programme mornings and afternoons both days for reasons of economy and security.

The following *Philharmonischen Konzerte* on February 20 and 21 were cancelled, as was the first of two Böhm concerts the first week of March, 1944.[163] Without a home, the Philharmonic shuttled between an assortment of performance venues throughout Berlin—the *Staatsoper*, *Titaniapalast*, the *Volksbühne*, the *Berliner Dom* and the *Beethoven Saal*, among others. Of varying sizes, locations were chosen based upon availability and the anticipated audience. Knappertsbusch concerts, for example, were larger draws than Robert Heger or Jochum concerts, and therefore took place in the more generous capacity of the Berliner Dom; concerts with lesser-known conductors such as were farmed out to locations such as the Berufsschule in Neu-Lichtenberg.[164] *Philharmonischen Konzerte*, meanwhile, demanding a better acoustic and more comfortable ambiance for their patrons, were lodged in the *Staatsoper*, despite its reduced seating capacity vis-à-vis the old Philharmonie. Beyond performing locations, a number of primarily foreign conductors cancelled their appearances in Berlin, compelling the orchestra to reimburse ticket-holders.[165]

Their orchestra's finances, programming and morale in shambles, with no place to perform, the RMVP decided to alleviate the situation by shipping the Berlin Philharmonic out on tour. Most remaining Berlin concerts were cancelled, and from the middle of March 1944, the orchestra was first sent on a sojourn to Scandinavia, returning briefly to appear with Knappertsbusch at Hitler's birthday celebrations in April, before embarking on an unscheduled six-week tour of France, Portugal, and Spain. A propaganda film was made during the orchestra's refuge in Iberia. The orchestra returned from the Mediterranean in June, passing through Paris the very week of the Allied D-Day Normandy landing, and was immediately put on summer vacation.[166]

During the summer of 1944, the Berlin Philharmonic once again profited from its privileged relationship with the regime. From the end of July to mid-September the RMVP arranged for Philharmonic members, along with their families, to take up "summer residence" in the relative safety of Baden-Baden. Instruments were stored in a secured location outside Pleissenburg bei Coburg (Bavaria), while the evacuated orchestra gave concerts for local audiences in backwaters such as Rastatt, Gagenau, and Lahr. The Philharmonic also made a number of broadcast recordings with Robert Heger during their extended holiday.

By the time the Philharmonic finally returned to Berlin in September 1944, not only had the physical landscape of their city transformed, but also Berlin's cultural plan. In fall 1944, all able-bodied workers at cultural institutions across Germany were mobilised for the losing war effort. Despite Göring's patronage, the *Staatsoper* orchestra and ensemble, as well as the Bruno Kittel Chor, the Philharmonischen Chor, among other Berlin institutions, were dissolved or massively reduced through service draft. Theatres and commercial music groups suffered a similar fate. The Philharmonic remained, quite literally, the only show in town.

Their long hiatus, however, had allowed administrators, bureau-crats, and politicians to work out the details of the Philharmonic's 1944-45 season. Though the first *Philharmonischen Konzerte* of the season took place at the then vacant *Staatsoper*, from December, most Philharmonic subscription concerts were moved to the Admiralpalast, as it was decided on the political level that in the *Staatsoper* "only private events, where no tickets are to be sold, should take precedence."[167] The *Staatsoper*, however, was also destroyed in January 1945, forcing the Philharmonic further afield in the final few months of the war.

Audiences too were shrinking, performances in general becoming more sporadic. The orchestra's principal activities concentrated on maximising its exposure. Radio broadcasts and mass concerts became the priority. Abendroth and Keilberth conducted a series of concerts in December and January. Furtwängler conducted the last *Philharmonischen Konzert* on January 22-23, 1945 before himself fleeing Germany. After that, the pieces of the Berlin Philharmonic's musical life came crashing together in rapid sequence: a *Trauerfeier* (memorial service) *im Kuppelsaal des Reichssportfeldes* (Reich's athletic grounds) with a new Chorwerk by Willi Traeder (21.2.45); a Hitler Jugend concert (24.3.45); a *Wehrmachtsbenefizkonzert* (benefit concert for the *Wehrmacht)* in Zossen (27.3.45); a performance of the Mozart Requiem in the Beethovensaal with the Lamy Chor— the Bruno Kittel Chor no longer existed (29/30.3.45);[168] a last Meistersinger *Vorspiel* for soldiers and the NSFO at the Berliner Olympisches Dorf (7./13.4.45); and the final concerts in the un-heated Beethoven Saal, including Brahms' *Deutsches Requiem* under Georg Schumann with the remnants of the Berliner Sing-Akademie (14.4.45).[169]

There is no record of what time of day these last performances occurred, or for whom they were intended. By mid-April, the Red Army was at the gates of Berlin. Able-bodied Germans had long since mobilised to the front. *Volkssturm* thugs ruled the streets, while those too young or too old to fight took refuge underground. The war had come home, and Philharmonic members were facing the terror themselves, experiencing the cycle of death and destruction their regime had unleashed first hand.[170] Colleagues were dying, families perished, homes were obliterated, and yet the orchestra played on.

In 1934-35, the Berlin Philharmonic performed for 151 702 people over 178 concerts.[171] In August 1936, the orchestra made its first appearance at the Nürnberg rallies, playing in one day for over half its total audience number from the previous year. At the height of its concertising activities during the Third Reich, not including mass events such as the *Reichsparteitage* or the Olympic Games, in 1940-41, the orchestra was attended live by a combined audience of 222 866 men, women and children, including 38 000 soldiers, and heard across the country on a weekly basis via radio broadcasts of the *Philharmonischen Konzerte*.[172]

Beside the sad final concerts under the Nazi banner, after the soldier and *Hitlerjugend* mass performances in late Winter and early Spring, the Berlin Philharmonic had one last command performance to play: On April 11, 1945, Armaments Minister Albert Speer convened the orchestra for a private concert in the Beethovensaal, a few meters from the bombed-out wreckage of the Philharmonie. Speer was a cultured man and profound music lover. The Berlin Philharmonic owed its salvation from almost certain decimation to him, after the Minister, reportedly in violation of Goebbels' own instructions, extended the orchestra's *Uk-Stellung*, saving the men from almost certain decimation. With a programme of Beethoven, Bruckner, and Wagner, the Berlin Philharmonic thanked its saviour, and took one final bow before a representative of the regime, which had brought the sound of the orchestra to millions.

Chapter 5

Unsere deutsche Musik: Programming

WHEN IT CAME TO MUSIC REPERTOIRE, the Nazis did not disguise their agenda—one derivative of an inconsistent blend of aesthetic appreciation, ideological principle and personal taste. The Nazis measured music according to politically-influenced interpretive criteria, namely the ideological framework which postulated a unity between 'high'-, *Volks*-, and *Unterhaltungs-musik*. The working theory privileged German classics, and those deemed among their contemporary heirs, as exponents of Germany's true, *Völkisch* roots. Translated into practice, the German 18th and 19th Century cannon, plus the works of living German composers writing in Romantic idioms, represented the bulk of the preferred repertoire. This grouping harmonised the pseudo-scientific historicist bias of continuity within a supreme German culture, with the fictitious struggle between mythological German values and foreign 'degenerate' influences. It also, not coincidentally, reflected the private tastes of the Party and later State curators.

Support for this music was iterated through the editorial bias of the Party-affiliated and State-controlled press, public sponsorship of festivals or events highlighting music representing the Nazi's postulated cultural values, and public endorsement through patronage of Hitler, Goebbels, Göring, Rosenberg, Ley, and others. From their speeches, political literature, and various media mouthpieces, what the Nazis liked and what they disapproved of, in musical terms, was common knowledge even long before they came to power. For this reason, there were remarkably few instances once Hitler occupied the Chancellery, where the government actually mandated what could or could not be performed. Anti-Semitic bias was a given, but sieving the rest of the repertoire also required little official assistance.

In the case of the Berlin Philharmonic, the first, most blunt reason for this definition of musical programming was direct political control. Overt political intervention in matters of Philharmonic programming was typically limited, however, to performances under explicitly Nazi auspices, such as Party functions, or State-sponsored events. This included Philharmonic appearances at the *Reichsparteitage* in Nürnberg, the various music and art events in Munich and Dusseldorf, or special anniversary celebrations. The tenor of these commissions characteristically defined parameters, with implied aesthetic preferences, but also remained somewhat open-ended. For example, in 1937, *Reichskulturverwalter* Hans Hinkel wrote to Karl Böhm:

> By request of the Reich's minister Dr. Goebbels you have been designated to conduct the introductory music (symphony) at this year's meeting of the *Reichskulturkammer* on the morning of November 26. Please get in touch with me concerning this matter as soon as possible and let me know about your proposals regarding the choice of repetoire.[1]

Circumstances designated the boundaries of expectation—the *Tagung* of the *Reichskulturkammer* was, after all, the RMVP's own party—while it was left up to the conductor to make specific suggestions. Böhm came up with a Schumann and Wagner programme suitably festive and compatible with the Nazis' requisites.

In 1943, Hitler requested hearing the Philharmonic with Furtwängler perform some of his personal favourites: "The *Fuhrer* desires Bruckner's symphony on the programme in connection with one of Beethoven's symphonies."[2] Objectively, these commissions were entirely within ministry, government or Party prerogative— they owned the orchestra, paid its bills, and were providing, in such instances, the forums in which the Berlin Philharmonic was to perform. It was indeed an extraordinary luxury to maintain such an instrument at its beck and call, but at least Hitler granted a choice of exactly which Bruckner and Beethoven selections the conductor and orchestra wished to offer.

Though political offices stipulating programmes was a clear abrogation of artistic freedom, the requests themselves, in terms of musical selections, were not out of keeping with the preponderance of the Philharmonic's typical repertoire. In 1935, for example, on 178 programmes, the Berlin Philharmonic performed Beethoven 85 times, Brahms 45, Bach 28, Händel 16, Pfitzner 15, Robert Schumann 20, Richard Strauss 29, Wagner 16, Weber 19, Bruckner 16, Haydn 26, Mozart 38, and Schubert 20 times. The only non-Germanic composer to break into double digits was Tchaikovsky with 18 performances.[3] These ratios did not change significantly over the following decade, with the vast majority of the repertoire drawn from the German 'canon'. The very need for ministry meddling, therefore, even after the orchestra's acquisition by the State, was rare: Nazi musical predilection and core Berlin Philharmonic repertoire were well harmonised from the outset.

This complementary effect was the result of a number of factors. First, the Berlin Philharmonic's principal concert series in 1933 were the 'popular' *Sonntags- und Dienstagskonzerte*, and the prestigious *Philharmonischen Konzerte*. Commercial considerations meant programming for popular concerts, in order to draw sufficient audience, necessitated remaining within well-known and accessible genres. A typical programme of this sort was given on September 24, 1933 under the baton of Heinz Bongartz: Wagner, *Meistersinger Vorspiel*; Mozart, *Eine kleine Nachtmusik*; Bach *Adagio und Fuge* aus *Suite g-moll*; Beethoven *Leonore Ouverture No.3*; Weber, *Vorspiel* zu *Euryanthe*; a selection of cello solos by Chopin, Faure and Popper; and Karl Goldmark's *Balletmusik* aus *die Königin von Saba*. These sorts of musical potpourri programmes offered little aesthetic risk because the Philharmonic could not afford to challenge or alienate a fickle middle-class audience which had many other choices for an evening's entertainment in 1930s Berlin. Though the Nazis could take exception with a handful of composers on racial grounds, aesthetically, the Philharmonic's popular programmes, which accounted for almost half the orchestra's Berlin concerts, generally conformed to the ruling Party's musical notions.

Popular programmes were not only attractive to middle and

lower class audiences. As a private enterprise up to 1934, the Berlin Philharmonic could also have its programming effectively shaped at the behest of individual wealthy patrons. For a sum, upper-class music lovers could hear the Berlin Philharmonic perform exactly what they liked: when a long-time Philharmonic patron named Paul Winkelsesser passed away, he left the orchestra a generous will of RM 40 000. The bequest, however, came with one condition:

> That on a day close to his birthday, in the middle of January, a concert be given in remembrance of him. The program was fixed and gave testimony to the musical taste of the deceased benefactor: Schubert's *Unvollendete*, the Double Concerto for two Violins by Bach and three movements from Beethoven's 9th symphony. This program will, as always, be performed on the memorial day.[4]

The tradition of Winkelsesser memorial concerts lasted until 1937, but more than its longevity, significant was correlation between a bourgeois Philharmonic patron's dearest "musikalischen Geschamck" for Schubert, Bach and Beethoven, and the musical values of Germany's new dictators.

The *Philharmonischen Konzerte*, meanwhile, were under Furtwängler's personal curatorium. Furtwängler alone was responsible for the concerts' programming, including selection of soloists, guest conductors and repertoire. As with the popular concerts, the conductor was to a certain extent bound by commercial considerations in programming the Philharmonic's main series too; the *Philharmonischen Konzerte* represented the orchestra's principal source of revenue, which could not afford jeopardising with adventurous programming choices. Berlin of the 1920s and 1930s, however, was a cosmopolitan and musically progressive environment, and the Berlin Philharmonic, though principally a bourgeois institution by organisation and patronage, was not strictly a bastion of conservatism. In 1920-21, the last full season of *Philharmonischen Konzerte* under Arthur Nikisch's leadership, the ten principal subscription concerts included a range of challenging repertoire: Walter Braunfels' *Phantastische Erscheinungen eines Themas von Berlioz*,

Mahler's *Seventh Symphony*, Ernst von Dohnanyi's *Violin Concerto*, an *Orchesterrondo* by Edouard Erdmann, and Erich Korngold's *Symphonische Ouverture Sursum corda*. Nikisch's choices reflected an embrace of 'modern' music without venturing too far into the radical avant-garde of, for instance, Webern or Varese.

Though his repertoire was considerably broader than the German romantic canon too, the thumbprint of Furtwängler on Philharmonic programming diverged subtly from that of his predecessor. In his first season as conductor of the *Philharmonischen Konzerte*, in 1922-23, among the ten concerts, Furtwängler conducted seven works by then-living composers: Sibelius' *En Saga*, Hans Pfitzner's *Ouverture to Das Käthchen von Heilbronn*, Glazounov's *Violin Concerto*, Richard Strauss' *Till Eulenspiegel*, Max Trapp's Second Symphony, and *Fünf Orchesterstücke Op.16* by Arnold Schoenberg. Although composers such as Stravinsky, Mahler, Prokofiev, Schoenberg, and Hindemith appeared in Furtwängler's repertoire over subsequent seasons, the conductor's programming choices, together with the character of his own compositions generally belied a distinct preference for broad romanticism. Furtwängler later explained his approach to programming thus:

> When someone asks why I keep bringing certain works of the 18th and 19th century to the stage, I can basically only respond with one thing: Because I [...] do not primarily make music as a curious wanderer through the literature or as someone with scholarly interests, but as an enthusiast. I perform the great works because I love them; the enthusiasm, the warmth, the sweetness, beauty, grandeur which this first-rate music and only it evokes in me is the source, the reason for all the music I make.[5]

Even as Braunfels, Mahler and Korngold were Jewish or part Jewish, it is safe to say Nikisch did not programme their works because they were Jewish; likewise, it would be specious to argue Furtwängler's choices deliberately avoided Jewish composers, Schoenberg aside.[6] The point was one of aesthetic judgement rather than ethnic bias. Each of the composers programmed by Nikisch in 1920-21 listed above were either banned outright or harshly criticised during the Third Reich not only for their parentage, but also for their progressive musical tendencies.[7] Furtwängler's repertoire, meanwhile, already in 1922, was largely well-suited to future Nazis guidelines. On the *Philharmonischen Konzerte* programme of 1932-33, bridging the end of the Weimar Republic and dawn of the Nazi Reich, were a total of six works by then-living composers: Prokofiev's *5th Piano Concerto* (with the pianist at the keyboard), a piece entitled *Variationen und Fuge* by Gottfried Müller[8], two short works by Karl Marx and Hugo Reichenberger, Richard Strauss' *Till Eulenspiegel*, and the premiere of *Mouvement Symphonique Nr.3* by Arthur Honegger.

Richard Strauss was a classic in his own time, venerated before and after 1933, whose tone poems were already well-entrenched in the symphonic repertoire. To many, he was the heir to Richard Wagner, and the Nazis could not resist his appeal, just as to a considerable extent, Strauss himself could not resist the appeal of the Nazis either.[9] Of the other contemporary composers performed in 1932-33, the Germans Müller, Marx and Reichenberger continued to enjoy performance, in Berlin and elsewhere, throughout the Third Reich. They represented a generation of German composers whose musical idiom remained firmly planted in the 19th Century. Müller became a Party member in 1933, and dedicated his *Deutsches Heldenrequiem* to Adolf Hitler.[10] Despite the grotesque dedication, the work was much admired not only by Goebbels, but apparently by Furtwängler himself:

> With the Fuhrer at a rehearsal of the BPO and *Kittel* Chor, Gottfried Müller *German Requiem*. He wrote it when he was 19 year old. The piece is still rather callow, but also vulcanic, skillfull, daring—modern, yet musical. Perhaps a significant talent for the future. The *Fuhrer* is quite taken. Also Furtwängler, who was also there, commented very positively. Müller is still young, not the least self-conscious or experienced at all.[11]

Of the foreigners on the 1932-33 programme, Honegger was not heard from in the Philharmonie again until after the war. Up to 1933, the French composer had maintained good relations with the Berlin Philharmonic—no fewer than seven of his pieces appearing on the orchestra's programmes over the previous ten years. Indeed, Honegger's *Mouvement Symphonique Nr. 3* was dedicated to the Berlin Philharmonic and Wilhelm Furtwängler. With his idiosyncratic Bach-influenced, harmonically-rich idiom, Honegger's music was modern, but inoffensive: there is no record of the authorities 'banning' performances in Germany. Yet while Debussy, Ravel, Roussel and Jean Francais among other French composers, continued to receive play on Philharmonic programmes conducted by the likes of Dimitri Mitropolous, Leo Borchard, and Herbert von Karajan, Furtwängler only conducted Honegger's music with the Berlin Philharmonic once more after the 1932-33 season: at the concert marking the orchestra's 70th Anniversary in 1952. Honegger's otherwise total absence from Furtwängler's repertoire in the 1947-54 period might well suggest musical rather than political choices behind his absence from 1933 to 1945.

Consideration of Prokofiev under the guidelines of Nazi musical protocol was more contentious: his music was adventurous, but not radical; he was famous, yet a Soviet citizen. He was heard twice in 1938-39. Later in 1939, Claudio Arrau performed the Third *Piano Concerto*, and in 1940, with the Molotov-Ribbentrop pact teetering, Heinz Stanske gave the German premiere of Prokofiev's *Violin Concerto Nr. 2*. Though the regime had a difficult time deciding what to do with him, Prokofiev's music was not proscribed until war with the Soviet Union in 1941 made it impossible to promote the music of an enemy composer. For reasons only he himself could answer, Furtwängler simply did not programme a single piece by Prokofiev after 1932-33. This was not a consequence of ideological prohibition, but personal choice.

The two examples, Honegger and Prokofiev, illustrate how political imposition was not the only means of harmonising culture under the Nazi yoke. Furtwängler's natural predilection for certain types of music already prepared the Philharmonic's main repertoire for an easy transition. Thereafter, a degree of if not outright self-censorship than at least malleable priorities, combined with Furtwängler's own transition from famous, middle-aged conductor to senior Teutonic legend, meant difficult cases could be marginalised, discarded, or easily replaced by German equivalents.

For the 1933-34 season, whether by choice or compulsion, Furtwängler programmed exclusively contemporary German composers to complement the *Philharmonischen Konzerte* steady diet of Beethoven, Brahms, Bruckner, Richard Strauss, Mozart, Bach, Haydn and Schubert. The composers were: Paul Graener, Max Trapp, Siegfried Müller, Hans Pfitzner and Paul Hindemith. Hans Pfitzner was second to Richard Strauss as the grand old man of German music, a noble vestige of 19th Century traditions; Graener was named vice-president of the *Reichsmusikkammer* in 1936; Trapp had been a member of the NSDAP since 1932; Siegfried Müller's music was popular throughout Germany after 1933; while in 1933, Paul Hindemith was regarded as a rising star among German composers. The uniform nationality of the five living composers might be pure coincidence, might be a sign of acquiescence on Furtwängler's part, or might rather be indicative of the conductor's conscious game of political tactics vis a vis the Nazi regime.

The previously cited Hindemith case of December 1934, is often mentioned as an aesthetic clash between Furtwängler and the Nazis.[12] The truth is more complicated. Furtwängler had long been a champion of Hindemith's music, and Hindemith a close musical friend of the Berlin Philharmonic. Though his music was too challenging for the tastes of Hitler or Goebbels,[13] it was not on musical grounds that Furtwängler and the regime came to quarrel. As Furtwängler wrote in his December 1934 letter of resignation:

> When the National Socialists finally infringed upon the nucleus of every aspect of music making and the freedom of performing art for the future generation—when I was forbidden to perform Hindemith for political reasons—I resigned from all my offices.[14]

Furtwängler quit because politics forbid the performance of Hindemith's new opera *Mathis der Maler* at the Staatsoper in Berlin, an unequivocal breach of artistic freedom. The *Mathis der Maler Symphony* was, however, premiered by Furtwängler and the Berlin Philharmonic in March of 1934, to public success while dividing critical opinion. Regardless, this performance certainly did not yield a ban.[15] The performance of the *Mathis* opera in fall, 1934 was forbidden by the *Reichsmusikkammer*. The RMK was founded by Goebbels in 1933 to control musicians and musical activities in Germany. Prior to their programming, all new works were subject to approval by *Reichsmusikkammer* supervisors in the *Fachschaft Komponisten*. Many leading Nazis, including those stacking the RMK may have disliked Hindemith's aesthetic, a fact which alone discouraged many orchestras and opera houses from programming his works,[16] but even the pettiest bureaucrat could neither ban Hindemith's work on racial grounds, nor qualitative grounds. Neither the music, nor the man was the problem. Authorities were exceptionally concerned about the opera's potent content: "Hindemith's *Mathis* is searching an answer to the matter of the position of art and the artist in times of political crisis."[17] The opera's central theme was challenging territory, and a provocation Nazi ideologues and bureaucrats, in a rare instance of agreement, could not permit.

The role of the artist in troubling times may well have been a question Furtwängler too was interested in pursuing in 1934-35, but his own resignation confirmed that the obstacle to performance of *Mathis der Maler* was "aus politischen Gründen" (for political reasons), not a conflict over artistic judgement. It appeared for some time, as if Hindemith would be rehabilitated, principally because his music was, in fact, not terribly adventurous.[18] Yet it was precisely because this was no aesthetic but rather a political fight, that Hindemith was not again accommodated. In the fallout, Hindemith left Germany for Switzerland, then Turkey, and eventually to the United States. Furtwängler, meanwhile, remained, where, in his letter of reconciliation with the regime in 1935, he answered Mathis' question: in Nazi Germany, the role of the artist was subservient to political authority. To *Mathis der Maler*, this position was unconscionable. Furtwängler, however, accommodated himself, at least musically, with ease.

Remarkable about the Hindemith episode is precisely how exceptional such instances of vulgar censorship truly were. Though the Nazi's *Gleichschaltung* policy extended to harmonising artistic activities with the tenets of National Socialism, in the case of the Berlin Philharmonic, there was no 'smoking gun' memo of 1933 or 1934, no meeting or other communiqué in which Furtwängler was instructed by Nazi authorities what or with whom he could not perform. Harmonisation was as much a matter of conditioning as dictate: an environment of hostility and suspicion made challenge unwelcome and discouraged risk, while advance publicity made known what sorts of choices would be most welcome. The general concordance of Nazi tastes with 'popular' audience inclinations provided potent motivation.

Once Furtwängler had divested himself of artistic control of the orchestra after the Hindemith Affair, his relationship with the Berlin Philharmonic remained close and influential, but limited. Artistic direction of the orchestra was overtaken by a series of political appointments, starting with Hermann Stange, then Hans von Benda, and finally Gerhard von Westerman. These men, acting as artistic directors, were responsible for planning what the Philharmonic performed, when, where and with whom. These decisions were made in consultation with Furtwängler, but also with regard to the commercial and political interests of the orchestra, and respecting the guidelines of the authorities which had appointed them. Stange, von Benda, and von Westerman each professed loyalty to the NSDAP, each was called to his office by the RMVP, and the first two were even contracted directly with the government, rather than to the orchestra. With the Philharmonic in such hands after Furtwängler's departure, there was no danger of musical programming diverging from the path of Nazi preferences. Music undesirable, for political, aesthetic, ethnic, or any other reasons, was simply never proposed by Philharmonic administrators appointed and paid by the Nazi Propaganda Ministry. Between this mechanism of indirect compliance, and the no less significant consideration of attracting audiences, it was neither in the administrators' interest, nor that of the orchestra, to bite the hands that fed them.

Already from Furtwängler's early days, the Philharmonic was for the most part treading on narrow, but solid ground. This pattern was merely codified by the orchestra's subsequent artistic directors. In 1938-39, slightly more than 50% of the Berlin Philharmonic's total performed repertoire consisted of the music of just six composers: Beethoven, Brahms, Bruckner, Haydn, Mozart, and

Richard Strauss.[19] Add to the list Wagner, and just eleven of the Philharmonic's seventy-seven public Berlin concert programmes (excluding *Honorar-Konzerte*) did not contain music by one of those seven men. [20] In 1938-39, the Bach family, Schubert, Schumann and Weber represented the next tier of programming options. As in 1934-35, Tchaikovsky was one of only two "foreign" composer in double-figures, with fifteen performances. The other was Berlioz.[21] Together, this cannon represented over 70% of all the music performed by the Berlin Philharmonic not just through the 1938-39 season, but during the entire Third Reich.[22]

In the crisis following Furtwängler's resignation, the Philharmonic was placed for artistic guidance in the "schützenden und fördernden Hände" (protecting and encouraging hands) of the *Reichsmusikkammer*,[23] the RMVP-founded entity for regulating German musicians and musical activities. In its consultant capacity, the *Reichsmusikkammer* executive, which included Paul Graener, Peter Raabe, and Heinz Ihlert, advised the Berlin Philharmonic directors on programming matters, promoting some composers, while discouraging others. This system of control and influence persisted also after Furtwängler's return. Despite the critical situation precipated by *Mathis der Maler*, even works subsequently proposed by the conductor were subject to official sanction.[24] With the weight of favour from the *Reichsmusikkammer*, meanwhile singularly unexceptional composers such as Emil Reznicek;[25] Arno Rentsch;[26] or Werner Egk [27] to prominence on Philharmonic programmes. These composers came to replace the Mahlers, Korngolds, and Schoenbergs on the fringes of the Philharmonic repertoire.

The creation of an administrative position with artistic control at the Berlin Philharmonic—an artistic director independent from principal conductor—meanwhile, also streamlined orchestra programming and planning immeasurably. With the Berlin Philharmonic administration integrated into the State bureaucracy, evolving priorities on the political side could be efficiently conveyed to the musical programmers. Such communication could not be construed as an infringement on artistic freedom, because they were bureaucrats making decisions on both sides. When, for example, a memo was sent from the RMVP to the Philharmonic regarding the suitability of the music of Stravinsky—"The performance of a Stravinsky piece is undesirable as it could set a bad precedent."[28]— the matter was raised as a procedural matter, an expression of concern rather than explicit dictate.

This cooperative manner was typical insofar as both sides could be flexible. In good bureaucratic fashion, efforts were made to regulate the symphonic repertoire, but standardisation was never more than a semblance, regularly disrupted by personal doubts, ideological inconsistencies, and mitigating political factors, among others. Stravinsky, for example, was a challenging case. Extremely famous, an outspoken anti-Semite, yet with a propensity towards progressive compositional styles not in keeping with the Nazis preferences, Stravinsky was difficult to categorise. Precedents on Stravinsky had already been set by the Berlin Philharmonic long before the above-cited memo: *Le Sacre du Printemps*, for example, was performed by the Berlin Philharmonic with Erich Kleiber in 1934. Kleiber left Germany shortly thereafter, but the orchestra played the *Firebird Suite* twice in 1937, under Robert Denzler and again with Oswald Kabasta, himself an NSDAP member, while Eugen Jochum conducted *Jeux de Cartes* in 1938, and even Furtwängler conducted *Le Baiser de la Fee* on a *Philharmonischen Konzert* program that same year. Such programming choices hardly constituted contest to Nazi hegemony. Rather, they described the ambiguity of the policy itself, and a flexibility on the part of the bureaucrats, combined with an understandable artistic need for some degree of musical variety.

Again, however, communications such as that regarding Stravinsky represented the exception rather than the rule. Stravinsky belonged to the remaining 30% of the repertoire comprised of contemporary German compositions sanctioned by the RMK, a handful of further exclusively contemporary music programmes in association with the Academy of Arts under the curatorship of composer and conductor, Georg Schumann, and concerts designed specifically to highlight the music of specific countries, such as Leo Borchard's 1936-37 French, English and Italo-Hungarian programmes, the 1937 *Schwedish-Norwegischer Abend*, the 1939 concert "unter dem Protektorat der Deutsch-Japanischen Gesellschaft", or the 1941

German-Greek exchange concert.

The purpose of isolating non-German and contemporary music on specific programmes served similar causes, namely, a reinforcement of German identity through juxapposition with other distinct traditions. New compositions debuted at the Academy of Arts concerts, like exotified "foreign" programmes, were held to the measuring stick of the heavily traditional Philharmonic canon.

Despite this conscious, 'othering' effect, recognition under these or comparable microscopes could earn repertoire a place in the orchestra's principal activities. For all such ideologically-motivated stratifying manouevres the practical requirement of presenting some degree of artistic variety on Philharmonic programmes over the years, necessitated occasional recourse to new and/or foreign sources. Within these narrow margins, there could still be room for a Stravinsky or Prokofiev piece from time to time, beside one by Otaka, Ekonomidis, or Heinz Tiessen, without putting the Philharmonic aesthetic signature at odds with Nazis norms.

Clearly, some composers were not programmable on ethnic or political grounds. Even with State supervision of programming activities, however, changes did not occur automatically on January 30, 1933. While Mahler, Schoenberg and Korngold were swiftly swept under the rug, Mendelssohn, for example, was conducted by *Philharmonic Kommisarischer Geschäftsführer* and NSDAP member Rudolf von Schmidtseck in December, 1933. RMVP favourite violinist Georg Kuhlenkampff performed the Mendelssohn Violin Concerto in March of 1935, two weeks before recording the same work with the Berlin Philharmonic, conducted by Hans Schmidt-Isserstedt.[29] As late as 1936, the Berlin Philharmonic also recorded excerpts from Mendelssohn's *A Midsummer Night's Dream* for the *Deutsche Telefunken*.[30] In the way of these activities, the RMVP evidently did not stand.

Mendelssohn, as part of the traditional German canon, posed the Nazis problems. Though performance of his music dwindled significantly compared to its frequency prior to 1933, it took years of ideological and musicological manipulation to finally justify official banning of Mendelssohn's music from Germany's concert halls. According to legend, the composer's bust was in fact never removed from the foyer of the Alte Philharmonie, even after his music ceased to be heard there.[31] It would be romantic to regard this fact, together with the partial persistence of Mendelssohn in the Philharmonic repertoire, as evidence of resistance. More likely however, these vestiges simply reflected the degree of ambivalence inherent in the system of ideologically-driven musical *Gleichschaltung*. Before each season, the Berlin Philharmonic Artistic Directors were required to submit their season planning to the RMVP. There is no evidence of forced revisions to these plans over the Philharmonic's eleven year subordinance to the Nazi State. This implies performances up to and including Mendelssohn as late as 1936 and Stravinsky in 1939, were given with the government's knowledge and consent.

By the start of the war, Philharmonic programming was by and large well harmonised with Nazi expectations and standards through a combination of ideological pre-conditioning, the force of commercial considerations, Furtwängler's musical preferences, the power of self-censorship, a form of musical affirmative action through the RMK, and the cooperative relationship between State bureaucracy and Philharmonic administration. 1939-40, however, imposed a new set of circumstances influencing Philharmonic programming. Principally, the war highlighted the distinction between music's artistic and semiotic, propagandistic properties. French music such as Debussy, Franck and Ravel, all featured on Philharmonic programmes up to 1939, promptly disappeared.[32] English and Russian composers also vanished from the programme, corresponding to the change in political climate. Musical choices needed to be tailored to the sensitivities of the moment.

Controls were tightened not just on music's origins, but also its character. In 1942, a memo was circulated by the RMVP:

> Hinkel then announced a decree of the minister to the effect that as regards "serious" music, no works are to be performed which have not already proven their value. New, problematic works should not be played.[33]

This message was directed towards all orchestras across Germany, not principally the Philharmonic. The implication was that *Gleichschaltung* was no longer simply a matter of translating ideological principles into musical programming, but further politicised music as motivational material. 'Problematic' pieces conflicted with the urgent socio-political need for organisation and order. It was in all likelihood Goebbels himself who ordered the Beethoven programme for radio broadcast coinciding with the march on Poland in 1939.[34] The occasion called for heroic music, to move and mobilise the nation, and no one but the Berlin Philharmonic could make it sound better. The traditional Philharmonic *Beethoven Zyklus*, re-formed by von Benda into a more diverse *Klassischen Zyklus*, was not insignificantly revived to its Beethovenian monopoly in 1939-40 and 1940-41. After 1939-40, the weight of Philharmonic programming tips even further towards Beethoven, Bruckner, Brahms, Strauss and Wagner.[35] The disruptive influence of experimental music, meanwhile, was strongly discouraged.

The regime's awareness of the suggestive power of music, however, was not limited to positive re-enforcement. The tightening of Hinkel's control over musical programming was intended less as a preventive measure against a resurgence of Mendelssohn or Hindemith or to fight the infiltration of jazz, but rather to address situations such as in 1941, when, of all composers, Mozart was forbidden. The reason: in Winter of that year Nazi armies were dealt a devastating blow on the Eastern Front, not by the Red Army, but by the Russian Winter. Goebbels and his ministry wished to avoid the embarrassment of having Hitler's military blunder immortalised in music. A performance of Mozart's *Requiem* under Furtwängler, therefore, was permitted for recording, but indefinitely forbidden from broadcast.[36]

As the war continued, government controls grew increasingly stringent, particularly with respect to radio programming.[37] Restrictions, however, whether imposed, voluntary, or achieved through a baleful dialectic between the two, were certainly not limited to the repertoire. The promotion of certain musical values at the expense of others, tinted by the lens of ideology and politics, also extended to world of performers—conductors and soloists alike.

On March 20, 1933, the Berlin Philharmonic was scheduled to perform the fourth in a five-concert subscription series under the baton of Bruno Walter. By this date, Walter would have been by no means the first Jewish musician to appear with the Philharmonic since Hitler's ascent to office. On February 6, 1933, Berlin Philharmonic concertmaster Szymon Goldberg performed the Beethoven Violin Concerto during a Furtwängler-led *Philharmonische Konzert*. Three weeks later, renowned violinist and pedagogue, Carl Flesch, played the Brahms concerto, also under Furtwängler's baton. That same night, February 27, 1933, a few hundred meters from the old Philharmonie, the German Reichstag was infamously set ablaze. On March 3, Otto Klemperer conducted Beethoven's *Missa Solemnis* with Szymon Golberg and Alexander Kipnis among the soloists. But by mid-March, the Nazis were making full use of the draconian measures of the *Verordnung des Reichspräsidenten zum Schutz von Volk und Staat* invoked in response to the Reichstag fire. In one act, the legal protections of the Weimar constitution were swept away. The SA and SS had free reign to violently target any opponent or opposition group of the new government. When the Nazis claimed victory in the legislative elections on March 5th, 1933, Hitler and his cohorts claimed the authority to impose themselves not only through violence, by also by wielding legal leverage. The upcoming Bruno Walter concert represented the occasion for Goebbels, his bureaucratic *eminence grise*, Hans Hinkel, and Walter Funk, the man who would emerge as the Philharmonic's key functionary within the RMVP, to take their stand.

The symbolism was all too ripe for the Nazis to resist: Bruno Walter, pupil of Gustav Mahler, music director of the Leipziger Gewandhausorchester and the Berliner Städtischen Oper, was very famous; the Philharmonic, meanwhile, the orchestra of the new Germany's capital, was teetering on the verge of bankruptcy; lastly, the concert was another production of the Wolff & Sachs agency, the Jewish impresario family behind the *Philharmonischen Konzerte*.[38] The resulting *affair* was a mock revolution exemplary of Nazi brutality and cunning, and set a precedent for the *Gleichschaltung* of Philharmonic programming.

Hinkel offered his account of the Bruno Walter episode to a Party newspaper thus:

QUESTION: HAS THE NSDAP OR ITS *KAMPFBUND FÜR*

> Question: has the NSDAP or its *Kampfbund für Deutsche Kultur /Fighting Coalition for German Culture* prohibited Bruno Walter's Berlin concert or made it impossible?
> Answer: No. We have never prohibited this concert or forbidden Herr Walter, whose actual name is Schlessinger, to conduct. However, it has proven impossible for us to go out of our way to provide security staff for the performance. As we have learned, the concert agency in charge cancelled the Bruno Walter concert on its own account. I may direct your attention to the fact that Richard Strauss received threatening letters from the USA as soon as he agreed to conducting in Bruno Walter's place in Berlin.[39]

The Hinkel's official explanation was, of course, highly cynical, but revealed the Nazis' brilliant strategy of igniting contained crises to achieve their desired result. The Bruno Walter concert was not cancelled by the regime, but was made impossible by circumstances of the regime's creation. Accounts of the affair vary, but clear is that unspecified threats to the concert were conveyed by Goebbels to Wolff & Sachs.[40] These threats were not necessarily of official Nazi disruption, but rather suggested certain ubiquitous groups in the new Germany may not welcome the conductor to the Berlin podium. Of course, the Nazis had their own squad of rabble-rousers, but in the new constellation of power, Party and government strategies could be deployed independently or complementary, as desired. Goebbels, therefore, was calling on government business, warning of unspecified disruptions being planned by the Party wing, or of movements merely encouraged by it.

This unspecified threat necessitated State security protection for the concert, which neither government nor Party, in characteristically sardonic fashion, declared themselves able to provide. Without necessary protection, for conductor, orchestra, producers, and audience in equal measure, the concert could not be sanctioned.

At this stage it was suggested, possibly by Walter Funk, that replacing Walter with a less 'controversial' choice would remove the security threat and alleviate the dilemma. It was noted, whether by a Nazi official, someone from Wolff & Sachs, or by Bruno Walter himself, that Richard Strauss was in Berlin at the time, and might be available. Louise Wolff objected—it was a Bruno Walter concert in Bruno Walter's own Philharmonic series, inviting another conductor would be absurd.[41] Walter, however, understood the ploy, declaring "I have no further business here," and departed Berlin that same afternoon.[42] Bruno Walter effectively cancelled himself. In quite justifiably doing so, however, he played directly into the Nazis' hands.

The precise way in which Richard Strauss came to take over the Bruno Walter Philharmonic concert is as obscure as it is historiographically belaboured, yet in the context of March 1933, the optics of the moment made for irresistible propaganda: 'abandoned' by Bruno Walter, the Berlin Philharmonic, in desperate times (the Walter concerts were also an indispensable source of revenue), was 'saved' by a true German hero. Not only was the concert saved, but Strauss also had the courage to ford into the breach despite supposed letters of protest from abroad referenced by Hinkel.[43] Lastly, and most spectacularly, Strauss donated the honorarium from his concert to the benefit of the struggling Philharmonic Orchestra.[44]

Strauss' magnanimous donation was no doubt made with the best of intentions, for the benefit of the musical institution in dire straights with which he had been associated since the early 1890s, and quite possibly out of respect for the colleague whom he replaced. Yet under the highly politicised circumstances of 1933, the Berlin Philharmonic, despite its still very uncertain future, was already acquiring the symbolic mantle it would wear comfortably for the next twelve years. The Nazis had chosen the Berliner Philharmonie as the ground for its musical standoff, with the Philharmonic orchestra cast as victimised *Volk*, and Bruno Walter and Richard Strauss unwittingly playing their respective roles as demon and saviour to a tee.

The model would replay itself many times over the following months and years, the Nazis capitalising on threat, misinformation, and naivety to transform the musical landscape most often through influence rather than force. Otto Klemperer, with his own three-concert Philharmonic series as leader of the *Philharmonischer Chor*, was the next to receive the Walter treatment. As recounted once again by Hinkel:

For the sake of a order in Germany, concerts, scheduled for several days ago, had to be postponed until further notice. For events of such kind, we could not put our SA and SS, which we need for more important things, at the disposal of Mr. Klemperer. After all, the German public has for quite some time been provoked by not a few Jewish bankrupters in the arts, so that, it may be regrettable, yet understandable, that Klemperer and Bruno Walter had to suffer for this public sentiment."[45]

As portrayed by Hinkel, Walter and Klemperer were merely 'incidental casualties' of the anti-Semitic fervour fuelled and justified by the Nazis. In the name of 'security measures', even those with no particular sympathy for the Nazi agenda could be convinced of the unavoidability of the changes afoot. For the 1933-34 season, Klemperer was replaced as conductor of the Philharmonischer Chor by Carl Schuricht. This was effectuated with less fanfare than the Walter-Strauss event, but with an equally disquieting sense of inevitability.

Carl Schuricht was the senior representative in a generation of conductors, including Eugen Jochum, Hermann Abendroth, Karl Böhm, and Herbert von Karajan, who made their marks during the Nazi years. It is impossible to speculate how their careers might have developed if Klemperer's forced vacancy had not left room Schuricht, if Jochum had not been there to replace Furtwängler after the Hindemith Affair, if Abendroth had not been gifted the Gewandhaus Orchestra after Bruno Walter, if Fritz Busch had not quit Dresden for Böhm to jump into the breach, or if Göring had not taken a fancy to the Kapellmeister von Karajan from Aachen. All were men of exceptional talent, who had already or would clearly have achieved impressive careers regardless of the conditions the Nazis provided. Clemens Krauss and Hans Knappertsbusch were also distinguished conductors much admired by prominent figures in Hitler's regime. Some were NSDAP members, others were not. Decisive, however, was not individual political conviction, but the potent formula of talent, ambition, and nationality. These men represented 'Germany's best', and were celebrated, traded, promoted, and peddled by Nazi elites like toys. They were favoured, and returned favours. Each had his base with a major German or Austrian orchestra or opera house, while common to all was also a protracted relationship with the Berlin Philharmonic.

During the Third Reich, the Berlin Philharmonic faced its share of 'Germany's worst' too. Prior to 1933, as a private enterprise, the orchestra could effectively be rented for publicity, marketing, or sheer vanity. The Nazi era eliminated the financial need for such occasionally embarrassing episodes, but replaced wealthy hacks with ambitious ones. Hermann Stange was the most glaring example of careerism pursued through political lobbying. Werner Richter-Reichhelm, Kurt Overhoff, Otto Frickhoffer, Hans Weisbach, and Heinrich Steiner, were among a handful of second and third rate conductors who, on account of NSDAP membership[46] also climbed ladders, knocked on the right political doors, and petitioned the powers at the *Reichsmusikkammer* diligently enough to win their crack at leading the Berlin Philharmonic. Most only did so once. Some did not even get their chance—the RMVP to Philharmonic management: "The invitation of the completely unknown radio orchestra conductor, Winter, should be abandoned."[47] Even nepotism had its limits.

Like the overtly political infringements on the Philharmonic's repertoire, appearances by lesser lights, whether achieved through political intrigue, hard work, or overestimation, were minimal. It was in the interests of the orchestra, its management, and the government, to ensure the Berlin Philharmonic continued to perform on the highest musical levels, sustaining the orchestra's excellence, and providing a forum for 'Germany's best' to shine. The regime elites themselves had no interest in hearing their prized instrument worn down by uninspired, provincial conductors. Thus, over the course of the Third Reich, a pantheon of conductors appeared with the Philharmonic with increasing frequency. In 1941-42 Abendroth, Böhm, Jochum, Knappertsbusch, and Schuricht each had their own series in the Philharmonic programme. At various times, each of these men maintained a more intensive working relationship with the Philharmonic, in terms of programmes per season, than even Furtwängler.[48]

Beyond regularly scheduled concerts, Hermann Abendroth, Karl Böhm and Hans Knappertsbusch were also the Philharmonic's most frequent collaborators at official *Reichsorchester* functions. To his credit, Furtwängler attempted to shirk participation in most of the more bombastic commitments of *Reichsorchestra* service, but the regime found more than adequate replacements. Though Abendroth was the only one belonging to the NSDAP, he, Böhm, and Knappertsbusch, in programming terms, were virtually interchangeable when it came to leading the Berlin Philharmonic on tour, for *Kraft durch Freude*, at the *Reichsmusiktage, Tag der Deutschen Kunst*, or in *Reichskulturkammer* events. Knappertsbusch conducted the Philharmonic on three occasions honouring Hitler's birthday; Böhm filled in for 1941, the same season he led Philharmonic tours to the Balkans, France and Spain; Abendroth, meanwhile, conducted *Sonderkonzerte* under the patronages of Göring and Goebbels in 1942 and 1943 respectively, to name just a few of their Philharmonic ventures.[49] The three delivered quality work, maintained traditionalist musical values, while physically and temperamentally epitomising aspects of Nazi ideals.

Carl Schuricht's two year tenure as conductor of the Philharmonischen Chor (1933-35) also kicked off an fruitful period of collaboration with the Berlin Philharmonic. He was often called on as a last minute replacement for indisposed colleagues, and filled the role of a 'poor man's Furtwängler' in terms of repertoire and seniority. The *Generalmusikdirektor* in Wiesbaden led the first *Philharmonischen Konzert* of the Furtwängler-less 1936-37 season. In 1937-38 he was entrusted with a series of 'modern' music concerts, including works by Stravinsky and Roussel, four *Klassischen Abende*, and the full six-concert Beethoven-Mozart series. A musical 'jack-of-all-trades', Schuricht conducted popular Philharmonic programmes for *Kraft durch Freude*, specialty contemporary music concerts, a Schumann cycle, and at the *Deutschen Reger Festes* in 1938. In 1941-42 Schuricht was rewarded for diligent service with a subscription series of his own.

Like Schuricht, Eugen Jochum's relationship with the Berlin Philharmonic was also precipitated by non-musical events. Jochum made his debut with the orchestra in 1932. His Philharmonic career took off, however, when the then-*Generalmusikdirektor* in Hamburg was chosen by a combination of artistic and political voices for the crucial task of conducting the first *Philharmonischen konzert* after Furtwängler's 1934 resignation. Jochum was also the first conductor authorised to tour with the Philharmonic in Furtwängler's absence. From then on, Jochum remained a regular figure on the Berlin podium, maintaining a four-concert subscription series from 1935-36 onwards, leading the orchestra in Scandinavia in 1938 and 1940, to Paris in 1942, and in a special concert at the *Reichspropagandaamt* in 1943.

Clemens Krauss, with his duties in Munich, Salzburg and Vienna appeared with the Philharmonic less frequently than most of his colleagues, but important occasions were found to do so: Richard Strauss' 75th birthday celebration in 1939, Sibelius' 75th birthday in 1941,[50] and the Berlin Philharmonic's big 1942 tour to France, Spain and Portugal, including performances for French workers, the Red Cross, the Nazi *Wehrmacht*, a charity concert—apparently—benefiting the poor of Lisbon, and a series of performances for Franco's Madrid elite. On the orchestra's tour to Iberia the following year featured two special opera performances in Salazar's Lisbon: *Tristan und Isolde* under Robert Heger, in the pit, quite possibly for the first time in its history, the Berlin Philharmonic.

The final addition to the pantheon of German conductors to find success with the Philharmonic was Herbert von Karajan. Von Karajan had been recruited to the Berliner Staatsoper from Aachen in 1937-38. The nature of von Karajan's meteoric rise remains couched in the ambiguities and intrigues of the Third Reich period. Charismatic and ambitious, the two-time NSDAP member coupled his natural assets with the political power of Göring's favour to catapult himself to the top of the class.[51] Von Karajan was called to conduct his first concert with the Berlin Philharmonic by Hans von Benda who "after two successful Karajan concerts at the *Philharmonie* led to negotiations with the Staatsoper, found it a matter of course to commit Karajan also to the Philharmonic."[52] The concert took place on April 8, 1938. The programme: Mozart *Symphony K 319*, Ravel's *Daphnis* and Chloe *Suite Nr. 2*, and Brahms *4th Symphony*. Von Karajan was just thirty years old.

As opportunistic as von Benda might have portrayed Karajan's engagement, it was neither an innocent move on the *künstlerischer Leiter*'s part, nor could its ramifications be entirely foreseen. The legendary 'Wunder-Kritik' (wonder critique) in which the Berlin music reviewer Edwin von der Nüll coined the phrase 'Das Wunder Karajan' in response to a Staatsoper performance of Tristan und Isolde almost single-handedly created a sensation where there previously had been none.[53] In the treacherous, intrigue-ripe, and press-controlled climate of Nazi Germany, such an astonishing outburst of unqualified praise was suspect. Furtwängler, among others, recognised a political motive behind the 'Wunder-Kritik', and sourced the promotion of the young Austrian to an alliance of Göring and his theatre director, Heinz Tietjen.[54]

"The case Herbert von Karajan," wrote Hans von Benda several months after the conductor's Philharmonic debut, "was, in the end, the real reason for my request for retirement [...] because Furtwängler had become obsessed with the idea that Karajan would henceforth be nothing more than a weapon, which General Director Tietjen would use against him until his ultimate demise."[55] Furtwängler and Tietjen had been on bitter terms since 1934, tracing back to conflicts at the Staatsoper, including the Hindemith Affair, and in Bayreuth, where the two were locked in a power struggle for artistic control. According to von Benda, von Karajan was a tool of personal attack, both in Furtwängler's personal war with Tietjen, and in the rivalry between Göring and Goebbels. Engaging von Karajan for the Philharmonic, von Benda claimed, provoked Furtwängler immensely, who called on high powers in the RMVP, in all likelihood Goebbels himself, to have the orchestra's artistic director sacked.

Painting himself as innocent victim, von Benda maintained he was simply looking after the Philharmonic's best interests in capturing a rising star to fill Philharmonie seats. If von Benda was also interested either in exacerbating a seemingly already tense relationship with Furtwängler, or in mixing in the Göring-Goebbels tussles cannot be accurately deciphered. It is unlikely, however, the man nominally in charge of Philharmonic programming arrived at the decision to hire von Karajan on his own. Beyond Göring's support, another of von Karajan's major professional advantages was the massive influence of his agent, Rudolf Vedder.

Already in 1933-34, Vedder had attempted to impose himself on the musical scene of Berlin by repossessing Wolff & Sachs Konzertagentur from its Jewish owners. The move failed, but over the following years, Vedder succeeded in assembling an impressive roster of conductors, including Clemens Krauss, Eugen Jochum, Paul van Kempen, Fritz Lehmann and Willem Mengelberg.[56] Vedder's success was founded upon shrewd talent scouting, and promotion of his artists through both musical and political channels. Vedder was not only an arts manager and later NSDAP member, but prodded his way into a senior position with the *Reichsmusikkammer*, heading from its inception, the *Konzertabteilung*. The conflict of interest running inherent in an agency while leading the very regulatory body for music agents was unsustainable, but Vedder parlayed his connections masterfully. He maintained good relations with bureaucratic and political elites, and later himself became a *SS-Sturmführer* with direct connections to Himmler. "Vedder often boasted," reported Hans von Benda's successor, Gerhard von Westerman,

> how easy it was for him to establish a young, obscure artist in almost no time, since he was able to impose him immediately in the most crucial positions in so many cities […] The mere fact that Vedder could so highlight conductors by way of his influence options resulted in other conductors striving to be represented by Vedder; these conductors were, of course, more than willing to grant [Vedder] considerable influence over the concerts he would arrange for them.[57]

Karajan was certainly not the first conductor furnished the Berlin Philharmonic by Rudolf Vedder, but perhaps the most apparent instance of the confluence between artistic programming and political intrigue. With his connections to Göring, Hinkel and Tietjen, among others, Vedder in all likelihood brokered the deal bringing von Karajan and the Berlin Philharmonic together, well mindful of the political as well as musical windfall.

After his first concert with the orchestra, despite a positive reception, von Karajan's relationship with the Philharmonic remained sporadic. Von Benda's insight into the suspicious, jealous, vengeful pathology of Furtwängler went some way to explaining the limited opportunities made available to von Karajan. Furtwängler's options to this extent were restricted, however, as he held no official position and no direct control over programming. Unlike the other politically-promoted hacks delivered the Philharmonic through nepotistic avenues, Furtwängler also had to recognise the genuine talent of his young rival. The only recourse the senior conductor had, he took— he engaged in his own proxy war, tapping his connections first to discharge von Benda, then turning his sights on Vedder. Gerhard von Westerman acted as Furtwängler's advocate on the perils when "a businessman and not an artist wields the decisive influence over Germany's musical life."[58]

Despite their remarkable effectiveness, Furtwängler's machinations only explained part of the hindrance to von Karajan enjoying a more extended partnership with what remained Berlin's leading orchestra. The other obstacle was the conductor himself. "Karajan make indescribable demands and wanted to conduct the PO at all costs," confirmed von Westerman, "but did not want to be put at the level of other conductors—he always insisted on a special status. Consequently he demanded a higher fee than [the twenty years his senior] Knappertsbusch. For these reasons a cooperation with Karajan could not be reached."[59] Fuelled by his own ambition and his agent's advice, Von Karajan effectively priced himself out of the Philharmonic market. He found conditions, if not the orchestra, more appealing at the Staatsoper, and thus began building his power base from Göring's tent.

Denied their goals, from 1939 through 1942, Vedder and von Karajan fought back, lining up along with Göring against Furtwängler and Goebbels. Their strategies included establishing an independent von Karajan subscription series with the Staatskapelle, and embarking on talent raids to lure Philharmonic players to the Staatsoper. The first move was designed to undermine the Philharmonic commercially, going head-to-head with the orchestra's secondary series (Böhm, Schuricht, Knappertsbusch).[60] The second efforts were aimed directly at sabotaging the Philharmonic's artistic standing. Concertmaster Siegfried Borries was successfully courted into switching to von Karajan's orchestra in 1940; a year later, Gerhard

Taschner, the boy-virtuoso newly arrived in Berlin, remained loyal to Furtwängler, and did not succumb. Vedder's connections were strong, von Karajan's champions effective, but Furtwängler and Goebbels represented a formidable power block. The Taschner case ended with Vedder's ejection from the *Reichsmusikkammer* in 1942 and the loss of his musical empire. Even then, '*Der Fall Vedder,*' remained inextricably linked to the Furtwängler-von Karajan rivalry, and a topic of strife and irritation lasting until long after the Third Reich's demise.[61]

Concerning soloists, the original draft of Furtwängler's 1934 contract as *1. Dirigent* of the Berliner Philharmonic Orchestra GmbH, in relation to programming choices, contained the following clause: "Die Bestellung von Nichtariern ist jedoch ausgeschlossen." ("The appointment of non-arians is, however, excluded.")[62] This anti-Semitic stipulation was not intentioned as a provocation, rather it was included as application of racialist *Gleichschaltung*' policy to the legal bindings between State, the Berlin Philharmonic, and its Principal Conductor. Furtwängler did not sign this document and the clause does not appear in subsequent contract drafts.[63] The deletion was in all likelihood effectuated through the conductor's recourse to Goebbels or higher. As always, however, the reason for Furtwängler's resistance to Nazi policy was not his particular love of Jewish musicians, but his absolute rejection of political interference in artistic affairs.

On this principle, Furtwängler went to war, inviting soloists such as Bronislaw Hubermann, Arthur Schnabel, and Fritz Kreisler—all Jewish—to perform with his Philharmonic during the 1933-34 season.[64] This act of open defiance was indeed daring, a challenging, hubristic poker match, attempting to call the regime's bluff. A defence of artistic freedom it was, a defence of Jewish musicians, however, it was not. Furtwängler was no anti-Semite (or at least no Nazi brand thereof), but his fight with the regime was not about racialist policy. Though he on numerous occasions attempted to wield his influence with the Nazis on behalf of colleagues on individual matters,[65] on the decisive issue of Philharmonic programming, Furtwängler's war was not a moral stance against anti-Semitism, but a defence of his own right to hire whom he wanted, when he wanted.

This forceful position raised the suspicion of many a Party functionary and bureaucratic clerk. "Können Sie mir einen Juden nennen, für den Furtwängler nicht eintritt?" ("Can you name me one Jew Furtwängler is not standing up for?") wrote a mocking bureaucrat to *Staatskommissar* Hinkel in July 1933.[66] Suspicion was the conditioned response to the fear on which Nazism fed and which its propaganda nourished. Furtwängler was not alone under the microscope of vitriol, and many suffered much worse fates. But as a high-profile, celebrated and self-proclaimed German artist of the highest rank, his sin of coddling Jewish artists was commuted to innocent accessory:

> It is regarded as an open secret that the driving force behind these preferences for Jewish artists is Furtwängler's Jewish secretary who, in intrigue with her mother, is said to strongly influence Furtwängler's artistic decisions.[67]

The official line in response to Furtwängler's stance twisted the story to amplify, rather than dampen anti-Semitic prejudice. Bertha Geissmar was labelled the pernicious, manipulating influence behind Furtwängler's rash artistic intentions, the case exhibited as yet another example of Jewish people corrupting well-intentioned German decision-making. The opposite, of course, was true: Furtwängler was using the persecution of Jewish musicians to launch his own attack on German decision-makers, a fight in which Geissmar was effectively caught in the cross-fire.

The damage, however, had already been done. After Bruno Walter's experience, along with that of Klemperer, Max Reinhardt, Arnold Schoenberg, and many other victims of the first wave of brutal ethnic cleansing unleashed on Germany by the Nazis, the inhospitable political climate frightened Jewish artists away. Furtwängler had a stake in challenging the regime, and felt secure enough in his stature to take the politicians, ideologues and bureaucrats on. Jewish musicians, meanwhile, had just had their identities as Germans, Austrians, or Poles stolen. In Nazi Germany, they were now Jews—Jews who did not belong. Furtwängler's fight was not theirs, and they would not be made puppets in a struggle which, whoever won, they would surely lose.

The Jewish soloists Furtwängler invited simply would not come. Violinist Fritz Kreisler, who debuted with the Berlin Philharmonic under Nikisch in 1899, and had lived in Berlin since 1924,[68] excused himself with the following comments:

> I cordially thank you for the invitation to play with the *Philharmoniker* under your direction, and especially for the distinction implied for me to be the first artist entrusted with resurrecting the ruptured bonds. Such a task would fill me with pride if I were convinced of being the right one for this mission. But that is not the case [...] I believe that merely the re-appointment of artists such as Bruno Walter, Klemperer, Busch etc. could obviously aid and improve the prospects for art in Germany and abroad, a matter which is as dear to me as to you. I am [however] intent on postponing performances in Germany until the right for all artist to pursue their activities in Germany regardless of descent, religion, or nationality has become a irrevocable fact. I put my trust in soon being allowed to play with you once more.[69]

Bronislaw Hubermann also rejected Furtwängler's entreaties to appear with the Philharmonic. Invoking the names of Toscanini, and Adolf and Fritz Busch, non-Jewish musicians who left or boycotted Germany, the violinist argued that negotiating with the Nazis, fighting them on their terms only legitimated their rhetoric, rendered their hatred conscionable:

> These examples of superior conscience [Toscanini, the Buschs', Paderewski] must keep their colleagues from committing grievous compromises. Even if the government statements, which you have called for, might constitute the limit of the currently achievable, I unfortunately still cannot regard them as a sufficient basis for me to again participate in German music life [...]
>
> You try to convince me that "one has to start in order to break down the dividing walls." Yes, if it were only about a wall in a concert hall! But the question of a more or less competent interpretation of a violin concerto is only one of the manifold aspects—and, God knows, not the most important!—that obscure the actual problem.

> In truth it is not about violin concertos, neither about Jews, it is about the most elementary conditions of our European culture: the freedom of the individual and his unequivocal personal responsibility, liberated from the fetters of castes and races![70]

Rather than assisting Furtwängler in calling the regime's bluff, Hubermann called Furtwängler's. Hubermann had identified Furtwängler's ethical Achilles heel: Furtwängler was an artist who prized music above all things. To him, it was precisely the violin concerto that mattered most. No doubt the conductor truly believed in the transcendental power of music, that "die eigentliche Aufgabe der Kunst [...] sei, die Menschheit über die Zersplitterung zu erheben" ("the essential purpose of art [...] is to elevate Mankind above fragmentation").[71] Nevertheless, he gravely miscalculated the scale of the rupture Hitler had unleashed. Hubermann saw the dangerous trap of skirmishing over trivial details while fear and authoritarianism destroyed tolerance and individual responsibility.

Furtwängler's response to ideological encroachment was to fight for preservation, for his artistic freedom, and by extension, for the autonomy of *his* orchestra. These aims he did, to a certain extent achieve, but they were concessions granted by the Nazis in exchange for legitimation of their venomous platform. Jewish soloists, meanwhile, refused to be made examples of, either as objects of the regime's scorn, or as peons in Furtwängler's face-off with Goebbels, Göring, Hinkel, Funk, and Hitler.

At his 1946 de-Nazification hearing, Furtwängler made great hay of his attempts to invite Jewish musicians to perform with the Berlin Philharmonic in 1933-34. "Gradually, the great foreign soloists are staying away," he reported, "The fulfillment of my programmes is becoming ever more difficult."[72] While Kreisler, Hubermann, and Arthur Schnabel refused to come, however, the Philharmonic's first season under Nazi rule was neither fundamentally altered through these cancellations, nor was it devoid of the presence of Jewish soloists. Indeed, between September 1933 and April 1934, Philharmonic concertmaster Szymon Goldberg appeared as soloist with the orchestra on five separate occasions, and solo-Cellist Joseph Schuster performed both Dvorak and Saint-Saens concerti with the Philharmonic. Meanwhile, Nicolai Graudan performed the Schumann *Cello Concerto* in the Philharmonie as late as November 1934, and appeared as soloist with Furtwängler on two *Philharmonischen Konzerte* programmes that same Autumn. Even 'Halb-Jude' Hans Bottermund played the Dvorak cello concerto with the Berlin Philharmonic in November, 1936, six weeks after sharing a programme with another so-called 'Mischling', bassoonist Karl Leuschner.[73]

The persistent presence of Jewish musicians in the Philharmonic was one matter, but featuring them prominently as soloists on concert programmes might well have represented an openly defiant stand. If these programming choices had symbolised Furtwängler's or indeed the orchestra's protesting of anti-Semitic laws and sentiments infringing on artistic liberty in the early years of Nazi rule, it would have been natural to cite them later, during the post-war period, as examples of conscious and conscientious resistance. This, however, was not the case. Performances by Goldberg, Schuster, Graudan, Bottermund and Leuschner represented part of the Philharmonic's longstanding tradition of showcasing its principal players. The fact the musicians were Jewish was coincidental to the persistence of this tradition after 1933. The fact of the tradition's continuation indicated not defiance, but reflected the uncertainty of both artists and regulators in accommodating to Germany's new cultural conditions.

The result of these uncertainties inferred a period of consolidation, between 1933 and approximately 1936, during which Philharmonic programmes offered a continuity of many previous traditions, and a free mixing of soloists and conductors ranging from Jewish instrumentalists and NSDAP members. Then on November 14 1933, for example, Joseph Schuster performed Saint-Saens' *Cello Concerto* with the Berlin Philharmonic. The conductor on the occasion was Helmut Kellermann, Pg.[74] The first Furtwängler *Philharmonischen Konzert* of 1934-35 featured soloists Nicolai Graudan, Siegfried Borries, and NSDAP loyalist, Walter Gieseking.[75]

Even once the Jewish musicians disappeared from the Philharmonic concert programme, it remains difficult to discern a pattern of obvious promotion of Party members and supporters at the expense of less politically favourable colleagues. Active Hitler supporters pianists Elly Ney and Winifried Wolf appear throughout the seasons with equal frequency as Edwin Fischer and Karolrobert Kreiten, the first a staunchly apolitical Swiss, the second a man subsequently denounced, imprisoned and murdered by the SS.[76] On February 26th, 1936, the Berlin Philharmonic performed a programme of Bach, Schumann and Ravel, at the piano, Wilhelm Kempff, after 1945 blacklisted by American authorities as a key cultural representative of the Nazi regime, on the podium, Dmitri Mitropoulos, an open homosexual. The 1938 Beethoven-Mozart Zyklus, conducted by Carl Schuricht featured Philharmonic leaders Röhn, Kolberg, and solo-violist Reinhard Wolf, but also the Frenchman Robert Casadesus, the Russian pianist prodigy Anna Antoniades, and Ukrainian pianist Lubka Kolessa, a friend of Bruno Walter's.

Foreign soloists were otherwise rare, but a row of foreign conductors appeared regularly with the Philharmonic during the Third Reich years. Beecham and Mengelberg both maintained long-standing relationships with the Philharmonic dating back decades. After the Nazis arrival to power, Beecham continued coming, first to conduct the Philharmonic, then on tour with his own London orchestra. Mengelberg, despite his association with the works of Mahler, was also a regular and highly-respected guest. In the years following, foreign guests tended to represent countries 'friendly' to the Reich, irrespective the political positions of the conductors themselves: Victor de Sabata, for example, from Italy, Hisatada Otaka from Japan, the Rumanian Georges Georgescu, and Vaclav Tallich from Czechoslovakia.

Naturally, for "Kraft durch Freude" events, Party spectacles, or Berlin Philharmonic command performances, it was ensured conductors and soloists would be German, and when possible, Party members. Such was the bill at the *KdF Wagner-Weber Abend* on January 31 1937, with conductor Erich Orthmann, Pg., and the card-carrying soloists Tina Lemnitz and Hans Hermann Nissen. Likewise, the Berlin Philharmonic's regular collaborators for their frequent Beethoven's Ninth offerings included the singers Watzke, Ludwig and Hoengen, as well as the Bruno Kittel Chor, whose leader, a close friend of Furtwängler, was a long-standing, committed member of the NSDAP.[77]

Despite such overtly political events demanding requisite programming decorum with respect to repertoire, conductor and soloists, musical quality remained the primary objective of each exercise. Undoubtedly, the politicisation of music and music programming in Germany under the Nazis came at a tremendous cost. German musical culture suffered irreparable damage as consequence of the Nazis' senseless anti-Semitic policies. The re-shaping, or perhaps rather, re-focusing of the repertoire likewise denied variety and stunted progressive musical growth. The Berlin Philharmonic, however, acclimatised handily to the new conditions, indeed revelled in its profile as leading exponent of its national musical culture, and received every encouragement to do so on the highest level. Inadvertently, the orchestra proved the Nazis points deftly, maintaining excellence without Walter, Klemperer, Schnabel, Kreisler, Huberman, Busch or Toscanini, bearing forth the flame of a German musical 'canon' devoid of Mendelssohn, Schoenberg, Mahler or Hindemith. "Hitler was the first to judge the artist according to his political orientation,"[78] testified Furtwängler in hindsight. Hitler's judgement, meanwhile, seemed to suit audiences and artists alike all too well.

Chapter 6

Vertreter seines Vaterlands:
The Philharmonic on Tour

> We refer specifically to our concert tours in the imperiled
> borderlands. Even during the occupation, we toured the
> Rhineland and the Saar region. The peoples' enthusiastic
> reception in these areas showed us that concerts
> performed by the orchestra of the Reich's capital were
> regarded as a symbol of loyalty to the Fatherland and the
> belonging together of all German peoples."
>
> – Lorenz Höber to the Prussian Finance Ministry
> January 27, 1931

SINCE ITS EARLIEST YEARS, the Berlin Philharmonic was always a
touring orchestra. Visits to cities across Germany and abroad, to
France, Great Britain, Scandinavia, Italy, Russia, and the Lowlands,
served the dual purpose of cultivating a prestigious international
reputation while providing a crucial supplement to the orchestra's finances. These two advantages converged in the Berlin Philharmonic's
worsening financial situation in the 1920s, when, to secure public
funding, the orchestra played the patriotic card, casting itself as an
indispensable cultural ambassador for the City of Berlin and all
Germany. The combination of exceptional musical quality, with international reputation, coupled with an embrace of the era's nationalistic rhetoric proved sufficient to draw the city of Berlin and the
German Reich into offering subsidy support. Even before 1933, the
Berlin Philharmonic was seen, and at least in part understood itself,
to be an effective organ of propaganda, bringing together Germans,
and broadcasting the best of Germany to the world.

Once the orchestra was subsumed under the Goebbels

Ministerium's yoke, however, this matter of pride and necessity became a matter of duty: at no other time in the Berlin Philharmonic's one hundred twenty-five year history did its musicians perform per season, as many concerts, in as many foreign lands, as during the Third Reich.

Indeed, the Berlin Philharmonic's tours were the most consistent aspect of its existence during the Third Reich. From its period of bankruptcy in 1933 to its concertising activities after the destruction of the Philharmonie in 1944, the orchestra kept travelling abroad. This consistency also pre-dated the Nazi's rise and succeeded Hitler's downfall. *Wehrmacht* and other specifically politically-mandated concerts aside, the objective of Philharmonic travels also remained consistent, only with the motivation slightly obscured: the main purpose of Berlin Philharmonic tours was always to impress foreigners with the greatness of German culture. The ratio of commercial incentive to missionary determination driving the operation was the only clear distinction drawn by 1933-34, and even then one readily compromised for gain.

The Berlin Philharmonic was well aware of its potential as an instrument of propaganda from early on. The quotation that begins this chapter was written by Lorenz Höber in 1931, as the orchestra was in the throes of yet another financial crisis. Even then, the orchestra understood its symbolic potential in two spheres: representing at once a domestic beacon for Germans to identify the superior accomplishment of their *Stämme*, while at the same time broadcasting to the outside world the best of German musical genius. Though the former role certainly had its place in Goebbels' vision of cultural propaganda, it was the latter possibilities which made controlling the Berlin Philharmonic such an appealing proposition.

The Berlin Philharmonic toured all over Europe during the years after the Nazi seizure of power. England every season 1933 to 1938; Holland 1933-35, 1937, 1940-41; France 1933-44; Italy 1937-38, 1941; Spain, 1941-44; Portugal 1941-44; Switzerland, 1933-34, 1938, 1941-42; the Balkans 1936, 1940, 1943; Hungary 1940, 1942-43; Rumania 1936, 1940, 1943; Scandinavia 1937, 1940-42; Poland 1941-44, among others.

Unlike in the past (and today), where concert tours were arranged often years in advance based primarily on commercial considerations, between 1934 and the orchestra's last foreign tours in 1944, weeks were set aside for travel in season planning, but the destinations to which Philharmonic would tour were often only determined on short notice. The orchestra's foreign tours were undertaken "at the behest of the minister" calculated to Goebbels' and the RMVP's assessment of the European cultural-political landscape. This could change at any time. As for example, Karl Stegmann reported in 1942:

> Only in the last few days was it decided that the Minister does not desire a deployment of the orchestra to Switzerland and Sweden—as had been planned—but rather a five week tour to Spain and Portugal.[2]

Nationalist ideology, even predating the Third Reich, divided Europe into an artistic battlefield, with the Berlin Philharmonic Germany's musical flag bearer. The objective was to magnify the propagandistic effectiveness of the orchestra, exhibiting Germany's finest qualities. This could be done either through the image of a musical conquest, or by creating the air of a cordial musical exchange. When the orchestra went to France, it was mobilised to crush French delusions of cultural ascendancy; when the orchestra played in Spain, Italy, or up until 1939 even in England, the orchestra was displayed to persuade friends and potential allies of the qualities of a superior race. The Berlin Philharmonic was a not-so-secret weapon, marshalled according to the imminent needs in the culture wars. And, to a great extent, it worked:

> The reviews of our concerts in the foreign press have shown our superlative artistic performance an extraordinarily effective tool of cultural propaganda.— "You philharmonic musicians," a foreign diplomat said to us last year in Reval, "are real dynamoes," and also the late ambassador v. Hoesch often described the orchestra, in Paris and then later in London, as the best German propaganda tool.[3]

The Berlin Philharmonic was selected as one of Germany's emissaries to the World's Fair in Paris in 1937. The Nazis also staged their own international cultural fairs, the *Reichsmusiktage* in Düsseldorf, the *Tage der Deutschen Kunst* in Munich and the 1936 Olympic Games in Berlin, where the Berlin Philharmonic played prominent roles. But it was abroad where the orchestra made its greatest impact, and it did so with pride, as violist Werner Buchholz celebrated:

> There can hardly be anybody who would not be convinced of the necessity of such concert and propaganda tours. Because this type of guest concert definitively represents propaganda in the truest and best sense of the word. Yet more than the international artists, in whom one sees primarily the phenomenally gifted individual, the performance of an entire orchestra with its artistic discipline and its racially conditioned timbre and specific style of playing takes on the role of a representative of its Fatherland, the cultural will and scope of which it conveys to the people of other nations [...] in this the BPO perceives its most noble duty to the Fatherland: as amabassador of German art and for the German people.[4]

The orchestra's foreign touring, therefore, was both the government's strongest use of the Berlin Philharmonic, and the ensemble's greatest source of pride, its superiority and distinctiveness on full display, trumpeted as the envy of the world. The orchestra's feeling of omnipotence in relation to its international profile was astounding. "The world has become so small," proclaimed the Philharmonic's own press, "that, if one day we hear a radio broadcast of the Berliner Philharmoniker from the *Zeppelin* or the *Hindenburg* high above the South Atlantic, we will not even be surprised."[5]

Mid-air performances for south-Atlantic migratory albatrosses aside, on tour, the Philharmonic performed for a range of publics and purposes, providing tastes of the finest in German culture to the widest possible audience. The orchestra averaged five concerts per week on tour, often travelling over night to ensure maximum exposure. The nature of each concert, open or closed, for locals or for Germans, elite or popular, was specified by the Propaganda Ministry.[6] The vast majority of concerts were public, often decorated with official attendance, but intended for the general pubic, or at least a certain class thereof, to be awed first-hand by the 'distinctive greatness' of German music.

After the start of the war, these public concerts were mixed with concerts for German soldiers in foreign territories, such as the autumn 1940 Lowlands tour for the benefit of the *Wehrmacht*, or when the Philharmonic paused in Bordeaux on its return journey from Spain to play under Arthur Rother for Nazi soldiers. The Philharmonic also appeared at local events on foreign territory, such as factory concerts, similar to those given in Germany. In 1942, for example, the orchestra gave a *Concert de Recreation* matinee under Clemens Krauss for the workers of Paris. The Schubert and Wagner programme reprised the *Wehrmacht* concert from the night before, and was repeated the following day in a public concert at the Trocadero.[7] The orchestra abided by a similar pattern in Warsaw the following year, repeating the same programme on consecutive days in the same location for different audiences: a public concert under Herbert von Karajan, repeated the next day "ausschlie sslich für Soldaten und Verwundete der Wehrmacht." ("Exclusively for soldiers and wounded of the German Army")[8] In 1942, while playing public and *Wehrmachtkonzerte* in Denmark, France and Poland, the Berlin Philharmonic also gave special concerts in each of those countries exclusively for *Auslandsdeutschen*—a combination of ethnic Germans living in Kopenhagen, Paris, and Krakau, together with representatives of the Nazi occupying authority.[9]

The Berlin Philharmonic's programmes on tour invariably consisted of German classics: Beethoven, Brahms, Wagner, Schubert, Richard Strauss. This repertoire at once reflected the concerts' propagandistic aim of promoting German culture while presenting the orchestra basking in its finest musical qualities. A remarkable number concluded with a Wagner highlight, typically the *Tannhäuser* Vorspiel or that of *Die Meistersinger*, indicated either on the programme proper or given as an encore.[10]

Programming, however, was more nuanced than pure musical-propagandistic bombast. Concerts abroad, like those in Berlin, were tailored to the interest-level of their audiences. Major symphonic concerts, such as those in Paris, London or Madrid, would typically comprise two full symphonies, a concerto and/or tone poem, plus a selection of overtures. Workers' and soldiers' concerts, meanwhile, were abbreviated to a single shorter symphony and some light, popular fare.[11]

The question of conductors was also a matter of both art and politics. In 1933-34, it was anticipated Furtwängler would lead all future concerts of the Philharmonic on tour. This assumption was cast in doubt with the conductor's resignation in December 1934. The Philharmonic visit to London planned for January 1935 was cancelled in the wake of Furtwängler's announcement. RMVP officials, in an attempt to turn the situation into a positive propaganda opportunity, tried to convince Sir Thomas Beecham to take over at least the London concerts,[12] but Beecham, not wishing to fall into Richard Strauss' ethical trap when he replaced Bruno Walter in 1933, declined. The tour was cancelled, and it took some time to clarify if and with whom the orchestra would travel with in future. With the exception of a single concert in the Haag under Jochum, the Philharmonic suspended foreign tours for the rest of the 1934-35 season.

In the larger scheme, however, Furtwängler returned to the fold relatively quickly, leading Philharmonic tours to England again already by winter 1935. Furtwängler later argued before his de-Nazification tribunal that once the war broke out, he never conducted the Berlin Philharmonic in an occupied country.[13] The merit of the case is somewhat suspect as he did conduct the Berlin Philharmonic in axis-partner Italy in 1941, and on tour to Sweden and Denmark in 1942, while again appearing in Nazi-occupied Denmark in 1942 and 1943 with the Vienna Philharmonic.[14] True, the Vienna Philharmonic was not the political symbol of the German Reich the Berlin Philharmonic was, but further appearances such as the 1944 opening of the German National Theatre in Prague with his Berlin orchestra where the guest list seemed highly dubious.[15]

Still, Furtwängler's reluctance to appear in politically loaded situations, particularly internationally with the Philharmonic, was a source of frustration for some bureaucrats.[16] "I have always taken the utmost care," reported von Benda to his ministry superiors, underscoring the delicate ethical line the conductor was walking, "to ensure that Furtwängler made as many tours with the orchestra as possible, especially those abroad."[17] The reticence of Furtwängler, who defended his actions performing abroad without his orchestra on the grounds that he appeared "only by personal invitation of me as an [individual] artist"[18] meanwhile, opened the door for other conductors to forge regular partnerships with the Berlin Philharmonic.

As scrutinised exports, Berlin Philharmonic concert tours demanded high artistic standards, not just from a propagandistic standpoint, but simply as a matter of musical pride. The orchestra and the regime found themselves in league in the paramount need for success on the international stage. Furtwängler remained the first choice, with the question left open "to what extent the orchestra [could] perform tours with other superior conductors."[19] If Furtwängler could not or would not lead the orchestra abroad, however, conductors of suitable stature were required to fill his shoes. There could be no place for error or cronyism the likes of Stange, Havemann or Reichwein representing the Reich to the world. Eugen Jochum, Clemens Krauss, Hans Knappertsbusch, Karl Böhm, Robert Heger, and later Herbert von Karajan, were among those drafted to conduct the Philharmonic on tour, and all stops were pulled out to ensure their cooperation.

Conductor choices were made by the Philharmonic *Künstlerischer Leiter*, with a dose of dalliance from the RMVP (a representative of Goebbels signed off on all conductor engagement decisions).[20] The selected conductors were just as duty-bound to perform for the regime as the orchestra. If necessary, the ministry would ensure a conductor's release from previous commitments to ensure its priorities were met:

> Telegram. German consul for Professor Knappertsbusch, San Sebastian. Directing urgent request on behalf of Ministry to conduct the Balkan trip from September 24 through October 16 STOP Please wire acceptance and indication of which obligations must be cancelled STOP

If necessary I authorize [the] ministry to intervene STOP
Program [to be] compile[d] from rehearsed repertoire.[21]

The touring procedure, like many instances of the regime's instrumental appropriation of orchestra, was at once explicit and
whimsical. In 1942, though the Philharmonic musicians before
dispersing for summer vacation had been informed of "a tour during all of September by decree of the RMVP."[22] The exact dates,
destinations, and with whom the orchestra would be performing
when they returned from holiday remained uncertain until just
shortly before the planned departure. Furtwängler managed to shirk
the government's wish he should lead the tour—"that was a certain arrogance on Mr. Furtwängler's part" recorded von Westerman
later—but not before ensuring the Philharmonic would under no
circumstances visit Istanbul, "because he only saw a purely political
purpose behind this concert."[23] The initial itinerary also called for a
visit to Athens which never materialised.[24] Not unexpectedly, in the
last minute, Furtwängler cancelled entirely, leaving the aperture into
which Knappertsbusch was again called.

The aforementioned *Vorbereitetem Repertoire* meant core German
repertoire familiar to both conductor and orchestra from recent
Berlin programmes. In the case of the 1942 Balkan tour, this included a Beethoven-Abend consisting of the Egmont-Ouvertürehe
First and Third Symphonies; and two mixed programmes contai-
ning Mozart's *Ein Kleine Nachtmusik* surrounded by Wagner excerpts, *Till Eulenspiegel* by Richard Strauss, and Liszt's *Les Preludes*
or Schubert's *Rosamunde* Ballettmusik, a Pfitzner Scherzo, and
the *4th Symphony* of Brahms.

Concerning soloists, both saving expense while representing
itself most proudly, the Berlin Philharmonic rarely travelled with
guests, rather performing concerti featuring members of the orchestra in solo roles. On the 1942 tour to Scandinavia, Concertmaster
Gerhardt Taschner played the Beethoven *Violin Concerto* with the
Philharmonic, while his colleague Erich Röhn played the Brahms
Double Concerto with solo-cellist Tibor de Machula. During the
Spain tour later that same year, Taschner and Röhn alternated performing the Bruch *Violin Concerto No.1*, while one programme saw

Röhn give a Mozart Violin Concerto before intermission, then played the solo in Strauss' *Ein Heldenleben* immediately after.[25]

On occasions where guest pianists or singers were engaged, such as for the September 1940 Philharmonic tour to France and the Lowlands, soloists were recognisable nationalist stalwarts—Elly Ney, Wilhelm Kempff, Rosalind von Schirach. A singular highlight was two special performances of *Tristan* under Robert Heger at the opera house in Lisbon in 1943.

Upon request, the Philharmonic also toured in reduced forces, in chamber music groups or as part of Hans von Benda's *Kammerorchester*. Von Benda created the *Kammerorchester der Berliner Philharmoniker* shortly after arriving to the orchestra in 1935. The founding of the chamber group served a number of personal and political purposes. First, to satisfy his own conducting ambitions without the misguided pomposity of his predecessor, Hermann Stange, von Benda assembled a modest group of about twenty-five Philharmonic musicians, programming principally Baroque music. The chamber orchester was further designed primarily for touring and recording purposes. In this way, von Benda could exercise his careerist ambition while avoiding the critical Berlin spotlight. Also, the *Kammerorchester's* founding was a political act, initiated by von Benda, but reflecting both ministerial volition and an attempt by the conductor to consolidate favour with the regime: "I recognised," explained von Benda, "the utility of a chamber orchestra of approximately twenty-five players for foreign propaganda, as it represents easy mobility and much lower costs than large orchestra."[26]

Through a conspiracy of mutual opportunism involving von Benda's self-promotion and the regime's thirst for cultural exports, the *Kammerorchester der Berliner Philharmoniker* became an active representative of the Philharmonic and the Reich abroad. The RMVP sponsored independent *Kammerorchester* tours across Germany and to Scandinavia and the Baltic, among other destinations. The success of the venture rose to a point where in 1938/39 the *Kammerorchester* gave more foreign concerts than the main Philharmonic orchestra.[27] After his dismissal from the Philharmonic in 1939, attributable at least in part to the success of his pet project, Hans von Benda continued travelling throughout with a re-branded

Benda Kammerorchester, composed of non-Philharmonic Berlin-based musicians.

The Berlin Philharmonic, meanwhile, maintained a pattern of touring in smaller groups too. The *Philharmonisches Quartett*, composed of Erich Röhn, Carl Höfer, Werner Buchholz, and Wolfram Kleber, travelled independently on a regular basis. They appeared alone, and on occasion in conjunction with other Philharmonic colleagues under the banner *"Kammermusikvereinigung der Berliner Philharmoniker,"* produced and organised by the orchestra *Geschäftsführung*. As example of this latter instance, in 1943, the Propaganda department of the Polish *Generalgouvernment* in Krakau requested "musical accompaniment [to introduce and conclude] a presentation by the Herr General Intendant Dr. Drewes," and turned to the Berlin Philharmonic for the requisite decorum.[28] Karl Stegmann offered the services of the Röhn Quartet plus a bass player and wind trio for a programme of Beethoven and Schubert. He further negotiated their travel terms and an honorarium of RM 2 000 for the one-day expedition.

This instance highlighted a number of key issues concerning Philharmonic international touring practices. In addition to the expected content of the programme, and the perhaps coincidental, but nevertheless explicit inclusion of the Party-member dominated Röhn Quartet among the group provided, most significantly, commission of the Propaganda Ministry did not necessarily imply gratis service. Indeed, at RM 2 000, the chamber concert fee was approximately one quarter the full orchestra per-performance rate.[29] Whether for commercial, propagandistic, or politically indulgent purposes, when the Berlin Philharmonic performed abroad, they were paid. Further, there were the matters of transportation logistics and accommodation.

Touring was lucrative business to the Philharmonic, with or without State subvention. When the January 1935 England tour was threatened by Furtwängler's resignation, Karl Stegmann wrote to the RMVP to avert the loss of this tour:

> As is well known, these trips abroad are the best
> propaganda for German culture, as the representatives

of the German Reich abroad agree. I would recommend attempting to at least carry out this tour, which has always had good financial results as well.[30]

Under the new system of orchestra funding after 1934, foreign touring was underwritten by the Reich, meaning travel, accommodation and incidental expenses did not appear in the orchestra's budgets. The orchestra would, to the greatest extent possible, make use of infrastructure provided by the Reich, and thereafter simply pass on additional bills to the government. The Philharmonic *Geschäftsführung*, principally Karl Stegmann, would handle negotiations. Either subsidies would be made available up front, based upon submitted estimates,[31] or reimbursement would be issued retroactively.[32] The security of these transfers eliminated the orchestra's financial dependency on concert revenue. So generous was the system towards the Philharmonic, in 1938/39, the orchestra paid over 6 000 Swiss Francs, 41 000 Italian Lire, and 57 000 French Francs collected from concert revenues back to the Reichsbank.[33]

Even late into the war, after the destruction of the Philharmonie, when touring became the Berlin Philharmonic's primary function, the system of strategic assignment, whereby the RMVP would direct the orchestra to perform in a given region and underwrite its expenses, persisted. In 1944, it remained assumed, "The orchestra will presumably continue touring," though the war crisis meant, "we cannot give more details about this as yet since these tours will require a special [underline original] subsidy from the Ministry,"[34] but estimates for which, under the circumstances, could not be provided.

The RM 170 000 *Reisekostenzuschuss* Goebbels granted the Berlin Philharmonic in 1936, supposedly at Hitler's own request,[35] meanwhile, was a wage supplement for members of the orchestra in recognition of "the artistic achievements and the special cultural-political significance of [Goebbels'] orchestra,"[36] not a travel subsidy to the institution. The *Reisekostenzuschu*ss and per diem *Tagesgelder*, both assessed on a per-head basis, were forms of travel-related funding issued the Philharmonic by the RMVP in addition to the large compensation sums offered to cover material costs, upwards of RM

100 000 per tour, for international touring.[37] The orchestra, there-fore, was in a fine position: the musicians receiving individual rem-uneration from the government bonus to their regular salaries, the orchestra making money from its performance either in the form of honoraria or from ticket sales, while the administration could write off all touring expenditures to the State's tab.

Of considerably more complexity and rancour was the is-sue of *Tagesgelder* for Philharmonic musicians whilst abroad. The *Reisekostenzuschu*ss was part of each musician's monthly salary. *Tagesgelder*, however, was assessed on a per diem basis, calculated according to estimates of living expenses in individual countries. Pride and celebration aside, it was not lost on the musicians of the Philharmonic that foreign tours were undertaken at the behest of the RMVP. "The day's work of touring orchestra members lasts practically from the early morning until late into the night," argued Stegmann on behalf of the orchestra, making the case for elevated recompense for State-commanded ardours.[38] In a wearying bureau-cratic farce, the RMVP would repeatedly attempt to set *Tagesgelder* standards for foreign countries, only to have their figures under-mined, either through a change in economic conditions (often pre-cipitated by the progress of the war), or political meddling.

Tagesgelder was, in theory, an expense independent from travel or accommodation, but paid out of the same pot of State money as the underwriting *Zuschuss*, and grew to an accounting hot-potato bet-ween the *Reichsfinanzministerium*, the *Reichswirtschaftsministerium* and the Propaganda Ministry, of which the Philharmonic was a part. The accounting branches naturally wished to keep down costs, while the political branches were keen to keep their premiere musical asset on the road.

Fixing costs was difficult as the circumstances of each Philharmonic tour so widely varied. At times, accommodation ex-penses would not be covered by the initial subsidy, at others, meals would be provided by hosting associations. Travel conditions were extremely variable. Estimates did not always cover real costs, and in the end, someone would be left out of pocket. The Ministry-assessed RM 27 per day per person outlay in Sweden in 1941, for example, was intended to cover expenses including hotel, while in Norway and Denmark on the same trip, accommodation was provided by the *Wehrmacht*, reducing the per diem to a minimal RM 13.80.[39] The following year, the Swedish rates remained the same, but the orchestra was given RM 18 per day, because though accommodation was again covered, meals were not.[40] The official 1942 RMVP-approved per diem rate for Greece was RM 18 per day, yet on his advance trip to Athens, Karl Stegmann remarked on the rampant inflation in the country his orchestra was shortly to visit: "A bottle of mineral water costs, depending on how the merchant wants to sell, 4-5 *Reichsmark*, a pair of shoes costs RM 1 500, a kilo of potatoes about 20; a bottle of wine RM 17; a pot of tea without biscuits RM 11; a lunch at the hotel RM 40. Thus it was clear from the start I could not make ends meet with a day rate of RM 18 + 30%."[41]

"Since France is a wine country," reported Stegmann on another occasion, "it is the custom to drink wine with the meals there. Expenses for wine are very high, because there is currently [1942] a wine shortage in France and prices have soared. A daily allowance of RM 14.50 would leave nothing for the daily needs of the orchestra members aside from meals."[42] Negotiations carried on endlessly. In some countries, amounts granted were just enough to cover necessities, in others, such as Spain, where standard RMVP war-time rates were a generous RM 32 per person, musicians could put their stipends towards fine meals and valuable souvenirs.[43]

Accounting minutiae aside, the problem was more fundamental. While the nature of bureaucracy perpetually attempted to impose regulation, the ideological agenda of the Nazi state sought to promote normative values. As in other aspects of the Berlin Philharmonic's experience, with the *Tagesgelder* issue, functional and instrumental directives conflicted. Though never explicitly denoted as a form of qualitative *Leistungszulage*, *Tagesgelder* rates were—at least in the minds of the Berlin Philharmonic *Geschäftsführung*, and reiterated by some in the RMVP—linked to the Tarifordnung der deutschen Kulturorchester. Wrote Karl Stegmann: "It is not acceptable for other touring orchestras to be offered higher daily allowances than the Berlin Philharmonic."[44] More than a simple matter of reimbursing expenses, to which any group sent abroad by commission of the government could reasonably have a right, the Philharmonic understood itself entitled to a higher standard of per diem comfort than other orchestras on the basis of its exigent schedule and qualitative merits. Though other German orchestras toured too, as Stegmann conceived it, *Tagesgelder* was not just a matter of pragmatic economics, but a form of reward for the Philharmonic's exemplary service—above and beyond Goebbels' *Reisekostenzuschuss*.

The incitement of Stegmann's case was once again precipitated by political interference in administrative affairs. The case also once again involved the Berlin Philharmonic's local rival, Göring's Staatsoper. In 1941 the Staatsoper gave a series of guest performances at the Opera in Paris. With some strings pulled up the political chain of command, the group received a tremendous RM 40 per diem. As word reached the Philharmonic, more details leaked out: in addition to their exorbitant daily allowance, the Staatsoper had stayed at the fancy Grand Hotel in Paris; in Italy the same year, the Staatsoper received RM 27 per day without hotel expenses, while being put up in "ein ausgesprochenes Luxushotel." ("a decidedly luxurious hotel")[45] This was clearly a form of petty intrigue: the juvenile squabbling between Göring and Göbbels spilled over into magnanimous prizes for their musical toys. To add insult to injury for the Philharmonic, it was further revealed that Goebbels' Deutsche Opernhaus Berlin, for its recent French, Dutch, Hungarian and Italian visits, had also received significantly higher per diem stipends than the supposed "Sendebote deutscher Kunst" ("Messengers or ambassadors of German art").[46]

Stegmann's case then, amounted to an ethical assertion that if political machinations should interfere with the bureaucratic process, it should at least be doled out along lines of quality and fairness, rather than childish tit-for-tat. Wrote the Philharmonic *Geschäftsführer* appointed to oversee the *Gleichschaltung* of Germany's Reichsorchester: "In our company, we enacted the principle of thrift and correct spending from the very beginning, especially with respect to the fact that, after all, we receive all of these benefits from public tax revenues."[47] He then submitted a retroactive bill for the RM 2 per person per day advantage received by the Deutsche Oper during its Paris last sojourn.[48]

This game persisted through the central war years, with complaints and recriminations volleyed back and forth unyieldingly. "It is a known fact that nothing remains hidden among musicians. Berlin musician soon know what happens in Munich and vice versa." [49] Perhaps respect for public funds did enter the minds of musicians and administrators as they bemoaned the prices of food, wine or tobacco abroad, but the first principle remained accountability—not to taxpayers, but within the system of German propagandistic exports.

Eventually, the system could no longer support such indulgences. By 1943-44, even as the Philharmonic's operating budget continued to expand, funds were more urgently needed elsewhere. In spring 1944, with the Philharmonie lost, the Philharmonic was sent out on tour, but this time with a warning: "In doing so, the daily expenses abroad must be kept at a minimum [...] and it should be noted that tour participants may not use money for the purchase of certain goods no longer available in the *Reich*." [50] Perhaps, finally aware their greatest privilege was simply to escape Germany, this time, the Philharmonic made no *Tagesgelder* fuss.

Despite the generous financial conditions for touring provided by the State, the Philharmonic *Geschäftsführers* continued to negotiate business terms with foreign impresarios and concert halls as the orchestra managers had done the years prior to 1933. What developed after the advent of the *Reichsorchester* was a curious sort of public-private partnership, whereby the orchestra would be delivered to a country by order of the German Propaganda Ministry, but then deal with local producers over fees, box-office shares and broadcast rights for public concerts.

Even in war and dictatorship, commercial interests played a role in such negotiations. For the RMVP-authorised fall tour of 1943 to Poland, Romania, Czechoslovakia, Croatia, and Hungary, for example, the Berlin Philharmonic was scheduled to appear in Budapest shortly after the Vienna Philharmonic had played at the opera house there. The orchestra's producing partner in Budapest was an entity called *Harmonia Genossenschaft für Künstlerische Belange Consorzio Musicale*. Karl Stegmann wrote to a Herr von Fischer, head of the private producing concern, demanding superior terms to those received by the Vienna orchestra, including a minimum two-thirds of box office receipts, and a guaranteed minimum take of Pengö 7 500, plus 10% of any broadcast revenues.[51] Fischer was conciliatory in response, affirming the deal with the Vienna Philharmonic was only a 60-40 split of profits, but cautioned that the success of the Viennese concert owed much to the presence of Furtwängler, which "was of course a big sensation for the Budapest public—as can also be appreciated by the increased ticket prices."[52] In commercial terms, audiences were willing to pay a premium for a star like Furtwängler, whom von Fischer put pressure on Stegmann to deliver. In the end, the Philharmonic received Pengö 7 500, while the Budapest public got Abendroth.

Depending on circumstances, the Philharmonic would either bargain for a share of box office receipts with a guaranteed minimum, or an outright appearance fee, usually in the neighbourhood of RM 8 000.[53] So unique was this constellation of propaganda, artistic excellence and commercial interest, business occasionally clashed with ideology. This was the case in Switzerland, were the producing partner of the Philharmonic's 1942 tour was a firm named Kantorowitz.[54] The Nazi regime's racist tenets were compromised likewise in Yugoslavia, where according to Stegmann, there existed "only Jewish concert promoters with whom the orchestra had to work, since there simply were no Aryan agencies of this sort."[55] The Philharmonic nevertheless travelled to Yugoslavia on a number of occasions. By virtue of its unusual status, the Berlin Philharmonic continued doing business with Jewish companies abroad throughout the period, demonstrating a remarkable hypocrisy on some level of administration. Whatever the Jewish concert promoters might have felt about producing events for the musical ambassador of Nazi Germany, at least in isolated cases, commercial pragmatics trumped ideological principles—effective propaganda was valued higher than anti-Semitic vehemence.

In addition to working with impresarios and private firms to arrange concerts abroad, the Philharmonic also coordinated with various State and Party organisations for technical and logistical support. Particularly during the war when large territories were controlled by German forces, the *Wehrmacht* and the *NS-Gemeinschaft*

"*Kraft durch Freude*" regularly provided invaluable assistance to the orchestra with food, transportation, accommodation and official travel documents (visas, permits etc.). These services were rendered gratis, with the orchestra 'piggy-backing' on communication and support lines established during invasion.

The *Wehrmacht*, and particularly "*Kraft durch Freude*" also co-operated with private travel agent firms in the sometimes elaborate plans it took to move a group of one-hundred musicians comfortably and efficiently across Europe.

By involving the *Wehrmacht*, KdF and other infrastructure already on the ground in foreign countries in the Berlin Philharmonic's touring plans—providing meals, transportation and paperwork, as in Paris, the Reich was able to produce an effective and economical synergy effect between branches of its expanding empire. This enabled the orchestra to tour more after the start of the war, further, and at substantially reduced costs.

The bureaucratic, technical, physical, and political logistics of Philharmonic tours were challenging. Some complications, instrument transport for example, were matters simply endemic to orchestra travel in any epoch. Others areas, such as police permissions, *Wehrpässe* and foreign transit visas, were obstacles specific to the rigorous restrictions on movement imposed by Nazi rule. Regulations were typically far less stringent outside Germany, where, with the help of consulates, visas could be issued at the frontier, and visitors' permits validated on location.[56]

Harder for a Philharmonic musician than entering into a foreign country was getting out of Germany. It was a three-step process for musicians to receive clearance for travel. As such, the procedures for certification began long before the planned tour departure, indeed, in many cases even before it was known where, when or with whom the tour would be taking place: "A Spring tour is foreseen; conductor and destination as of yet, unknown. We ask, however, to check passports already now and to report in the event a passport will expire [within the next six months]."[57]

Musicians were responsible for maintaining a valid passport, which meant not only renewing them before expiry, but keeping up with regulations which periodically rendered documents prematurely invalid.[58] The passport was required for presentation to the musicians' local *Polizeirevier* along with a special letter issued by the RMVP. This letter read:

> To the police department in charge. [name] is a member of the BPO and as such obliged to participate in a journey to [destination] as ordered by *Reichsminister* Goebbels. We request to grant the above mentioned the special exit permit and confirmation thereof in writing. [59]

The *Polizeirevier* would perform a background check to ensure the musician had a clean criminal record, and was denunciation-free, before issuing a statement, in a sealed envelope, consenting to their participation in the tour.

Musicians were then required to obtain '*Wehrurlaub*' from their local *Wehrbezirkskommando* or *Wehrmeldeamt*. Though issued letters from Goebbels confirming their *Verdoppelte Uk-status*, most Berlin Philharmonic members were still, by health and age, officially eligible for draft. It was therefore compulsory to be registered with and reachable by the military authorities at any time. Musicians were reminded of this requirement to foreclose all contact information also before holidays.[60] Because *Uk-Stellung* was dispensed at the discretion of local WBKs, *Wehrurlaub* and permission to leave Berlin for concertising purposes was not necessarily a pro-forma matter. Occasionally, the Philharmonic administration or RMVP would need to intercede to ensure the orchestra could travel in its entirety.[61]

With their valid passports, letters from the *Polizeirevier*, *Wehrurlaub* authorisations from the *Wehrmeldeamt*, and up to 12 passport photos,[62] the orchestra musicians could finally submit their documents to the Philharmonic offices. A secretary in the orchestra management was then responsible for forwarding the collected material, together with a formal travel itinerary and official group list to the central *Polizeipräsidium*. After reviewing all submitted material, the *Polizeipräsidium* would issue the orchestra and accompanying staff with official exit visas.[63] Under no circumstances could spouses, children, or other relations travel with the orchestra. Musicians were reminded that: "We cannot forward passports to police headquarters if they are not provided on time; in these cases, individuals willhave to deal with the trip and the associated efforts themselves."[64] It is not known if musicians ever missed deadlines for this elaborate procedure, but they certainly had reminders and incentives not to.

The vast majority of the Berlin Philharmonic's travel was by train. Exceptions were 'overseas' journeys by ship to England in 1935-38, and by plane to Scandinavia in 1941.[65] Otherwise, the orchestra's travel plans consisted of a tangled web of intra-European railway connections. Train travel was consistent, cost-effective, but slow. During war time, the trip from Berlin to Munich lasted over nine hours,[66] Budapest to Vienna five,[67] Barcelona to Valencia ten. The orchestra travelled by a combination of public railway, specially-hired trains, and military transport trains. Depending on availability, schedule, and cost, when travelling on public railway the orchestra would travel in second-class, third-class or sleeper cars. [68] For accommodation in sleeper cars, musicians were often asked to pay a supplemental fee.[69] By public transportation where seating availability was not guaranteed, the orchestra would sometimes travel in different classes aboard one train, or be divided into groups taking a series of scheduled trains. Special train services, meanwhile, could be booked for long routes, such as those to Spain, by travel agents, to ensure the orchestra could travel complete.

During the war, the Berlin Philharmonic was mobilised like a military unit, and made use of a network of German military transport spanning most of Europe. They frequently travelled in military transport trains, which were among the more comfortable forms of transportation. During its 1942 tour to Poland, Austrian and the Balkans, for instance, the Berlin Philharmonic travelled exclusively on trains provided by the *Wehrmacht*.[70] *Wehrmacht* trains typically had dining facilities, which was not a certainty on public transportation, and, depending on space and presentation of the requisite documentation, beds. [71] *Wehrmacht* trains also had priority on congested rail lines, ensuring the orchestra would arrive on time.

The orchestra's dense concert schedule put a premium on making connections. It was common for the Philharmonic to travel the same day as a concert. When not relying on the *Wehrmacht*, the orchestra could still call on privilege from other public service siblings, such as the *Reichverkehrsministerium*, or the *Reichsbahndirektion*, to whom they owed much thanks:

> Back in Berlin safe and sound, I would like to again express my sincere gratitude for taking such good care of the *Berliner Philharmoniker* whilst in your region. Even the return trip from Vienna was managed in such a way, that we indeed reached the scheduled train to Berlin— if at the last moment—after all, whereby all other difficulties which could have arisen in Vienna, were dealt with most efficiently."[72]

Originally, responsibility for travel arrangements was assumed by Bertha Geissmar, who had essentially run the Philharmonic's touring affairs out of Furtwängler's private secretariat from 1922 to 1933. From 1933 to 1934, Geissmar continued managing touring matters as an unofficial, yet salaried, member of the orchestra administrative staff. After Furtwängler's resignation and Geissmar's reluctant emigration, travel organisation reverted to the Philharmonic's senior administration. In many cases, after 1933, the Berlin Philharmonic travelled to many of the same places it had visited before the Nazis came to power. For these excursions, travel, accommodation, programming, and business arrangements were relatively uncomplicated, and could be handled by telephone or written correspondence. When the orchestra was commissioned to tour to unfamiliar countries, such as Greece, or Portugal, a representative of the Philharmonic administration, usually Karl Stegmann, but occasionally Gerhardt von Westerman or even Lorenz Höber, would make advance trips to negotiate and organise.

The Philharmonic's accommodation situations on tour varied widely. Options included private billets, private hotels, occupied hotels, rented railway cars, and military facilities. Musicians were typically lodged in double or triple rooms.[73] Accommodation usually depended on who was paying. When the principal objective was a *Wehrmachtsreise*, there would be little or no revenue to offset costs. The *Wehrmacht* would therefore provide lodging "zum Teil sehr miserabel" ("sometimes utterly miserable"),[74] for the orchestra during its trip. For prestigious visits to England or Italy, where the Philharmonic could be guaranteed income from concert ticket sales, hotels were booked. In Portugal in 1942, a part of the orchestra was billeted with the German community of Lisbon, a not entirely appealing proposition to many:

> In order to reduce hotel expenses, the German community in Lisbon has offered to host approximately 30 members of the orchestra with them in private homes [...] I now call upon the solidarity of all orchestra members and urgently ask 30 gentlemen of the orchestra in the name of our common interest to VOLUNTARILY apply for these private lodgings so we can make use of this friendly offer by the German community in Lisbon.[75]

These hosts were background checked, and according to recollection, at least some were *überzeugter* (genuine) Hitler supporters.[76]

Travel naturally grew more difficult during the war, but the facts were handled euphemistically. "Herr Reichsminister Speer" wrote Karl Stegmann to Furtwängler in 1942 through Lord Mayor Liebel (Nuremberg), has informed us that all of our concert tours are to be considered essential to the war effort."[77] Despite such guarantees, things grew more difficult. The 1943 Italy tour was "cancelled due to travel-related difficulties."[78]

The musicians were deliberately kept in the dark as to the gravity of the evolving military situation and how the war was adversely effecting their travel plans.[79] In 1943 and 1944, the Philharmonic journeys to and from Iberia were precarious: "Unfortunately I am currently not in a position to go into details of the current difficulties of this trip in front of the assembled orchestra; difficulties which have meanwhile become much more significant and numerous, both in Germany and in the countries to be visited."[80] On the Eastern Front too, by 1943-44 the tide was sweeping in:

> On our way back we were unfortunate insofar as the majority of the orchestra was forced to make a detour via Ostrowo, arriving with substantial delay in Posen, and did not have time to catch their breath before the

concert. But those are factors which, quite simply, the fifth year of war brings with it.[81]

Through good and bad times, Berlin Philharmonic concerts were always important events. Whether public concerts, performances for soldiers or at closed events for dignitaries, the orchestra's appearances were reported enthusiastically by local and international press—both controlled and free. Paying audiences forked out handsomely for the chance to hear one of the world's greatest orchestras, and were seldom disappointed. Overt propagandistic fanfare or regalia was seldom a part of public concerts abroad, the choice of repertoire and quality of performance sufficient to draw and persuade the public of the objective's justification.

The distinction between audience's genuine admiration and their succumbing to the bluff of political propaganda was almost impossible to draw. This fact was not lost on either the government or the orchestra. Wrote Karl Stegmann in a memo to his superiors at the RMVP in 1939, "The best propaganda remains the kind that does not obviously reveal itself its intentions." [82] The Philharmonic made a point of ensuring its musical quality, and the Reich facilitated its exposure far and wide, capitalising, for the most part subtly, before the eyes of the foreign public. In truth, the typical Berlin Philharmonic appearance in a capital of Europe looked scarcely different before and after 1933. Only on occasions of distinctly political or ideological dimension, such as the World's Fair, the opening of Deutsches National Theater in Prague, or performances with elite Nazi attendance was Nazi paraphernalia explicitly unfurled.

While the press in occupied lands during the war was heavily controlled, a new dimension of the Philharmonic's integration into the State propaganda machinery was the broadcast of orchestra exploits abroad to audiences at home, either through radio transmissions or via glowing reports of the orchestra's triumphs in the German media. In many respects, Philharmonic concerts were of greater propaganda value inside Germany, where comments such as "once again a triumph of German music in France "[83] held special resonance. Often, the German press framed Philharmonic exploits in political terms at best implicit, and often not at all present in the orchestra's actual appearances abroad. In 1942, for example, "The people of Portugal now know what German music means to the world. This victory, achived by the *Berliner Philharmoniker* on neutral ground between the wars and that front, which has lately been named the "invisible" by an English paper, will be remain unforgotten in Lisbon."[84]

Though the Philharmonic's performances were usually presented to local audiences as benign, purely musical delights, the orchestra was not always welcomed warmly in foreign countries. Political consciousness in some European centres understood the musicians and their appearances as ambassadors of a heinous regime. Berlin Philharmonic concerts were picketed and protested on a number of occasions. In Paris, just months after Hitler's ascension to the chancellery, a group called the "Ligue Internationale contre l'Antisemitisme" (The International League Against Anti-Semitism) stormed a concert during intermission, and dropped pamphlets from the balconies. The messages read:

> *Vous, qui venez d'ecouter avec emotion cette belle musique, vous, qui etes l'elite du public Parisien, songez que 700.000 hommes, femmes et enfants, sont condamnes a mourir de faim dans un pays civilise! Nous vous adjurons de fair tout ce qui est humainement possible pour que cesse ce crime monstrueux! Malgre notre decision de poursuivre et d'intensifier le boycottage de l'Allemagne Hitlerienne, nous n'avons pas voulu trouble la manifestation musicale de ce soir, organisee bien avant les evenements actuels, et dont les dirigeants ont courageusement proteste au nom de l'art, contre ces exactions abominables. Joignez vous a nous, et a tous les hommes de coeur, pour fletrir au nom de la dignite et de la conscience humaine, ce retour a la barbarie et pour sauvegarder la Paix du Monde.*[85]

In their message, the protesters recognised the menace of Hitler's Germany, but did not yet directly equate the Berlin Philharmonic with the Nazi regime. Rather, the concert was used as a pretext for a demonstration warning of impending barbarism in Europe, addressed to an educated class of French concert goers, but issued with respect for the unpartisan nature of a musical performance, particularly one organised "well in advance of events."

In 1935, two and a half years into Hitler's rule, the Berlin Philharmonic travelled to England. In London, their concerts were met with demonstrators from a group called the 'German Anti-Fascist Musicians'. Their manifesto read:

> A WELCOME: AND YET! We welcome the members of the Berlin Philharmonic Orchestra as representatives of a country whose civilisation was formerly among the highest in the whole history of mankind [...] Under the greatest conductors it has brought old man modern German music to people of other countries, and demonstrated the highest standard of German orchestral playing. In this way, this Orchestra, through its visits abroad, has succeeded in obtaining many admirers of Germany and its civilisation and will naturally do so also on this occasion [...] Progress and liberty stand today in such danger that we must not forget, in listening to the glorious major march of the Egmont Overture the hundreds of thousands of upright men confined in the horrible goals of German Fascism, tortured by loneliness and terror. AND YET—These men did nothing but try to save honour of the great German people. They stood, and still courageously stand, against a regime which has betrayed the real will of people for peace, and has destroyed a great civilisation for the benefit of a few individuals [...] Let the musical experience of hearing the Berlin Philharmonic Orchestra be a commemoration of these anti-fascist heroes. Honour by your applause the unknown anti-Fascist, whether he sits before you at this moment among the Orchestra, or whether he is carrying on in Germany, Italy, Austria etc. his dangerous underground work against War, Reaction and the Destruction of Civilisation.[86]

This protest, like that in France earlier, did not interrupt the musical proceedings, but made use of a Philharmonic concert as a pulpit to send a larger political message. The London protest even went several steps further. Not only did the German Anti-Fascist Musicians (composed quite possibly of German exiles and/or Communists) not equate the orchestra with the regime, it suggested its performance should be received as a harbinger of resistance. Further still, the group suggested members of the orchestra could themselves have been dissidents, not just through their acts in performance, but by undertaking "dangerous underground work" too. The suggestion that Beethoven should be a sentinel against totalitarianism, and musicians, by connection to such art, somehow innately attuned to the struggle for freedom, was echoed by figures from Furtwängler to Thomas Mann. Whether the musicians of the Berlin Philharmonic in any way felt their performance of the Egmont Overture was a symbol of protest against the regime which had ensured the orchestra's existence, paid their wages, and had sent them to England in the first place, cannot be known. From the Philharmonic's point of view, however, the contradiction between the Nazi political agenda and the preservation of Germany's "great civilisation" was not so stark. Through their support for the orchestra and its touring activities, the Berlin Philharmonic's experience would have largely seen the Nazis as beneficial to the great civilisation of which the Philharmonic was a leading vessel.

The equation of the Berlin Philharmonic Orchestra with the Nazi Reich was only fully formed with the war. From its extensive touring, the orchestra became known as the "Vorkämpfer der Fallschrimjäger" (avant garde—in the military sense—of the paratroopers),[87] prompting threats to the security of Philharmonic concerts in unoccupied territories. An aggressive protest campaign in Belgrade led to the scuttling of the Philharmonic's 1940 appearance there and their scheduled performance in Zagreb later that week. The demonstrators warned: "The *Berliner Philharmoniker* are giving their first concert in Belgrade on May 8, 1940. This is the same Philharmonie which gave a concert on March, 15, 1939 in Prague and, a few days prior to the German attack, in Oslo and Copenhagen. The arrival of the 118 German musicians is a bad omen of political and military conquest. The sound of combat vehicles and military transports can be heard behind the enchanting sounds of their instruments."[88]

No longer impartial entertainers offering beautiful, inspiring music, the shape and even the sounds of the Philharmonic now bore menace. And the music itself was impacted. In occupied countries, security for Philharmonic concerts was overseen by German forces, as it had been in Germany since 1933. The orchestra reportedly never experienced problems in the Lowlands, for example, or in Poland. In unoccupied territories, however, protests continued. In Vichy France in 1942, protests were staged interrupting the orchestra's performances. Upon returning to Berlin, Gerhard von Westerman was required to file a comprehensive report: "Subject: report of the concerts of the *Berliner Philharmoniker* in Marseille and Lyon on May 17th and 18th, 1942. [...] These concerts were the first German cultural events in unoccupied France since the armistice. Both concerts were great artistic successes. The sold-out houses both responded with enthusiastic applause, which, however, took on a demonstrative note towards the ends of the concerts."[89] "Demonstrative" in this case, meant in Marseille, protesters in the galleries had staged a noisy mass walkout while the orchestra performed. In response, security was tightened for the Philharmonic's next concert in Lyon. This, however, did not solve the problem, as Gerhard von Westerman reported:

> Unfortunately, in Lyon, police protection was carried out in a very conspicuous manner. All entrances to the concert hall were blocked by police at approximately 40 meters distance at the street crossings. The audience could only access the concert hall in one spot by producing their tickets and their IDs. In front of the police cordon, larger crowds had gathered in several places, jeering loudly or singing the Marseillaise. Some smaller military battalions were engaged to disperse the crowd. Still, the demonstrations continued during the concert. We realised during the ticket sale for the concert in Lyon that all tickets had been bought by Jews and Communists.[...] In the morning before the concert, pamphlets were distributed around town threatening to disturb the concert [...] Likely these indications were the reason for the extraordinary but ultimately rather embarrassing police presence.[90]

Whether the protesters in Marseille and Lyon were demonstrating against the Nazi regime in general or specifically the presence of the Philharmonic is not clear, but after receiving von Westerman's report, the RMVP suspended all further German cultural exchange with unoccupied France.[91]

Finally, on tour with Furtwängler in Switzerland in 1942, both conductor and orchestra received a first bitter taste of the polarising debates which would come the characterise the ethical ambiguities of their respective fates in the post-war era:

> Furtwängler is a Prussian *Staatsrat* by Goebbels' [sic] grace. But we do not want such State officials presenting us with State-sanctioned art, even when it concerns Furtwängler. You may think: As long as the Nazi comes along with Brahms and Bruckner, he cannot be so bad. But this is just what Herr Goebbels wants. That's why the "Department Switzerland" exists in the Berlin Ministry of Propaganda. The dead composers are defencelessly forced to let their works be engaged in the service of the refined National-Socialist foreign propaganda apparatus. And that's why they enlisted the help of a Jewish concert agency in Zurich!
>
> Furtwängler: an exponent of slavish dependence! Toscanini: a free genius! Long live Toscanini!![92]

This protest was one of the first to identify the subtlety with which the propaganda system operated, a system wherein Furtwängler and any Berlin Philharmonic musician could be virtually interchangeable. Whether or not the concert agency run by a man named Kantorowitz was part of the disingenuous propaganda ploy, or if rather commercial and pragmatic factors brought about the unexpected partnership, the prosecuting advocate acknowledged the artists' qualitative merits, but urged his Swiss audience to rouse itself from naivety. Furtwängler and, for example, Lorenz Höber, were no more indelibly Nazis than Bruckner or Brahms, yet the genius of the Nazi system created a culture of dependency whereby musicians' identities were subsumed into a machinery which politicised all it produced. The Third Reich politicised art by binding music and musicians materially and spiritually to the State. Hence, the representation of Furtwängler, and by extension his orchestra, here, as a slave of the Nazi regime, completed the transformation of the Berlin Philharmonic in the international critical view, from exponents of beauty to manifestations of evil.

This critical view, meanwhile, was not the prevailing opinion. The Berlin Philharmonic was, for the most part, extremely well received in foreign countries, not just by dignitaries, idolising fans and jubilant music critics, but by music-lovers and disinterested locals alike. In contrast to the vast majority of Germans, the opportunity to travel for the members of the orchestra, was a luxury. Philharmonic players were able to make acquaintances, meet foreign relatives, and purchase goods unavailable in Germany. This latter benefit was particularly popular with the musicians, who would wait anxiously for ruling on their import allowances before stocking up on coffee, spices, jewlery, or other gifts for friends and family back home.[93] Many musicians also had friends and family abroad, who would be keen to know the news from Germany. Musicians were used to courier parcels and messages. Likewise, on tour Philharmonic musicians had access to foreign news sources, some controlled, some not. Even during the war, they could visit beautiful cities and enjoyed freedom of mobility.

As far as their meetings with locals, Werner Buchholz's somewhat biased account from recalled:

> Almost a hundred gentlemen are always along for the trip and each one of them makes some kind of personal contact along the way, and thus has unlimited opportunity to convey a better and more vivid picture of our Fatherland to the representative of the foreign nation, who is mostly informed by the biased press. Because it is an often experienced and psychologically explicable fact that the artist is met with extraordinary trust, due to his profession he is regarded to be rather above things; one does not suspect him of political passions and therefore deems his evaluations and views independent and objective. Especially the *Philharmoniker* have frequently had opportunity to experience unforgettable testimony of true hospitality and cordial sympathy in contact with other peoples.[94]

On an individual basis, it is unlikely the majority of Philharmonic musicians were interested in duping foreigners into believing they were politically unaffiliated while feeding them pre-fabricated lines about the spendors of the 'Vaterland.' Still, orchestra members were aware they were ambassadors for Germany, and their expected comportment was commensurate. They were required to dress appropriately at all times, and to behave with dignity.[95]

In contrast to Buchholz's account, moreoever, musicians in fact did not fraternise extensively with locals. In addition to prohibitions like language barriers and the orchestra's gruelling schedule, musicians' activities were monitored. There are no records of an orchestra 'informant', nor did the orchestra travel with any government appointed supervisor, rather, it would seem, musicians governed themselves with utmost caution, while the Party-member executive (Kleber, Schuldes, Woywoth, as well as Stegmann) kept a close eye on things. Orchestra discipline was a function of limitation and intimidation. Musicians were reminded in the coded language of the day, "it is the natural duty of all members to comply with these measures without protest and to follow the orders of the management or those of their representatives unconditionally." [96]

At the same time, to minimise contact with outsiders, the orchestra ate most meals together, and social events, such as post-concert receptions, were always by invitation only.

So well obedient and well-managed was the orchestra, some suspected that rather than having informants within its ranks, the orchestra itself was in the business of spying on others. So much was suggested to Furtwängler at his de-Nazification tribunal that, "under the circumstances it might be supposed that such tours could have been widely used for the purposes of espoinage." Such suggestions were even insinuated by the Nazi press, where the satirical *Illistrierter Beobachter* published a cartoon with the note:

> The BPO has now been transformed into a branch of the secret service. It will soon make a concert tour to neutral countries. We have evidence that most of the orchestra's members belong to the Gestapo. The use of the orchestra for espionage purposes is especially clever since the "artists" will have the opportunity to come into immediate proximity with highest ranking persons, which would be otherwise impossible for normal spies.[97]

Though perhaps intended as humour, the sketch played on the exceptional nature of the Philharmonic's touring activities, while correctly recognising the enviable opportunities the musicians enjoyed. It also reified the concordance of the orchestra's mandate with the interests of the regime.

Privately, however, musicians were fortunate able to make and maintain contacts abroad. Particularly as the war dragged on, news from the outside kept musicians informed. This news did not always come from the press, but often from acquainances with access. Switzerland represented a bastion of somewhat free-information. It was there musicians heard say for the first time in 1942, "Für Euch ist dieser Krieg verloren" ("For you this war is lost.").[98]

Not just the musicians, but Philharmonic administrators too made use of connections forged in the process of touring for private purposes. Writing to the *Oberbereichsleiter* of the *Regierung des Generalgouvernements für den Distrikt Warschau*, a Herrn Schmonsees, offering thanks for facilitating the orchestra's passage through Poland, Karl Stegmann took the opportunity to broach with the *Oberbereichsleiter* a personal matter regarding the safety of his son, a German soldier wounded on the Eastern Front.[99]

On the orchestra's 1944 tour to France and Spain, a private film production company made a film for the RMVP. "It will be a hit," wrote Goebbels in his diary after the initial discussions, "I have already thought out the whole scenario."[100] The result, entitled 'Philharmoniker', was premiered in Berlin in December, 1944. It was a feature film, staring some of the most notable actors of the day embedded in the Berlin Philharmonic Orchestra. Of greater interest than the film's storyline, was its backdrop showing the orchestra impressing hundreds of French and Spanish onlookers with performances of Beethoven and Bruckner. In a remarkable sense, the film captured the unique and terrifying semiotics of the moment: an artwork of artwork—a propaganda film made of propaganda.

Epilogue

Heirs to a *Reichsorchestra*

On December 14, 1933, the Deputy Mayor of Berlin, Dr. Sahm, wrote to the RMVP, complaining that of 109 employees, the Berlin Philharmonic did not count a single disabled worker.[1] According to the letter, a deal was brokered in fall of 1933 to see the orchestra employ two disabled people among its musical and administrative staff. Since that time, however, only one had been installed.[2] Sahm was losing patience.[3] In 1933, in the process of subsuming by one bureaucracy—the RMVP—the Berlin Philharmonic was being hounded by another: the government of Berlin. In fact, one bureaucracy was harassing another to influence the orchestra in a trivial matter of red tape. Yet characterised here were many of the themes that would play themselves out in the experience of the Berlin Philharmonic over the coming years.

First, the notion of bureaucratic process, which for all its inflexibility, recognised, indeed insisted upon due process. Once a private, independent entity, the Berlin Philharmonic had never before been beholden to imposed standards, models, practices, policies. From 1933, with the State securing its long-term stability, the orchestra was forced to adjust to the legal commitments and functional implications attendant to employment in the public service. The translation of policy into pragmatics was something to which the orchestra, along with the rest of Germany, had to acclimatise, with the radicalisation of policy after January 30, 1933. To be sure, political and ideological pressures abounded, but while the public service was controlled by Nazi officials, bureaucratic functionalism mitigated a portion of their ideological ferocity; the language of discourse evolved, but pragmatic problems consistently required effective solutions. Adherence to due process, as in the legal acquisition of the Berlin Philharmonic GmbH shares, the formalisation of a new orchestra constitution, the interposition of a management class, the ratification or dissolution of contracts, even the commitment to handicapped employees within the orchestra organisation, were all part of this banal, yet fundamental, transformation.

Secondly, the politicisation of values. As Dr. Sahm's letter spelled out, providing a public service was not a matter of public account-ability but public example, an appraisal of symbolism above utility. How exactly a busy musical ensemble was meant to accommodate a disabled member was not made clear, but the Berlin Philharmonic's duty was to obscure that fact—to provide a symbol to society of 'true German values' by engaging a couple of veterans. Practically, this was near preposterous, but translated to the national or international stage, the orchestra was elevated to a symbol of Germany—the best of German culture, even as that culture was consuming itself in vio-lence and hatred.

Thirdly, the chronic system of influence peddling symptomatic of the circuitous power relationships and 'cronyistic' culture surround-ing the Berlin Philharmonic during the Third Reich. Dr. Sahm wrote to the RMVP to exercise influence over the Berlin Philharmonic regarding hiring of the disabled. Furtwängler spoke to Goebbels's RMVP to have Hans von Benda dismissed as *Künstlerischer Leiter* in 1939. A musician of the Philharmonic contacted Furtwängler to get rid of Hermann Stange in 1935. Stange wrote to just about everyone to get a job, anywhere. The interdependency of such a system made it ripe for exploitation. The Berlin Philharmonic in many cases fought against the outcomes of this system, but ultimately exploited the al-liance of ideological values, political ambitions and artistic sensibili-ties which put it at the top of the musical world.

In 1939, the RMVP developed a plan to further transform the Berlin Philharmonic. Proposed was the "transformation of the GmbH into a direct Reich's service branch."[4] The plan called for "a conversion of the present GmbH structure similar to what has been done with our State theatres,"[5] putting the musicians directly in service of the Ministry and disbanding the even illusory orchestra independent entity. The plan was to be kept secret,[6] but Stegmann heard of the initiative, and wrote to the Ministry privately:

> One of the orchesta's most important duties is to
> presents concerts abroad as a part of German cultural
> propaganda. The best propaganda, of course, remains
> that which does not openly reveal its intentions. For this
> reason, the external form of our organisation as a GmbH
> was very appropriate, as the orchestra could be viewed as
> a private [as opposed to a State] company.[7]

Stegmann's point was well made: why tamper with a well-working machine? It may indeed have been a sign of the Philharmonic's successful integration, that bureaucrats were left drafting gratuitous memos proposing superfluous measures—an example of bureaucrats creating policy rather than sustaining it. In any event, whether the orchestra got wind of the proposal, or if Furtwängler was notified of the plans afoot, the Ministry, of its own accord, shelved the operation within several months. As Stegmann argued, dissolving the GmbH would not improve organisational efficiency and only harm the Philharmonic's effectiveness as an instrument of propaganda. Goebbels would have agreed.

When Furtwängler resigned from the Philharmonic in December 1934, many both within and outside the orchestra thought it was the beginning of the end. Lorenz Höber, for example, was convinced that without Furtwängler's protection, "[the Philharmonic] would have become a Nazi orchestra, and would have certainly suffered an artistic decline."[8] In 1934, both consequences were distinctly possible, but these were not the regime's intentions. The Nazis had no use for yet another mediocre Nazi orchestra; it would have precisely defeated Goebbels' purpose to fully consolidate and repress the Philharmonic. Rather, the Nazis wished to encourage the Berlin Philharmonic's uniqueness, and let it and Furtwängler enjoy their small favours in exchange, however reticent, for cooperation.

When Otto Klemperer returned to Berlin in 1947, Philharmonic musician Erich Hartmann recalled the conductor's dour demeanour. "Perhaps," speculated Hartmann, "that as a Jew who had been compelled to leave Germany, he was unhappy having to face an orchestra which had enjoyed privileges of the Nazi times—even if it was never a Nazi orchestra itself."[9] Klemperer's psychology aside, in his recollection, Hartmann recognised the orchestra's post-war ethical dilemma: the Berlin Philharmonic was to an exceptional extent cherished, groomed and protected by the Nazi regime. That the Berlin Philharmonic was, at the same time, not a Nazi orchestra, by spirit, constitution, or membership, was also true. The Berlin Philharmonic, however, did not have to be a Nazi orchestra to serve its purpose to the regime—in fact, it was desirable that it not be. And the regime went to great lengths to protect and promote the exceptionality of its prized musical asset.

As the Third Reich drew to a terrible end, however, the immunity the Berlin Philharmonic experienced from the horrors the Nazi regime wrought upon Germany and Europe finally evaporated. The writing on the wall became visible through the Winter of 1943-44. The disturbing ambivalence of the situation was expressed in a RMVP memo dated January 3, 1944:

> *Geschäftsführer* Stegmann has reported that in the attack of November 22nd, the office building [of the orchestra] completely burned down. The administration of the Philharmonic Orchestra has subsequently been based in a private home [...] we cannot anticipate that a more appropriate space can be made available until the conclusion of the war [...]

This is followed by a highly cryptic passage concerning the 'special circumstances' of the moment bringing 'uncertainties' which 'can be viewed from different perspectives', the result of which 'remain ambiguous'.[10]

Pragmatism was replaced by opaque, elliptical language which captured the state of precariousness, almost disbelief, of the moment. The destruction of the Alte Philharmonie three weeks later was but the most tangible symbol of the Philharmonic's vulnerability. Many musicians were bombed out of their homes. "It was difficult," recalled double bass player Erich Hartmann, "for us to grasp it all."[11] And yet, the privileges lavished upon the orchestra did not cease. In the summer of 1944, orchestra members were evacuated out of Berlin, to the relative safety of Baden-Baden.[12] The musicians' instruments were later transported to Bavaria for safekeeping. In the fall of 1944, most cultural institutions were shut down as men and resources were shifted to fighting losing battles, but not the Berlin Philharmonic. Under the protecting hand of Albert Speer, the *Uk-Stellung* for Philharmonic musicians remained in force, even as militia thugs forced children with rocks into the streets of Berlin to be blasted by Red Army tanks. Through a combination of ingenuity and hubris, the Berlin Philharmonic grafted itself so tightly to Germany's cultural and political frame that its pulse kept beating right to the very end. The end itself was not glorious, but for the Philharmonic, came quickly, and passed.

The last concerts of the Berlin Philharmonic under the Third Reich took place on the second week of April 1945—Beethoven, Wagner, Weber and Brahms in the unheated Beethoven-Saal adjacent to the wrecked Philharmonie. Furtwängler had fled to Switzerland several months before. The final performances were led by Robert Heger and Georg Schumann with Gerhard Taschner, Siegfried Borries, Tibor de Machula, and soprano Gertrud Rünger among the soloists. The last piece the Philharmonic performed was a symbolic and sentimental choice, Richard Strauss' *Death and Transfiguration*. Ten days later, Hitler was dead.

On May 4, 1945, four days before Germany's unconditional surrender, the *Wehrmacht* surrendered Berlin to the Red Army. From approximately April 17 until just after this date, the Berlin Philharmonic dispersed, some musicians joining the militia voluntarily, others were forced to, while a number fled the city altogether. In the period from winter 1943 to April 1945, the Berlin Philharmonic lost six members directly to the war: violinist Alois Ederer and timpanist Kurt Ulrich perished in Allied bombing raids, violist Curt Christkautz was abducted by the Nazi *Volkssturm* and died somewhere on the Eastern Front, and three men—violinist Bernhard Alt, bassist Alfred Krüger, and bassoonist Heinrich Lieberum took their own lives by suicide. Violinist Hans Ahlgrimm was added to the list of Philharmonic war fatalities when he perished in the final siege on Berlin in April 1945. In the lawless wilderness of the Capital after Germany's defeat, oboist Willy Lenz and harpist Rolf Naumann also met untimely ends when beset upon by a brutal mob outside the

capital.[13] Anton Schuldes, trumpet-player and NSDAP member, reportedly volunteered for active military duty during the final weeks
of the war. In 1947, he was officially declared a casualty of war, in all
likelihood one of the thousands of German POWs who disappeared
in Soviet prison camps and were never heard from again.[14]

After the cessation of hostilities, Philharmonic musicians immediately attempted to contact their colleagues. Without telephone,
post or other communications, the local pockets of orchestra members living in neighbourhoods such as Schöneberg, Wilmersdorf and
Steglitz, were quickest to reconnect. Those living in eastern districts,
or the musicians who had fled Berlin altogether, remained out of
touch for days or weeks.[15] A number of informal meetings in the
days following Germany's surrender established the majority of the
orchestra had survived, along with an assortment of instruments and
sheet music rescued, salvaged or hoarded away. A poignant, though
unlikely deliberately symbolic aspect to these early meetings was
their location—the Wilmersdorf home of clarinettist Ernst Fischer
and his Jewish wife, Edith.[16]

The survival of the Philharmonic in May of 1945 was by no
means assured. Indeed, the orchestra's future was severely threatened.
Political authority in Berlin was weak, cultural administration was
non-existent. The Berlin Philharmonic had no home, no status, no
money. The orchestra was simply a community of slightly fewer than
one hundred shell-shocked, world-class, unemployed musicians with
a severely tarnished name. They had been prominent cultural emissaries for a regime which had brought terror, horror and ruin. If they
were to survive, it remained up to the sovereignty of this group to
define what the orchestra should be, how it should be directed, and
who should be in it.

In this time of crisis, the Berlin Philharmonic's greatest assets came to the fore: its collective combative spirit and the group's
shrewd political judgement. The former quality assured that the
community would regroup and persist. They were not a Nazi orchestra. The Philharmonic had existed before 1933, had fought through
deeply trying times, and the colleagues were determined to see their
orchestra outlive the Nazi tyrants. At the same time, if the orchestra
were to survive, the orchestra had to be proactive. Hitler's musical

ambassadors were a stained bunch. In the torrid change of currents following the dictator's demise, the Berlin Philharmonic was in serious danger. For individual and collective consciences, but also as an urgently pragmatic matter, the orchestra needed to seize the earliest possible moment to distance itself from former times, to redefine itself before it was identified and tarred by others in the tide of anti-Nazi revulsion which was sure to follow.

Though largely intact, sufficiently equipped, and eager to resume its activities, before doing so, the musical community faced numerous problems: where would the Berlin Philharmonic perform? Who would pay them? Under whose authority could such events take place? Who would conduct them? And most significantly, who or what was the Berlin Philharmonic in post-Hitler Germany? To answer these questions, the orchestra was compelled return to its self-governing roots.

A complete return of the Berlin Philharmonic to a state of self-governance, however, was out of the question. The reasons were two-fold: first, every action, gathering and movement in the Berlin of May 1945 required explicit authorisation. The authorities were numerous and individually tenuous. In order to begin their rebuilding, the Philharmonic required representatives, and the cooperation of an alliance of partners. Second, the once proudly autonomous private orchestra collective, by conscripting itself to public service under the Nazis, had forfeited a piece of its independence. The orchestra community still represented the institution's head and torso, but the GmbH no longer provided the legs to power it. After eleven years in public service, the Berlin Philharmonic needed the assistance of public authorities to redefine itself, not least to prevent it from tearing itself apart.

Of immediate concern, however, was how to re-establish the orchestra as a functioning musical entity. The details could be arranged thereafter. Instrumental to this reconstitution were two figures whom the orchestra had long relied upon. The indefatigable Lorenz Höber took up the reins once more as the musicians' spokesperson and organisational leader. In the early days and weeks after the capitulation, it was not possible to speak of 'government' per se, but Höber assumed responsibility for liaising between the orchestra and the array of local, municipal, regional, military, and occupying authorities on the Philharmonic's behalf. Höber's first success was the procurement of permits for the orchestra to meet, and letters of passage for orchestra members to travel, by bicycle, to Wilmersdorf for said gatherings.[17] This was arranged within a week of the capitulation.

Ever the politically savvy group, the Philharmonic also turned for assistance to the man still nominally their *1. Geschäftsführer*, Gerhard von Westerman. Westerman was, by all accounts, not a Nazi in the zealous mould, but an NSDAP member nonetheless, and had been appointed to the Philharmonic with Goebbels' personal blessing. The orchestra could not have been unaware of the moral precariousness in soliciting and accepting Westerman's help, yet their collective pragmatism made him an obvious choice. Westerman's managerial competence was much appreciated by the musicians, but during the first weeks of May 1945, Berlin was still under complete Soviet occupation. Gerhard von Westerman was born in Riga, Latvia, and spoke fluent Russian (his German always remained tinged with a Baltic accent). The Berlin Philharmonic, therefore, made use of their Nazi-imposed self-styled *Intendant* to negotiate directly with Soviet officials, in their own language. The Philharmonic's letters of passage were bi-lingual.

Pragmatism, astute politics, and linguistic skills again played a role in the Berlin Philharmonic's search for a musical leader. Furtwängler remained the orchestra's undisputed father figure, but his fate was far from clear. In the meantime, the orchestra wished to make a statement, and to make it quickly. To do so, they needed both a conductor and a messenger. The choice of Leo Borchard was no coincidence. Borchard had a long relationship with the Philharmonic dating back to a Haydn-Beethoven-Brahms concert on January 3, 1933. He had been a regular and well-regarded guest with the orchestra throughout the Nazi years until, in 1943, when he was blacklisted by the *Reichsmusikkammer*.[18] Thereafter, Borchard joined the German resistance.[19]

Borchard was familiar with and to the orchestra, and a name known to Berlin audiences. Further, in political terms, as a resister and victim of Nazism, he was able to project a stark moral break from the Philharmonic's recent past. Another ace, raised in St. Petersburg by German parents, Borchard was spoke Russian perfectly, making relations with the Soviet authorities all the cosier. Finally, at the end of the war, Borchard was already in Berlin, meaning, without waiting for Furtwängler, Böhm, Jochum, Karajan, or other notable conductors who had dispersed as the Third Reich crashed to a close, Borchard could be enlisted promptly, and the Philharmonic could, as the expression goes, 'hit the ground running'. Borchard was the ideal candidate for the Philharmonic's ticket to resurrection.

Through their collective will and cunning, and with the triumvirate talents of Höber, Westerman and Borchard, the Berlin Philharmonic gave its first concert in the Titania-Palast in Steglitz on May 26 1945. The programme: Mendelssohn's Overture to *Einsommernachtstraum*, the A Major Violin Concerto by Mozart, with Ulrich Grehling as soloist, and Tchaikovsky's Symphony Nr.4. The choice of Mendelssohn was, naturally, significant, indeed symbolic. By account, orchestra trombonist and music librarian Friedrich Quante had kept the parts stashed away, saved from Nazi barbarism, awaiting the day Mendelssohn could be heard again.[20] Framing itself with Mendelssohn and Borchard, the Philharmonic was making a convincing case for its post-war legitimacy.

The first post-war concert was a triumph, but playing again was just the beginning. Many musicians who had suffered under the Nazis saw the need for restitution. Violinist Erich Bader, a cardcarrying socialist before 1933, apparently argued for an immediate purge of NSDAP members, or at least the aggressive ones, from the orchestra.[21] Other orchestra members were more conciliatory, recognising the ethical eggshells on which they all were walking. Both sides had their successes and failures in a virtual civil war over the Philharmonic's new course.

The precise nature of the discussions between Philharmonic members as they first met in the new era are lost to history. Clear is only that certain musicians either did not wish to, or were not invited to participate in the orchestra's post-Nazi constitution. Whether for political, personal, musical or career motivations, Concertmasters Erich Röhn and Gerhard Taschner, violist Reinhard Wolff, solo-cellist Arthur Troester, and trumpet player Adolf Scheerbaum were among those who did not return. The patterns in such departures are not evident. Some musicians decided to leave unilaterally, others may have been forced out by resolutions of the collective. Some, such as Wolff, were NSDAP members, others, such as Troester, were not. Scheerbaum was a Party member, but was also apparently in too poor technical form to remain principal trumpet with the Philharmonic anyhow. [22] Taschner, meanwhile, already on a special contract with the Philharmonic since late 1944,[23] had only joined the orchestra for the *Uk-Stellung* protection in the first place, so was now free to pursue his career as an independent soloist. Röhn, Troester, and Reinhard Wolf quickly jumped to more stable and lucrative positions in Hamburg.[24]

Other colleagues were also removed from the orchestra by political authorities as the process of so-called 'de-Nazification' took shape. Debates within the orchestra raged, both between musicians, and among musicians lobbying for the ears of the political representatives who intervened with executive authority to oversee the Philharmonic's disengagement from its twelve-year association with the Nazi State. These included municipal officials and investigators of the Allied powers. Before the end of May 1945, violinist Alfred Graupner, bassist Arno Burkhardt, violist Werner Buchholz, cellist Wolfram Kleber, and violinist Hans Woywoth were all suspended from the Philharmonic for their Nazi activities. So prompt were these men's extractions, it could have only been by orchestra members themselves denouncing their colleagues that the process was so expedited. Graupner and Burkhardt were subsequently restored in short order.[25]

The Berlin Philharmonic's legal status and jurisdiction, meanwhile, remained unclear. Successfully canvassed by Höber and von Westerman, the municipal government of still Soviet-controlled Berlin agreed to assist the orchestra financially, and the Titania Palast was made available to the Philharmonic on a provisional but open-ended basis.[26] With its first concerts, the orchestra made a successful beginning at disengaging itself from the recent past, but in June 1945, it was still too early, and the occupying powers were otherwise too busy, to examine the Philharmonic file in detail. Until such time, the authorities entrusted the orchestra to Leo Borchard, whose political, as well as musical credentials were indubitable.

Borchard was given *carte blanche* and the legal authority to handle all aspects of Berlin Philharmonic affairs responsible only to his own judgement:

> Until a final decision, Herr Borchard will be charged with the artistic and general direction of the Berlin Philharmonic, including conducting its concerts. Herr Borchard is conferred the right to remove all members of the orchestra who were, as former members of the NSDAP, politically active.[27]

Borchard was remarkably lenient in execution of his right to cut Party members adrift. He must have been the crucial sounding-board for the orchestra's internal debates, but acted with prudence and restraint. The established and politically active NSDAP members—Buchholz, Kleber, and Woywoth, among others, though musical colleagues, were not only morally discredited, but their continued presence threatened the Philharmonic's efforts to reform. It is not clear if their departures were sanctioned first by Borchard, public authorities, or the orchestra community itself. All eventually found employment elsewhere in Berlin, but the ends of their Philharmonic careers effectively coincided with the demise of the regime to whose leading Party they belonged.

Official de-Nazification policies, enforced by Berlin's four occupying powers took some months to institute. All Germans were required to fill out lengthy questionnaires on their various activities, allegiances, and affiliations during the Third Reich. These questionnaires were reviewed by local authorities. As public servants in Hitler's Reich, Philharmonic musicians were further subject to personal interviews by Allied investigators. As the Soviets pulled back to the eastern sector, the Berlin Philharmonic, with its temporary offices established in Berlin-Steglitz, was transferred to American jurisdiction. This meant orchestra musicians were subject to at least two sets of questioning, first based upon zone of residence, second through their employment. The resulting system produced a myriad of inconsistencies.

In several cases, orchestra members were requested to testify on each other's behalf. The first violinist Johannes Bastiaan, for example, submitted a statement in defence of his section colleague, Hans Gieseler, who had been a member of the NSDAP since 1934.[28] In relation to Gieseler's political allegiance, Bastiaan attested to his colleague's complete trustworthiness and openness to all kinds of political discussion. Furthermore, according to Bastiaan's testimony, Gieseler never attempted to impose his opinions or intimidate others.[29] With the help of Bastiaan's seemingly credible testimony, Gieseler, despite his tarnished record, was never suspended from his activities with the Philharmonic.

Discerning between 'good' and 'bad' Nazi-Party members was a perilous affair, morally and bureaucratically. Referring to colleagues Alfred Graupner and Arno Burkhardt, Erich Hartmann wrote "these two never did anyone the least harm. They were great artists and true colleagues."[30] Artists and friends these men might have been, but distinguishing grades of Nazi obfuscated the courage and integrity of those who resisted joining the Party at all. This morally challenging problem was further compounded by the subjective and uncoordinated nature of the individual assessments. Individual investigators in the various sectors maintained differing opinions on degrees of culpability, and the scales of retribution varied between American, British, French, and Soviet sectors.

Some, like Gieseler, also Friedrich Quante, Herbert Teubner, never suffered adverse consequences for their Party membership. Other Philharmonic players, such as trombone player Heinz-Walter Thiele, also had suspect records but were assessed more harshly. An NSDAP member since 1933, Thiele was investigated and sentenced by American authorities. He was banned from working in the city's American sector and had his membership in the Berlin Philharmonic summarily ended, effective immediately.[31]

Decisions were reached by sector authorities, then communicated to the Philharmonic, which in turn was responsible for notifying its own members. Similar letters, on Berlin Philharmonic stationery, went out to a total of at least nine orchestra members. Like Graupner and Burkhardt, Heinz-Walter Thiele was suspended from his Philharmonic activities, but pursued a right to appeal. Upon review, Thiele was reinstated.[32] In other cases, such as Philharmonic hornist and former NSDAP member Georg Hedler, authorities were not so lenient. Though by no account a rabid Nazi, Hedler's most prominent role during the Third Reich had been a brief tenure on the orchestra *Vertrauensrat*. This, it would seem, was enough to doom his future with the Philharmonic. Either his appeal failed, or he did not even try. Hedler was released from the orchestra after 24 years service, at the end of December, 1945.[33]

The uncoordinated, sectoral de-Nazification process, meanwhile, did not necessarily mean expelled Philharmonic musicians were left unemployed. Musicians were banned from performance in one sector or another—Thiele, for example, before his reinstatement, was black-listed from performance in the American zone—but in principle could seek jobs in other sectors of the capital. Indeed, there was a demand for players of Philharmonic calibre elsewhere in Berlin. So, Georg Hedler found a position elsewhere in the American sector with the RIAS Sinfonie Orchester, violist Werner Buchholz landed in the Soviet-controlled *Staatsoper Unter den Linden*, and former Philharmonic *Obmann*, Wolfram Kleber, ended up in the cello section of the Deutsche Oper orchestra in the British zone.[34] Of the Berlin Philharmonic's approximately twenty Nazi Party members during the Third Reich, two died in the war. Seven left the orchestra, either voluntarily or by compulsion in 1945-46. Another three were suspended by Allied investigators in 1945, then later reinstated. The remaining musicians were absolved through the de-Nazification process.[35]

The investigating authorities, however, were not only interested in hunting down Nazis. As Furtwängler's prolonged de-Nazification procedure illustrated, the fact of Party membership was only part of the larger issue. British and American investigators were mindful of semiotics, both in terms of Nazi appropriation, and to themselves make examples of Nazi complicity. Furtwängler was called to commission on the basis of "having been guilty of disseminating Nazi and fascist ideologies."[36]

Once the initial sweep on Party-members was completed, the Berlin Philharmonic was also examined on the basis of its service to the Nazi State. Judged by the criteria of complicity rather than individual political allegiance, the Berlin Philharmonic suffered two further casualties. The first was Friedrich Mayer, cellist and founding *Vorstand* of the Kammeradschaft der Berliner Philharmoniker. At war's end, Mayer found himself in Steinhude, Niedersachsen.[37] From Steinhude, he went to Munich. By the time Mayer had made the necessary arrangements to get to Berlin, however, the political atmosphere had changed. His cooperation with the Nazi regime in his capacity as *Kammeradschaft Vorstand* was held for suspicious. Recognising the difficult situation,[38] Mayer abandoned his hopes of returning to Berlin and the Philharmonic. Rather, he remained in Munich, where an old friend from former times, Hans Knappertsbusch, helped secure for the cellist a place in the Bayerischer Staatsorchester.[39]

The Philharmonic's final loss to the de-Nazification guillotine was perhaps the hardest. On April 4 1946, American authorities suspended from his duties as violist and orchestra *Geschäftsführer*, Lorenz Höber.[40] This was a devastating blow. The judgement was appealed, but a little over one year later, British authorities concurred with their American colleagues:

> You are hereby notified that, because of your previous adherence to a political organisation, you are forbidden from participating in public performances or to contribute to any other public activities in the British sector.[41]

Lorenz Höber, leader, stalwart and champion of the orchestra, had never been a member of the Nazi Party. The 'political organisations' to which he belonged were the *Reichsmusikkammer*, universal to all performing musicians during the Third Reich, and the Berlin Philharmonic Orchestra. Specifically, Höber's investigating officer indicated the charge: "The a/n was a member of the board of directors of the Berliner Philharmonischen Orchestra G.M.B.H."[42] Stripped of his position and his dignity, within six months of this sentence, Lorenz Höber, aged 58, was dead.

"An orchestra is like a people; each has his place, must do his best and adhere to the will of the collective."[43] This line was attributed to the fictional Wilhelm Furtwängler in the first script draft of *Die Philharmoniker*, Goebbels' testament to the tautological nature of propaganda. Beyond the implicit message praising voluntary, collective subordination, the phrase could also be applied to the totality of the Berlin Philharmonic's experience during the Third Reich. The quote also captured the forces that brought about Lorenz Höber's tragic downfall. Through exceedingly difficult times, Lorenz Höber led and served the Berlin Philharmonic with extraordinary devotion. From his position, he did his best in the service of his musical community. The orchestra collectively too, tried its best to do good—for its audiences, for its country, for itself. And surely Germany as a whole had no interest in unleashing havoc, terror, war and genocide on itself, let alone on the world. Yet, "an orchestra is like a people," the Berlin Philharmonic, like the German people, lashed itself to a political structure—the Nazi State—which embraced the collective wholeheartedly, then led it down a path of unspeakable horror. Though the Nazis spoke in a language of force, the Philharmonic experience revealed the dialectic into which the Nazi State could be drawn. For being such a fine leader, engaging, confronting, and working with the Nazis to assure his orchestra's success, Lorenz Höber paid a tragic price.

Höber's legacy, however, remains indelible. The transformations undergone by the Berlin Philharmonic during his leadership established the foundations upon which the orchestra has existed ever since. Höber guided the orchestra from private collective to public service in 1933-34. Though the cooperative GmbH was forever dissolved, Höber ensured the self-governing character of the organisation remained its fundamental feature, even under totalitarian conditions. To this day, the musicians of the Berlin Philharmonic retain ultimate sovereignty over the orchestra's direction.

While a champion of self-determination, Höber had the foresight to recognise the cooperative model could not fulfil the orchestra's artistic and institutional ambitions. He also had the good sense to resist discarding public partnership after the RMVP experiment went so badly awry. Among Höber's final acts as leader of the Berlin Philharmonic musicians, was securing the City of Berlin as the orchestra's principal financial guarantor in 1945.[44] This legal and financial relationship with the City of Berlin endured until the founding of the Stiftung Berliner Philharmoniker in 2002.

When the Nazi State absorbed the Berlin Philharmonic in 1934, Lorenz Höber was *Orchester Vorstand* and *Geschäftsführer*.

Politics, pragmatics and ideology demanded a reorganisation in the administrative structure of the institution, but Höber, with his skill and knowledge, was indispensable. He remained the musicians' voice throughout the *Reichsorchester* period. On the administrative side, what he accomplished alone required at least two appointees to replace. The creation of *Intendant* and *Kaufmännischen Direktor* positions was a direct consequence of the precedent set by Höber's multifaceted portfolio. Both positions, advents of the Nazi era, are now entrenched in the Philharmonic's institutional structure, with the orchestra *Vorstand* as immediate peer.

As *Orchestervorstand*, Höber was not only responsible for the managing the musicians' affairs, but for representing the orchestra community to management, government, the press or the public. When the Nazis decided to shift the Philharmonic's representation to a more favourable group, they created a *Vertrauensrat*. In the post-War era, the *Vorstand* was restored as official spokesperson of the collective, but the *Vertrauensrat* was reformed into the so-called *Fünferrat*. The *Fünferrat*, once stacked with Party members, inherited many of the internal matters previously the *Vorstand*'s responsibility. It continues to exist as the primary conduit of mediation within the orchestra community.

Throughout the Third Reich, Höber was never content to abdicate the Berlin Philharmonic's independent tradition. Though not evidently his personal initiative, Höber was nonetheless instrumental in establishing the orchestra's own sphere of self-determination in the Kammeradschaft der Berliner Philharmoniker. While the Nazi regime sanctioned the creation of this association, and then only after much deliberation, as an outlet for political agitation and ideological dissemination, the *Kammeradschaft* long outlived Goebbels' intentions. Renamed the *Philharmonische Gemeinschaft*, the association has continued its social and valedictory activities uninterrupted since 1937.

Rather than reject the advents, compromises and impositions of the Third Reich, the Berlin Philharmonic, like an organism, integrated its experience into its post-war composition. For all these reasons, is not only the legacy of Lorenz Höber, but indeed the Berlin Philharmonic's entire twelve year Nazi odyssey inexorably linked to the orchestra's present and future.

On August 23, 1945, Leo Borchard was killed by a jittery American soldier at a British-American checkpoint in the divided capital. It was Philharmonic violinist Hermann Bethmann who proposed the thirty-three year-old Rumanian conductor Sergiu Celibidache as Borchard's successor.[45] Unlike Borchard, Celibidache had no background with the orchestra. The Philharmonic, however, had already re-established itself, and was making inroads with local and military authorities for permanent status. Celibidache was a fresh face for a new start. The orchestra's supervising authorities could not but agree. It was even an advantage he was not German. His musical ideas were a stark contrast to the orchestra's traditions. Degrees of curiosity and apprehension aside, the Philharmonic musicians realised only Celibidache, or one like him, could help the orchestra move forward while leaving room for the anticipated return of Furtwängler.[46] Though a risky, even somewhat radical choice, Celibidache represented the necessary completion of the Philharmonic's process of disengagement from its Nazi past, while pointing a way to the future.

On December 1 1945, Celibidache was crowned by the American authorities "licensee" of the Berlin Philharmonic Orchestra. The conductor was entrusted with responsibility for all aspects of Philharmonic affairs, principally, but not exclusively limited to musical matters. Celibidache was a sort of midwife, appointed to wean the orchestra from its previous habits. On his watch, the final purge of the orchestra, including Friedrich Mayer and Lorenz Höber, was completed. Mahler and Schostakovich, among other composers, were restored to the repertoire. Bruno Walter and Otto Klemperer made their reluctant returns. The Berlin Philharmonic went on tour—not to Madrid, Paris, Bucharest or Stockholm, but to Potsdam, Leipzig, then, Lübbeke and Bünde. It was, indeed, a new era.

In December 1946, Furtwängler passed his German de-Nazification hearing and was cleared to return to the podium in Berlin. Coincidentally, from the 1st of January, 1947, Celibidache was joined by violinist Richard Wolff and cellist Ernst Fuhr as joint-"Licensee" of the orchestra. With the first judgement, the Berlin Philharmonic's musical and spiritual leader was exonerated; of greater significance,

with the investiture of Wolff and Fuhr, American authorities restored the orchestra its collective honour. The Berlin Philharmonic
had proven itself mature enough to share in controlling its destiny.

On May 25, 1947, two years to the day after the Philharmonic's
first post-war concert under Borchard, Wilhelm Furtwängler returned to the podium of the Berlin Philharmonic. It was a deeply
emotional event. Conductor and orchestra had experienced so much
together, the memories must have been acute, both fond and painful.
At the same time, conductor, orchestra, and the world had changed.
While Furtwängler had successfully defended his past, the Berlin
Philharmonic had moved on. Furtwängler was no longer the man in
charge. Celibidache held the confidence of the American authorities,
if not the full enthusiasm of the orchestra. A number of key players
from Furtwängler's orchestra were gone, the orchestra's aesthetic was
changing. Moreover, the Berlin Philharmonic had learned a fundamental lesson: its greatest asset was its collective strength. For two
tumultuous years, the orchestra had survived without Furtwängler,
through challenges every bit as threatening as those of the early
1930s. The orchestra remained grateful to the conductor for the benevolence he had procured and conferred, but in the post-war era,
the musicians resolved to proceed differently.

Rather than a lesson, one might say the Berlin Philharmonic was
simply reminded of what it had always been: a self-governing orchestra community born of rebellion. After the senior conductor's return,
the ensuing power struggle between Furtwängler and Celibidache
was virtually inevitable,[47] but, as ever, the orchestra looked out for
its own interests first. Furtwängler represented the old, beloved, but
bitter-sweet past; Celibidache was the inspired choice of the moment, but did not personify the Berlin Philharmonic's destiny. The
Berlin Philharmonic's post-war reformation came to completion in
1954, with the orchestra's own election of the man the musicians
believed "the artistic personality who may be best suited to continue
the traditions of the Berlin Philharmonic"[48]—Göring's protégée,
Furtwängler's nemesis, the anti-Celibidache,—Herbert von Karajan.

A number of powerful forces schemed together to influence
this outcome, particularly those linked to Germany and the Berlin
Philharmonic's Nazi past.[49] Though under pressure from many sides,

with this collective decision, the orchestra again chose to hitch its wagon to an ethically questionable, but politically, commercially, and musically astute selection. A replay of the ill-fated *Reichsorchester* experiment? No. In 1954, the Berlin Philharmonic was not dealing from a position of vulnerability. Erected upon the rubble of Goebbels' *Sendebot der deutschen Kunst*, by integrating its past with reforms breathtaking in both speed and guile, the orchestra had succeeded in retaining its singular reputation while inflating to a level of institutional maturity where the Berlin Philharmonic could assimilate even a two-time member of the Nazi Party as chief conductor and suffer no damage.

When the Berlin Philharmonic mounted its first tour to North America in 1955, concerts were protested vigorously by demonstrators who would not let the world forget events a decade before. Their beef was not, however, with the orchestra, as during the "avant garde of the paratroopers"[50] war years, when the Philharmonic became increasingly, and justifiably, identified as an instrument of Hitler's poisonous Reich. Rather, anger was directed towards former NSDAP members von Karajan, and the orchestra's new old manager, Gerhard von Westerman, who had finally achieved his coveted *Intendant* title in 1952.[51] Mythology, instinct, cunning, and a radical sense of self-determination allowed the orchestra to craft an image exempt from acrimony. Communal determination wedded to collective ingenuity. In this respect, the musicians of the post-war Berlin Philharmonic resembled their *Reichsorchester* and cooperative GmbH ancestors— heirs to a visionary heritage.

Endnotes

Archival sources with abbreviations:

BArch = Bundesarchiv (German Federal Archives), Berlin
R55 Reichsministerium für Volksaufklärung und Propaganda
(Reich Ministry for Public Enlightenment and Propaganda)
R56I Reichskulturkammer (Reich Chamber of Culture)
NS18 Reich Propaganda Leadership of the NSDAP
RKK Personel files

BArch (BDC) = former Berlin Document Centre
RK Reichskulturkammer/Reichsmusikkammer
PK Personel files of the Reichsministerium
für Volksaufklärung und Propaganda

GStA = Geheimestaatsarchiv (Prussian State Arcives), Berlin
IB 2281-2287 Prussian Finance Ministry

ABPhO = Archive of the Berliner Philharmoniker e.V.
A Personal correspondence
F Photo collection
G Orchestra lists
P Programme collection
Z Personal documents

ZBZ = Zentral Bibliothek Zürich (Zurich Central Library)
FN BF to BO Furtwängler Estate, Letters and Documentation

PJB = Private collection Johannes Bastiaan
PKS = Private collection Klaus Stoll
PWK = Private collection Walter Küssner
PPM = Private collection Peter Muck
PCH = Estate of Carl Höfer
PHW = Estate of Heinz Wiewiorra

Chapter 1

1   GStA BPhO Höber to Höpker-Ashoff Preussische Finanzministerium, 27.1.31; BArch R55/1146 BPhO Höber to Reichsminister des Innern, 11.7.31

2   BArch R55/1144 Berlin Magistrat f. Kunst to Reichsminister des Innern, 9.12.26: "Bei der überragenden Beduetung des Philharmonischen Orchesters für das Berliner und auch für das gesamte deutsche Musikleben ist es unser Bestreben, die Fortführung des Orchesters unter Aufrechterhaltung seines guten Rufes, das beste Orchester Deutschlands und eines der besten der Welt zu sein, zu ermöglichen…"

3   BArch R55/1133 Bürgermeister München to Reisministerium des Innern, 6.2.30

4   BArch R55/1133 Reichsminister des Innern an Oberbürgermeister Scharnagl (München), March, 1930

5   BArch R55/1144 Preu. Min. f. Wissenschaft, Kunst und Volksbildung and RMVP, 30.7.33

6   ibid.

7   BArch R55/1145 Niederschrift betr. Philharmonisches Orchester, 23.5.29

8   BArch R55/1145 Abgeändertes Statut des BPhO, 1929; Avgerinos, G., 70 Jahre Einer GmbH, p.45

9   BArch R55/1145 Berlin Magistrat f. Kunst to Reichsministerium des Innern, 25.6.29

10 ibid.

11 BArch R55/1145 Abgeändertes Statut des BPhO, 1929

12 ibid., Part B, Paragraph 2

13 ibid., Part C, Paragraph 8

14 Avgerinos, G., 70 Jahre Einer GmbH, p.45

15 BArch R55/1145 "Von den neuen Geschäftsanteilen der BPhO GmbH, welche durch den Kapitalerhöhungsbeschluss von geschaffen worden sind, übernimmt das Deutsche Reich, vertreten durch den Herrn Reichsminister des Innern, hiermit einen Geschäftsanteil zum Nennwert von RM 14 400 […]" undated draft, 1929

16 BArch R55/1146 Reichsminister des Innern to Reichsfinanzminister 19.1.33: "An der Erhaltung unseres qualitative besten Orchestern hat das Reich nicht nur aus allgemeinen Grunden ein besonderes Interesse, sondern auch as sehr beachtlichen aussenpolitischen Grunden."

17 BArch R55/1133 Reichsminister des Innern Vermerk, 19.8.30 "Der Zuschuß des Reichs für das Berliner Philharmonische Orchester fällt infolge der beschlossenen Sparmaßnahmen aus"; BArch R55/1146 Finanzamt Börse 14.12.32: "die vorgesehene Übernahme eines Geschäftanteils durch das Deutsche Reich von diesem abgelehnt worden ist."

18 BArch R55/1145 BPhO Höber to Reichsministerium des Innern, 11.7.31

19 BArch R55/1146 Reichsminister des Innern to Reichsfinanzminister 19.1.33; BArch R55/1146 Oberbürgermeister Sahm to Reichsministerium des Innern, 23.1.33

20 BArch R 55/1146 Überbürgermeister Sahm an RMdI, 7.2.1933

21 BArch R55/1137 RMdI Dr. Donnevert, Vermerk, 17.3.33

22 BArch R55/1146 RMVP v.Keudell Betrifft: Philharmonisches Orchester, 6.4.33

23 BArch R55/1146 Herrn Staatssekretär, Vermerk, 6.4.33

24   ibid.: "Aus sachlichen und aus innenpolitischen Gründen spreche ich mich gegen eine Überlassung des Phiharmonischen Orchesters aus."

25   BArch R55/1146 Vermerk über die Besprechung betr. Philharmonisches Orchester, 19.4.33

26   ibid.

27   BArch R55/1146 BPhO Höber to RMdI, 11.5.33

28   BArch R55/1146 BPhO Höber to RMdI Pfundtner, 7.4.33

29   BArch R55/1146 RMdI Wöllke 10.5.33: "Das Propaganda-Ministerium hat erklärt, kein Geld zu haben und im übrigen gemeint, dass, solange das Orchester noch inoffiziel bei uns sei, wir auch dafür sorgen müßen."

30   BArch R55/1146 BPhO Höber to RMdI, 11.5.33: "In einer gestrigen Sitzung im RMVP wurde von Herrn Ministerialdirektor Greiner festgestellt, dass das Berliner Philharmonische Orchester etatrechtlich noch dem Reichsministerium des Innern unterstellt ist."

31   BArch R55/1146 Oberbürgermeister Sahm to RMVP 13.5.33: "Wie ich durch Herrn Präsidenten Laubinger erfahren habe, wird die Reichsunterstützung für das Orchester künftig nicht im Reichsministerium des Innern, sondern in Ihrem Ministerium bearbeitet warden."

32   BArch R55/1146 BPhO Höber an RMdI, 11.5.33

33   BArch R55/1147 RMVP v.Keudell, Vermerk, 12.6.33

34   BArch R55/1147 BPhO Höber, Wolff to RMVP, 30.5.33

35   ibid.

36   GStA IB 2287 Oberbürgermeister Sahm to Pr. Finanzministerium 22.10.33; The RMVP could not secure a budget for the orchestra from the Ministry of Finance until Winter, 1933

37   BArch R55/1147 BPhO Höber to RMVP v. Keudell, 30.6.33

38   BArch R55/1147 Schröder Tatsachenbericht X.2.34

39   BArch R55/1147 RMVP to RMF, 17.5.34

40   BArch R55/1147 RMVP v. Keudell to BPhO, 21.2.34

41   BArch R55/245 Höber Bericht, undated

42   Goebbels Tagebucher, 27.7.36

43   see Prieberg, Kraftprobe; Kater, The Twisted Muse; Shirakawa, The Devil's Music Master

44   BArch (BDC) RK WO002 Deutscher Prüfungsausschuss, Rücksprache mit Herrn von Westerman, 9.5.46

45   Muck, P., Einhundert Jahre BPhO, Band III

46   BArch R55/245 Höber Bericht, undated

47   BArch R55/1145 Vertrag, BPhO-Furtwängler, 1929

48   ibid.

49   see Haffner, H., Furtwängler, S.120- 126

50   BArch R55/1145 Vertrag, BPhO-Furtwängler, 1929

51   ibid.

52   BArch R55/1147 Furtwängler Abschrift, 1.8.33

53   BArch R55/1148 Furtwängler re: Reichssparkommissar, 22.3.34

54   BArch R55/1148 Furtwängler, Arbeitsgebiet und Arbeitseinteilung der Geschäftsführung, undated 1933

55   BArch (BDC) RKO002 RMVP v. Keudell Vermerk, 12.4.34

56   ibid.

57 BArch R55/1148 RMVP von Keudell Vermerk, 14.3.34

58 Geissmar, p.107. In her memoires, Geissmar recalled the tone of a telephone conversation with Havemann: "Ich habe gerade das Programm für das Wiener Brahmsfest gesehen. Bilden Sie sich ja nicht ein, dass das Brahmsfest in dieser Form stattfinden wird! Naturlich ist die Auswahl der Solisten auf Ihren jüdischen Einfluss zurückzuführen..." The artists in question were violinist Bronislaw Hubermann, pianist Arthur Schnabel, and cellist Pau Casals, among the most respected musicians of the era. Casals, meanwhile, was not Jewish. More bizarre, Austria in 1933 was still an independent country, outside the sphere of at least direct Nazi authority, and certainly beyond Havemann's reach. For these reasons, the attack was most clearly personal, and just one of many Geissmar had to endure.

59 BArch R55/1147 BPhO Bedarfs-angeldung, 30.6.33

60 Geissmar, p.183

61 Muck, P., Einhundert Jahre BPhO, Band II, p.105

62 Geissmar, p.106

63 BArch (BDC) RK 002 RMVP v. Keudell, Vermerk, 14.3.34

64 see Stegmann, Stange, Benda

65 BArch R55/1147 RMVP v. Keudell, Vermerk, 11.4.34

66 Avgerinos, G., 70 Jahre Einer GmbH, p.64

67 Muck, P., Einhundert Jahre BPhO, Band III

68 BArch R55/1148 Furtwängler, Arbeitsgebiet und Arbeitseinteilung der Geschäftsführung, undated 1933

69 ibid.

70 see Chapter 2: Berliner Sinfonie-Orchester merger; Jewish musicians and their wives

71 BArch R55/1148 Furtwängler, Arbeitsgebiet und Arbeitseinteilung der Geschäftsführung, undated 1933

72 BArch R55/1147 Vertrag, 1.4.34: "Alle künstlerischen Angelegenheiten sind im Einvernehmen mit dem Haupt-Dirigenten, Staatsrat Dr. Furtwängler, zu regeln; Dr. v. Schmidtseck steht dem Orchester als Dirigent zur Verfügung. Er leitet alle offiziellen Veranstaltungen des Orchesters, soweit sie nicht von Staatsrat Dr. Furtwängler geleitet werden."

73 ibid.

74 Barch (BDC) RK O002 Furtwängler, Handschriftlichter Brief, 4.12.34

75 BArch R55/1148 BPhO Stegmann to RMVP Funk, 19.12.34

76 BArch (BDC) RK 002 RMVP v. Keudell, 12.3.34

77 Walter Funk was later promoted by Hitler to Reich Economics Minister; at the Nurnberg Trials in 1946, Funk was sentenced to twenty years in Spandau Prison.

78 BArch R55/245 Von der Geschäftsleitung der Berliner Philharmonisches Orchester G.m.b.H., 12.10.35

79 BArch (BDC) RK 002 RMVP v. Keudell, 12.3.34: "Konzession an das Orchester wird dem an sich nicht vertretbaren Wunsch von Herrn Furtwängler, nach einem aus Orchestermitgliedern bestehenden "Führerbeirat" sachlich Rechnung getragen."

80 ibid

81 ibid.

82 ibid.

83 BArch (BDC) RK 002 RMVP v. Keudell, Vermerk, 14.3.34

84 BArch (BDC) RK 002 RMVP v. Keudell, 12.3.34

85 ibid.

86 BArch (BDC) RK 002 RMVP v. Keudell, Vermerk, 14.3.34

87 Not to be confused with Otto Müller, Philharmonic harpist and orchestra Vorstand from 1895 to 1930

88 BArch (BDC) RK 002 RMVP v. Keudell, Vermerk, 14.3.34

89 BArch R55/1147 RMVP v. Keudell, Vermerk, 11.4.34

90 BArch R55/197 Dr. Ing. Freiherr von Schleinitz, Reference, 8.5.34

91 BArch R55/197 Senatspräsident Dr. Seeliger, Reference, 7.4.34

92 ibid.

93 BArch R55/197 RMVP Dr. Ott, Vermerk, 28.5.34: "Herr von Schmidtseck hatte am 14. Mai gewisse Bedenken gegen Wehe geäußert, die ein gedeihliches Zusammenarbeiten nich gewährleistet erscheinen lassen." The precise nature of these reservations are unknown.

94 BArch R55/197 RMVP to Pg. Wehe, 28.5.34 : Wehe's notification read: "Sehr geehrter Pg. Wehe! Unter Bezug auf die persönliche Besprechung beim Ministerium und Ihre Unterredung mit Herrn Staatsrat Furtwängler muß ich Ihnen zu meinem Bedauern mitteilen, daß ich von Ihren Diensten als Geschäftsführer der Berliner Philharmonischen Orchester G.m.b.H. leider keinen Gebrauch machen kann. Die Wünsche des Herrn Furtwängler waren nach einer bestimmten Richtung hin so ausgeprägt, daß wir glaubten, uns ihnen nicht verschließen zu können."

95 BArch (BDC) RK O0024 BPhO Schmidtseck to RMVP Ott, 24.5.34

96 BArch (BDC) RK O0024 Reference 16.5.34

97 BArch (BDC) RK O0024 Deutsche Angestellenschaft Stegmann reference, 17.5.34

98 BArch (BDC) RK O0024 Die Deutsche Arbeitsfront, Stegmann reference, 1.6.34

99 BArch (BDC) RK O0024 Deutsche Angestellenschaft Stegmann reference, 17.5.34

100 ibid.

101 ibid.

102 BArch (BDC) RK O0024 RMVP Ott to Stegmann, X.5.34: "unter Vorbehalt jederzeitigen Widerrufs"

103 BArch (BDC) RK O0024 Vertrag between BPhO and Karl Stegmann, 12.6.34

104 BArch (BDC) RK O0024 NSDAP Beschluss Karl Stegmann, 1.7.36

105 BArch (BDC) RK O0024 Stegmann Bericht, X.2.37

106 BArch (BDC) RK O0024 RMVP to Oberste Parteigericht der NSDAP, 10.11.36

107 BArch (BDC) RK O0024 RMVP Funk to den stellvertretenden Gauleiter des Gaues Gross-Berlin der NSDAP Görlitzer, 10.2.37: "Herr Stegmann ist im Jahre 1934 zum Geschäftsführer der Philharmonischen Orchester G.m.b.H. mit der besonderen Aufgabe bestellt worden, im Betrieb die Partei und ihr Programm zu der gebotenen Geltung zu bringen und in wirtschaftlicher Hinsicht Ordnung zu schaffen. Herr Stegmann ist beiden Aufgaben gerecht geworden. Ich kann insbesondere bestätigen, dass ich ihn bei seinen Arbeiten stets als ehrlichen und überzeugten Nationalsozialisten kennen gelernt habe. Sein Ausschluss aus der Partei würde wohl auch dazu führen, dass er seine Stellung als Geschäftsführer der Philharmoniker aufgeben müsste. Das würde aber für den Betrieb einen schweren Verlust bedeuten."

108 BArch (BDC) RK O0024 Abschrift Adolf Hitler, 31.5.38

109 An example of Stegmann expressing political opinions privately is quoted by Franz Jastrau in his testimony at Furtwängler's de-Nazification hearing in December, 1946: "Im Jahre 1937 war ich in England Zeuge, wie Mr. Huld, der dortige Manager [...] und Herrn Dr. Furtwängler [...] mit Herrn Stegmann, unserm Nazimitglied, eine Unterredung hatte [...] Herr Huld sagte "Lieber Stegmann, Sie sollten nicht nur in England und Schottland Torneen machen, Sie sollten in unsere ganzes Kolonien gehen, aber wenn das nicht aufhört mit Hitler da drüben, dann müssen wir davon Abstand nehmen." Herr Stegmann als Nazi moserte so ein bisschen, er sah dann Herrn Doktor an und sagte: "Ich weiss, Herr Doktor, Sie halten von der ganzen Sache nichts." BArch (BDC) RK WO002 p.96

110 BArch (BDC) RK O0024 RMVP Greiner, Vermerk, 4.6.34

111 BArch (BDC) RK O0024 BPhO Schmidtseck to RMVP Ott, 24.5.34

112 BArch R55/951 Gesellschaftsvertrag des BPhO GmbH, 18.6.34

113 ibid., Section 13: "Über die Genehmigung der Bilanz beschliesst die ordentliche Versammlung der Gesellschafter auf Vorschlag des Aufsichtsrates; Die Genehmigung der Bilanz schliesst die Entlastung der Geschäftsführer und des Aufsichtsrates in sich."

114 ibid., Section 7

115 ibid., Sections 7 & 8

116 BArch BDC RK002 RMVP v Keudell, Vermerk, 14.3.34; Responding that Schuricht would be "zu groß" for his deputy, Furtwängler suggested the Kapellmeister Papst from Hamburg as an alternative to von Schmidtseck, again a 'weak' figure.

117 BArch (BDC) RK O0024 Deutsche Angestellenschaft Stegmann reference, 17.5.34

118 BArch X Vertrag Entwurf, 20.7.34

119 In December, 1932, Hindemith played the solo part in Berlioz' Herold in Italy; appearing on the same programme was Prokofiev's 5th Piano Concerto with the composer at the keyboard.

120 NL Furtwängler; Furtwängler an Göring, 7.7.34; Prieberg, Handbuch, s.1776

121 Prieberg, Handbuch s. 2992-3000

122 BArch (BDC) RK O002 Abschrift, An den Herrn Reichsminister für Volksaufklärung und Propaganda, 4.12.34

123 BArch (BDC) RK O002 Abschrift Goebbels to Furtwängler, 5.12.34

124 ibid.

125 BArch R55/1148 BPhO Stegmann to the Vorsitzenden des Aufsichtsrates der BPhO, 19.12.34

126 BArch R55/1148 BPhO Stegmann to RMVP 2.1.35

127 Muck, P., Einhundert Jahre BPhO, Band II, p.115

128 BArch R55/1148 BPhO Stegmann to the Vorsitzenden des Aufsichtsrates der BPhO, 19.12.34

129 BArch R55/1147 RMVP Schmidt-Leonhardt, Vermerk, 11.12.34

130 BArch R55/1148 BPhO Stegmann to the Vorsitzenden des Aufsichtsrates der BPhO, 19.12.34

131 ibid.

132 ibid.

133 ibid., BArch (BDC) RK O002 Furtwängler to Funk, 1.3.35

134 see Chapter 5

135 BArch R55/1148 RMVP to RMK Ihlert, 17.1.35

136 BArch R55/1148 Jung to Goebbels, 3.1.35

137 ZBZ Furtwängler Nachlass B F:48 to RMVP Funk, 23.7.35

138 BArch R55/1148 RMVP to RMK Ihlert, 17.1.35

139 BArch (BDC) RK N39 Stange to Hinkel, 6.5.33

140 ibid.

141 ibid.: "Heimgekehrt vermochte ich mich nicht gegen die jüdische Front in meinem Vaterlands durchseten; konnte nicht einmal ein mir auf Befürwortung des Deutschen Gesandten in Sofia aus repaesentativen Gründen zugesagtes Gastspiel an der Staatsoper Berlin erhalten, während gleichzeitig sich Gelegenheit zu mehrfachen Gastspielen eines namenlosen ausländischen jüdischen Dirigent fand, der an einer Deutscehn staatlichen Bühne fest angestellt war."

142 BArch (BDC) RK N39 Hinkel to Emil Georg von Strauss (Deutsche Bank), 26.8.33

143 BArch (BDC) RK N39 Stange to Goebbels , 14.6.33

144 ibid.

145 BArch (BDC) RK N39 Hinkel to Emil Georg von Strauss (Deutsche Bank), 26.8.33

146 BArch (BDC) RK N39 Stange to Hess, 3.11.34

147 ibid.

148 BArch R55/1148 RMVP to RMK Ihlert, 17.1.35

149 BArch R56I/109

150 BArch (BDC) RK N39 Havemann to Hinkel, 22.5.35

151 BArch R55/1148 Niederschrift über eine Besprechung in der Reichsmusikkammer am 2.1.35, 3.1.35

152 ibid.

153 BArch R55/1148 RMK Ihlert to RMVP Funk, 4.1.35

154 ibid.

155 Muck, P., Einhundert Jahre BPhO, Band II, p.117

156 ibid.

157 BArch (BDC) RK O0024 RMVP Funk to BPhO, 31.7.35

158 BArch (BDC) RK N39 Stange to Dr. Daube Richard Wagner Festwoche, Detmold, 25.4.35

159 BArch (BDC) RKO002 Furtwängler to RMVP Funk, 1.3.35

160 ibid.

161 ibid.

162 BArch (BDC) RK N39 Reichsmusikerschaft Havemann to Hinkel, 22.5.35

163 BArch (BDC) RK N39 Stange to Hinkel, 6.5.33

164 BArch (BDC) RK N39 Reichsmusikerschaft Havemann to Hinkel, 22.5.35.: "Heute erklärt Herr Stange, dass er niemals der SPD angehört habe. Herr Dr. Mahling ist bereit, diese ihm gegenüber von Herrn Stange gemacht Äusserung eidesstattlich zu versichern. Dies ist der zweite Fall—ähnlich wie im Fall Gräner—dass Aussage gegen Aussage steht. Es soll sich auch ein dritter Fall dieser Art mit Herrn Prof. Stein zugetragen haben."

165 BArch (R. Strauss) RMK, Ihlert, an RKK, Hinkel, 22.5.35, Prieberg, Handbuch, S. 6779

166 BArch R56I/93 Hinkel to Funk 22.7.35; Stange was replaced by the composer Max Trapp

167 BArch (BDC) RK N39 Reichsmusikerschaft Havemann to Hinkel, 22.5.35

168 ibid: "dem Urteil des Herrn Dr. Furtwängler dem Herrn Reichsminister Dr. Goebbels gegenüber anschliessen, der Herrn Stange sowohl künstlerisch als auch menschlich für ungeeignet halt."

169 BArch (BDC) RK WO002 de-Nazification preliminary report, 12.46, p.103

170 BArch (BDC) RKO002 Furtwängler to RMVP Funk, 1.3.35

171 BArch R55/1148 BPhO Stegmann to RMVP Funk, 19.12.34

172 Muck, P., Einhundert Jahre BPhO, Band III

173 Avgerinos, G., 70 Jahre einer GmbH, p.105

174 "Nach der Machtergreifung hat sich B. überraschend schnell umgestellt und sich als Nationalsozialist ausgegeben. Ausgesprochen nachteilige Tatsachen wurden seither über ihn nicht bekannt. Als Mitglied einer Freimaurerloge oder logenähnlichen Vereinigung ist v. B. in den bisher hier ausgewerteten Verzeichnissen nicht erfaßt. Auszug aus dem Strafregister wurde nicht eingeholt" (Eintragung auf der RMK-Karteikarte von Benda, SS-Oberscharführer Schleier, undatiert = 1934. Quelle: BA Namensakte von Benda), Prieberg, Handbuch, S. 374-75

175 BArch (BDC) RK NO002 von Benda to RMVP p.11, undated 1939

176 ibid, p.10

177 BArch (BDC) RK NO002 von Benda, Bericht, undated 1939

178 BArch (BDC) RK NO002 von Benda to RMVP p.6, undated 1939

179 BArch R55/197 Bericht des Künstlerischen Leiters 1938/39

180 BArch (BDC) RK NO002 von Benda, Erklärung, 18.12.39

181 ibid.

182 ibid.

183 BArch (BDC) PK T0051 RMVP Leiter der Personalabteilung to Goebbels, 9.6.39

184 BArch (BDC) RK NO002 von Benda to RMVP p.9, undated 1939

185 BArch (BDC) PK T0051 RMVP Leiter der Personalabteilung to Goebbels, 9.6.39

186 ibid.

187 ibid.

188 BArch R55/197 Bericht des Künstlerischen Leiters 1938/39

189 BArch (BDC) RK NO002 von Benda to RMVP p.9, undated 1939: "Mit Zustimmung meines damaligen Aufischtsrats Vorsitzenden [Funk], und mit Wissen und dem Einverständnis von Dr. Furtwängler habe ich diese Aufgaben mit einem Kammerorchester aus Mitgliedern des Berliner Philharmonischen Orchesters fortgesetzt."

190 Muck, P., Einhundert Jahre BPhO, Band III; ibid.

191 BArch (BDC) RK NO002 von Benda to RMVP p.1, undated 1939

192 ibid., p.4

193 ibid., p.11

194 ibid., p.1

195 BArch (BDC) RK WO002 Furtwängler de-Nazification, transcript, p.11

196 BArch (BDC) RK WO002 Vermerk über die Unterredung mit Herrn v. Westermann bei Herrn Schmidt, Furtwängler de-Nazification, 7.12.46

197 BArch (BDC) PK T0051 RMVP Leiter der Personalabteilung to the Herrn Minister, 26.8.39

198 Goebbels to von Benda, 22.12.39, reproduced in Muck, P., Einhundert Jahre BPhO,

Band II, p.148

199 BArch (BDC) PK T0051 RMVP Leiter der Personalabteilung to Goebbels, 9.6.39

200 BArch (BDC) PK T0051 RMVP to Westerman, 31.5.39

201 BArch (BDC) PK T0051 RMVP Leiter der Personalabteilung to Goebbels, 9.6.39

202 BArch (BDC) PK T0051 RMVP Vermerk 26.7.39: "Da über die künftige Verwendung des Geschäftsführers von Benda noch nicht entschieden ist, kann seine Abberufung als Geschäftsführer noch nicht erfolgen. Die Berufung des neuen Geschäftsführers von Westerman geschieht zweckmässigerweise gleichzeitig mit der Abberufung von Bendas."

203 BArch (BDC) PK T0051 RMVP to den Herrn Minister, 20.6.39; BPhO Westerman to RMVP 11.12.39; RMVP Vermerk, 19.1.40

204 BArch (BDC) RK WO002 Deutscher Prüfungsausschuss, Rücksprache mit Herrn von Westerman, 9.5.46

205 Avgerinos, G., 70 Jahre Einer GmbH, p.105-06

206 BArch (BDC) PK T0051 RMVP Leiter der Personalabteilung to Goebbels, 9.6.39

207 see Muck, Avgerinos

208 see Chapter 2

209 BArch (BDC) PK T0051 RMVP Leiter der Personalabteilung to Staatssekretär Hanke, 23.6.39

210 ibid.

211 ibid.

212 ibid.

213 BArch (BDC) RK N0047 RMVP Vermerk, 29.6.39

214 BArch (BDC) PK T0051 Naumann to Herrn Leiter Pers. 29.8.39

215 Muck, P., Einhundert Jahre BPhO, Band II, p.118

216 BArch (BDC) PK T0051 BPhO Westerman to RMVP Kohler, 11.9.39

217 ibid.

218 Muck, P., Einhundert Jahre BPhO, Band II, p.181

219 BArch (BDC) RK WO002 Deutscher Prüfungsausschuss, Rücksprache mit Herrn von Westerman, 9.5.46

220 BArch (BDC) PK T0051 Abschrift NSDAP Kreisgericht I Berlin, 11.3.40: "Der Parteigenosse von Westerman ist beschuldigt worden, mit dem Parteigenossen Jacob Meyer in gleichgeschlechtlichen Beziehungen gestanden zu haben."

Chapter 2

1 Avgerinos, G., Das BPhO: 70 Jahre Einer GmbH, p.47

2 Muck, P. 100 Jahre BPhO, Sonderdruck, p.17

3 Muck, P., Einhundert Jahre, p. 88-89

4 BArch R55/1146 Lange to RMdI 29.3.31

5 Muck, P., Einhundert Jahre BPhO, Band II, p.91

6 BArch R55/1146 Lange to Dr. Zweigert, RMdI 14.4.32

7 Avgerinos, G., 70 Jahre einer GmbH, p.47

8 BArch R55/1146 Aktenvermerk 27.4.32

9   Volks or popular concerts were not defined by repertoire, but ticket prices. Volks concert admission would typically be less than 50% the price of a subscription concert.

10 BArch R55/1146 Lange to Aufsichtsrat 4.6.32; Avgerinos, G., 70 Jahre einer GmbH, p.54

11 BArch R55/1147 Furtwängler to Sahm 24.4.33

12 ibid.

13 BArch R55/1146 Min.Rat v. Keudell Vermerk 12.6.33

14 Avgerinos, G., 70 Jahre einer GmbH, p.54

15 BArch R55/1148 Neander to Bald 10.11.33

16 Avgerinos, G., 70 Jahre einer GmbH, p.57

17 BArch R55/1147 Schröder Tatsachenbericht X.2.34

18 ibid.

19 Avgerinos, G., 70 Jahre einer GmbH, p.60

20 BArch R55/1147 Schröder to Hitler, 18.1.34

21 BArch R55/1147 Schröder Tatsachenbericht X.2.34

22 BArch F55/1147 Furtwängler to Sahm 24.4.33

23 BArch R55/1147 Schröder Tatsachenbericht X.2.34

24 BArch R55/1147 Oberbürgermeister Hafemann to RMVP, 11.1.34: "[...] das Ausscheiden dieser Orchestermitglieder nicht auf Wunsch der Stadt, sondern des Berliner Philharmonischen Orchester und das Deutschen Reiches erfolgt ist."

25 BArch R55/1147 Reichsversicherungsanstalt für Angestellte to BPhO, 9.12.33

26 BArch R55/1147 Heyl to RMVP, 27.11.33

27 BArch R55/1148 Neander to Nationalsoialister Kriefsopferversorgung, 10.11.34

28 ibid.

29 BArch R55/1147 Schröder Tatsachenbericht X.2.34

30 BArch R55/1147 Schmidt-Leonhardt Betr. Philharmonisches Orchester, 15.2.34

31 BArch R55/1147 Schröder to RMVP, 13.11.34

32 BArch R55/245 Deutsche Revisions-und-Treuhand-Aktiengesellschaft (DRuTA) Nachprufung 14.10.35, p.28

33 BArch R55/1146 Hafemann to BPhO Höber, 22.4.33

34 ibid.

35 ibid.

36 Deutsche Allgemeine Zeitung, 11. April 1933, reprinted in Ursachen und Folgen: Eine Urkunden- und Dokumentensammlung zur Zeitgeschichte, Band IX, Das Dritte Reich, p.484

37 ibid., p.446

38 Goebbels Tagebuch, 11.5.33

39 BArch R55/1146 BPhO Höber to Bürgermeister Hafemann, 26.4.33

40 ibid.

41 PKS Telegram Arnold Schoenberg to Furtwängler, 29.5.33: "Da beurlaubt wurde erbitte ihre intervention bei minister wegen marz eingebrachten gesuches barablosung meines vertrags"; BArch (BDC) RK W002 Furtwängler petitions on behalf of Carl Flesch, Schoenberg, Bernhard Sekles, Georg Dohrn, 10.7.33

42 see Evans, R.; Kater, M., Shirakawa, S.

43 NL Furtwängler; Furtwängler to Dr. Goebbels, Paris, 1.5.33, in Prieberg Katalogue

44 BArch R55/1147 Schröder Tatsachenbericht X.2.34

45 Prieberg, Handbuch, S. 1749

46 Geissmar

47 BArch R55/1138 Furtwängler an den Vorstand des Nationalorchesters Mannheim, 29.5.33

48 Nachlass Furtwängler, Furtängler an Dr. Goebbels, Paris, 1.5.33, in Prieberg Handbuch, S. 1748-49

49 BArch R55/245 Deutsche Revisions-und-Treuhand-Aktiengesellschaft (DRuTA) Nachprufung 14.10.35, p.13

50 ABPhO Z Gold, Landsberger an BPhO, 5.57

51 BArch R55/1147 Abschrift BPhO Schmidtseck to General-IntendantMeissner, Städtische Bühne Frankfurt, 23.10.34

52 BArch R55/197 RMVP Kohler to BPhO, 17.1.35

53 BArch R55/197 RMVP Vermerk Verträge, 18.4.35

54 BArch R55/197 Vertrag BPO Borries, 1.2.35

55 BArch R55/197 RMVP Rüdiger Vermerk, 18.1.35

56 ibid.

57 BArch R55/197 BPhO to RMVP, 17.8.35

58 ibid.

59 BArch (BDC) RK RO009 Präsident der Reichsmusikkammer Raabe to Graudan, 19.8.35: "verlieren Sie mit sofortiger Wirkung das Recht zur weiteren Berufsausübung auf jedem zur Zuständigkeit der Reichsmusikkammer gehörenden Gebiete."

60 BArch (BDC) RK O0024 BPhO von Benda, Stegmann to RMVP Hinkel, 21.8.35

61 Arch (BDC) RK WO002 Furtwängler de-Nazification, von Benda testimony, p.57: "Als ich im Sommer 1935 zum Philharmonischen Orchester kam, war noch ein jüdischer Geiger im Orchester. Ich hatte nur noch die Abwicklung seines Ausscheidens durchzuführen. Er bekam 16.000 oder 18.000 RM Abfindung und davon einen grossen Teil in Devisen."

62 BArch (BDC) RK O0024 BPhO von Benda, Stegmann to RMVP Hinkel, 21.8.35

63 ABPhO Z 1936-3, Erklärungsformblatt "Arischer Nachweis" Karl Rammelt, 10.8.36

64 BArch (BDC) RK O0024 BPhO von Benda, Stegmann to RMVP Hinkel, 21.8.35

65 BArch R55/197 Projektierter Inhalt des Vertrages mit Konzertmeister Kolberg, 1.12.34

66 BArch R55/197 RMVP Kohler to Hanke, 17.8.38

67 ibid.

68 BArch (BDC) RK WO002 Furtwängler de-Nazification, Fischer testimony, p.77

69 Prieberg, Handbuch, S. 7904

70 Aktennotiz auf der RMK-Karte; Quelle: BA Namensakte Wolff; in Prieberg, Handbuch, S.7904

71 interview with Erich Hartmann, 13.2.2005

72 Goebbels Tagebuch III, Eintrag vom 3/VIII/37. S. 222-223

73 BArch R55/197 X to RMVP, handwritten, 22.9.39

74 BArch R55/197 BPhO Stegmann to RMVP 13.10.39

75 BArch (BDC) RK O0024 BPhO von Benda, Stegmann to RMVP Hinkel, 21.8.35

76 Deutsche Allgemeine Zeitung, 11. April 1933, reprinted in Ursachen und Folgen: Eine Urkunden- und Dokumentensammlung zur Zeitgeschichte, Band IX, Das Dritte Reich, p.484

77   BArch R55/245 Höber Bericht X.X.1934

78   BArch R55/197 BPhO von Benda to RMVP, 29.11.37

79   R55/245 BPhO Höber History, undated 1935

80   BArch (BDC) RK N37, according to his NSDAP records, Anton Schuldes only joined the Party in January, 1934; this does not mitigate his Nazi activities prior to that date.

81   Avgerinos, G., 70 Jahre einer GmbH, p.60

82   BArch R55/1147 Schröder Tatsachenbericht X.2.34

83   Kleber, W., "Deutsche Orchestermusiker rufen auf!", reprinted in Dümling, A., Entartete Musik, p.59

84   ABPhO G1 Listen, 1946; The BDC of the Bundesarchiv contains so-called Blaue and Gelbe Registers, which contain the NSDAP Party registrations of approximately 6.6 million individuals, representing roughly 70% of the Party's total membership. Cross-referencing with this catalogue, therefore, offers a broad but significantly incomplete guide.

85   Hellsberg, C., Demokratie der Könige: die Geschichte der Wiener Philharmoniker, S. 464: "In Verbindung mit dem "Umsturz" waren 14 Mitglieder der Partei beigetreten, zu denen 25 weitere Kollegen kamen, welche diesen Schritt schon vor 1938 vollzogen und nach dem Verbotsgesetz des Jahres 1933 teilweise sogar illegal der NSDAP angehört hatten. Der hohe Anteil von 36 Prozent an Parteimitgliedern stieg bis Ende 1945 auf rund 42 Prozent [...]"

86   interview with Johannes Bastiaan, 02.05

87   ibid.

88   ABPhO BPhO Stegmann to Kormann, Hauptabt. Propaganda der Regierung des Generalgouvernements, Krakau, 25.9.43; ABPhO, Poster Bachsteinsaal, Streichquartett des Berliner Philharmonischen Orchesters, 3.12.36

89   see Chapter 1

90   BPhO Rundschreiben 17.4.37, quoted in Avgerinos, G., 70 Jahre Einer GmbH, p.63

91   PJB, BPhO Rundschreiben Nr.11/38, 22.12.38

92   ibid.

93   Hartmann's name also appears with a Pg. on the Archive of the Berlin Philharmonic list of 12.6.46

94   PJB BPhO Rundschreiben Nr.11/38, 22.12.38

95   PJB BPhO Rundschreiben No.6/38, 14.11.38 (some discrepancy as the Rundschreiben is dated 14. November, while the meeting is called for 26. October)

96   PJB BPhO Rundschreiben Nr.17, 24.11.39

97   ibid.

98   Avgerinos, G., 70 Jahre einer GmbH, p.63

99   PJB BPhO Rundschreiben No.36, 15.12.41; An die Herren Mitglieder des BPhO, 24.8.42; BPhO Rundschreiben Nr.X: "Wir sehen uns daher in diesem Falle gezwungen, bei Nichteinhaltung dieses Termins Ordnungsstrafen zu verhängen."

100   PJB Rundschreiben No.9/38, 5.12.38

101   ibid.

102   Avgerinos, G., 70 Jahre einer GmbH, p.64

103   BArch R55/951 BPhO Dienstordnung, 4.1939

104   ibid.

105 BArch R55/951 BPhO Stegmann to RMVP Sondertreuhänder f.d. Deutschen Kulturorchester, 14.4.39

106 BArch R55/1147 Schröder Tatsachenbericht X.2.34

107 BArch R55/197 Diburtz and Fuhr, 14.2.36

108 BArch R55/197 Diburtz and Fuhr, 6.4.36

109 ibid.

110 ibid.

111 BArch R55/197 RMVP memo im Hause, Betr.: Kameradschaft der Berliner Philharmoniker, X.4.36

112 ibid.

113 BArch R55/197 Gründung der Kameradschaft der Berliner Philharmoniker, 17.4.38

114 BArch R55/197 BPhO von Benda to RMVP, 11.6.38

115 BArch R55/197 BPhO von Benda to Herren Mitglieder des Berliner Philharmonisches Orchester, 11.6.38

116 BArch R55/197 BPhO von Benda to RMVP, 11.6.38

117 BArch R55/197 BPhO von Benda to Herren Mitglieder des Berliner Philharmonisches Orchester, 11.6.38

118 BArch R55/197 RMVP Vermerk 11.6.38

119 BArch R55/197 RMVP Kameradschaft der Berliner Philharmoniker e.V. (Gründung), 7.2.38

120 ibid.

121 BArch R55/197 NSDAP (Berlin) to BPhO, 24.6.38

122 PJB BPhO Rundschreiben Nr.3/28, 3.9.38

123 ibid.

124 BArch R55/197 BPhO Stegmann to RMVP Meyer, 9.9.38

125 PJB Westerman, An die Herren Mitglieder des BPhO, 9.12.42

126 ibid.

127 PJB BPhO Rundschreiben Nr.14, 24.11.39

128 Hartmann, E., Die Berliner Philharmoniker in der Stunde Null, S.16

129 Those who suggest some Nazi plot to starve the orchestra into submission fail to see the Philharmonic 'take-over' in the larger, factual, perspective presented in Chapter 1, see Potter, Pamela, The Nazi ›Seizure‹ of the Berlin Philharmonic, or the Decline of a Bourgeois Musical Institution (National Socialist Cultural Policy hrsg. G. Cuomo, 1995)

130 ABPhO from Philharmonisches Blätter, 1937, Musik als Propagandamittel by Werner Buchholz

131 PJB Rundschreiben No.9/38, 5.12.38

132 ABPhO Westerman an Furtwängler 19.2.44

133 ABPho Westerman an Furtwängler 7.9.42: „Am vorigen Mittwoch veranstaltete das Ministerium für uns einen Presseempfang im Auslandsklub. Trotz beispielloser Hitze war dieser Empfang, zu dem die Berliner und die gesamte Auslandspresse erschienen war, sehr gelungen. Ich sprach kurz über das Programm, überreichte die sehr hübschen Prospekte und unsere Kammermusik spielte [..] Es war ein eindeutig grosser Erfolg."

134 PJB Rundschreiben Nr.10/38 BPhO von Benda to die Herren Mitglider des BPhO, 21.12.38

135 PJB BPhO Rundschreiben Nr.1/39-40, 26.7.39

136 BArch R55/197 BPhO Stegmann to RMVP, 8.12.37

137 BArch R55/246 Gehälter der Orchestermitglieder, 1.2.42

138 BArch R55/197 BPhO Stegmann to RMVP, 10.6.39

139 BArch NS18/1173 Aktenvermerk Betr. Musikinstrumente der Philharmoniker, 4.5.42

140 BArch R55/853 Reichswirtschaftsminister to RMVP, 3.12.42

141 BArch R55/853 RMVP Nachtrag, 21.1.43, concerning the purchase of an instrument collection from a Graf Hartig in Rome, informants in Italy conveyed to the RMVP "daß Graf Hartig nicht in seinem Ortsbereich wohnhaft ist und daß er [the informant] über dessen jüdische Abstammung nur von einem Mitarbeiter aufmerksam gemacht wurde."

142 BA NS18/1173 RMVP Trissler to Hausen, 5.5.42

143 ibid.

144 PJB BPhO Programm Spielzeit 1942/43, 2.43

145 BArch NS18/1173 RMVP Telefonnotiz Berlin, 5.5.42

146 BArch R55/853 Vertrag Entwurf, Wortlaut für junge Künstler, Wortlaut für bewährte Künstler, 1943

147 PJB BPhO Rundschreiben No.13, 9.11.39

148 PJB Bescheinigung, Reichsverteidigungskommissar, 14.5.45

149 BArch R55/586

150 BArch R55/198 Taschner, Protokoll, 1.6.42

151 BArch R55/197 BPhO Furtwängler to RMVP, Betr. Hornist Ziller, 17.9.38

152 ibid.

153 PJB BPhO Rundschreiben Nr.12, X.X.39

154 ibid.

155 PJB BPhO Rundschreiben Nr.X 20.8.42

156 PJB Der Reichsminister für Volksaufklärung und Propaganda, 8.7.42

157 PJB BPhO Rundschreiben Nr. 14, 24.11.39

158 Kurt Ulrich, Alois Ederer, and Oskar Audilet

159 PJB BPhO An das zuständige Polizeirevier, 19.5.44

160 BArch R55/247 BPhO Westerman to RMVP, 23.9.44

161 PKS Furtwängler to Westerman, 25.6.44

162 BArch R55/198 Taschner Protokol, 1.6.42

163 ibid. This document reads like a Kafkaesque farce: bureaucrats bouncing Taschner back and forth between departments, changing appointments, waiting rooms, contradictions, connections, contacts, threatening telephone calls, accusations, cursing, fighting, Furtwängler's role. Taschner's Uk-Stellung was finally secured in February, 1942 in time for the Philharmonic's tour of Scandinavia, where Taschner performed as both concertmaster and soloist.

164 ABPhO Westerman an Furtwängler: „Generalfeldmarschall Keitel soll dem Führer persönlich Bericht über den Fall Taschner erstattet haben. Da General Schneider persona grata im Führerhauptquartier sein soll, ist der Entscheid so ausgefallen, dass man dem Wunsch der Wehrmacht, die sich schwer beleidigt fühlt, nachgibt und Taschner, wenn auch nur pro forma und für kurze Zeit, Soldat werden lässt. Ich weiss nicht, was man für Taschner tun könnte. Der Minister soll in dem Punkt Künstlerreklamationen weniger im Zusammenhang mit Taschner als wegen verschiedener Vorkommnisse in Filmkreisen

sehr schlecht zu sprechen sein. Wenn man andererseits direkt den Versuch machen sollte, an Generalfeldmarschall Keitel heranzutreten, dürfte sich der Minister mit Recht übergangen fühlen. "

165 PJB BPhO Rundschreiben Nr. 9, 19.9.39

166 ibid.

167 PJB BPhO Rundschreiben Nr. 6, 26.11.42

168 PJB Stegmann and Höber, An die Herren Mitglieder des BPhO, undated

169 PJB Höber, An die Herren Mitglieder des BPhO, 7.10.42

170 ibid.

171 ibid.

172 see Hartmann, E., Die Berliner Philharmoniker in der Stunde Null

173 Avgerinos, G., 70 Jahre einer GmbH, p.66

174 ABPhO Westerman an Furtwängler, 3.2.45

175 Interview with Erich Hartmann, 17.3.2005

176 Avgerinos, G., 70 Jahre einer GmbH, p.66

177 BArch (BDC) RK WO002 Vermerk Besprechung in Sachen Dr. Wilhelm Furtwängler, 9.12.46

178 PJB RMVP Schnellbrief, 12.3.45

179 PJB Bescheinigung, Reichsverteidigungskommisar, 14.5.45

Chapter 3

1   BArch R55/951 BPhO Stegmann to RMVP, 25.11.38

2   Avgerinos, G., 70 Jahre einer GmbH, p.36-37

3   ibid.

4   BArch R55/1144 Magistrat Berlin to Reichsminister des Innern, 9.12.26

5   Avgerinos, G., 70 Jahre einer GmbH, p.45

6   ibid., p.40

7   BArch R55/1146 Bericht über die Prüfung der Bilanz der BPhO 31.3.31

8   BArch R55/1145 BPhO Höber to Reichsministerium des Innern, 19.7.31

9   BArch R55/1145 BPhO Höber to Reichsministerium des Innern, 19.7.31

10 BArch R55/1145 der Reichsminister der Finanzen to Reichsminister des Innern, 27.9.29

11 BArch R55/1146 Bericht über die Prüfung der Bilanz der BPhO 31.3.31; rather than the city contributing RM 360 000 and Reich RM 120 000, the patchwork subsidies totaled RM 356 100 and RM 118 700 respectively.

12 Ibid.

13 BArch R55/1146 Abschrift der Reichsminister des Innern, 19.4.32

14 BArch R55/1146 Bericht über die Prüfung der Bilanz der BPhO 31.3.31

15 Avgerinos, G., 70 Jahre einer GmbH, p.46-47

16 BArch R55/1146 Wirtschaftsplan der Berliner Philharmonisches Orchester, 31.7.33

17 BArch R55/1146 BPhO Höber to Reichsministerium des Innern, 7.4.33; BArch R55/1146 Reichsminister des Innern to Reichsfinanzminister, 19.1.33

18 BArch R55/245 Deutsche Revisions- und Treuhand-Aktiengesellschaft, Report, 14.10.35

19 BArch R55/1147 BPhO Bedarfs-Anmeldung, 30.6.33

20 BArch R55/245 Deutsche Revisions- und Treuhand-Aktiengesellschaft, Report, 14.10.35

21 BArch R55/1146 BPhO Höber to Reichsministerium des Innern, 7.4.33

22 BArch R55/1146 RMVP Wöllke memo, 10.5.33

23 ibid.

24 BArch R55/1147 BPhO Höber to RMVP, 31.7.33

25 BArch R55/1147 BPhO Höber to RMVP, 30.5.33

26 BArch R55/1146 RMVP Wöllke memo, 10.5.33

27 BArch R55/1147 RMVP to Reichsminister der Finanzen, 31.7.33

28 GStA, IB 2281, Oberbürgermeister Sahm to Preussische Finanzministerium, 22.9.33

29 BArch R55/245 Deutsche Revisions- und Treuhand-Aktiengesellschaft, Report, 14.10.35

30 BArch R55/1147 RMVP von Keudell memo, 21.2.34

31 BArch R55/245 Deutsche Revisions- und Treuhand-Aktiengesellschaft, Report, 14.10.35

32 BArch R55/1148 Furtwängler to RMVP re: Reichssparkommissar, 22.3.34

33 ibid.

34 BArch R55/245 Deutsche Revisions- und Treuhand-Aktiengesellschaft, Report, 14.10.35

35 Barch R55/245 Zuschüsse des Ministeriums für Volksaufklärung und Propaganda für das Geschäftsjahr 1934/35

36 BArch R55/1147 BPhO Abschrift an den Herrn Reichsfinanzminister, 28.6.34

37 Barch R55/245 Zuschüsse des Ministeriums für Volksaufklärung und Propaganda für das Geschäftsjahr 1934/35

38 R55/1146 BPhO to RMVP Betr. Geldbedarf zum 1. Feb. 1935, 22.1.35

39 ibid.

40 Barch R55/245 Zuschüsse des Ministeriums für Volksaufklärung und Propaganda für das Geschäftsjahr 1934/35

41 ibid.

42 BArch R55/197 Bericht des kaufmännischen Leiters 1938/39

43 BArch R55/197 Haushalt—Voranschlag des Berliner Philharmonischen Orchesters, 3.39

44 BArch R55/247 BPhO Accounting 1939-40

45 BArch R55/246 Rechnungshof des Deutschen Reichs, Einnahmen und Ausgaben der Berliner Philharmonischen Orchester GmbH für die Rechnungsjahre 1938 und 1939, 15.4.42

46 BArch R55/247 BPhO Accounting 1939-40

47 BArch R55/246 BPhO Bilanz 1941-42

48 BArch R55/246 BPhO Gewinn—und—Verlustrechnung am 31. März 1943

49 BArch R55/1148 BPhO Stegmann to RMVP Greiner, 2.1.35

50 PJB BPhO Philharmonische Blätter 1936/37, Nr.1, p.6

51 BArch R55/245 Zuschüsse des Ministeriums für Volksaufklärung und Propaganda für das Geschäftsjahr 1934/35; BArch R55/247 Erläuterungen zu den Einnahmen, 1939; BArch R55/247 Erläuterung zu den Einnahmen, 1944

52 BArch R55/197 BPhO Bericht des künstlerischen Leiters 1938/39

53 BArch R55/247 Erläuterungen zu den Einnahmen, 1939

54 PJB BPhO Philharmonische Blätter 1936/37, Nr.1, p.6

55 ibid.

56 BArch R55/245 Zuschüsse des Ministeriums für Volksaufklärung und Propaganda für das Geschäftsjahr 1934/35

57 BArch R55/197 BPhO Bericht des künstlerischen Leiters 1938/39

58 BArch R55/197 BPhO Bericht des künstlerischen Leiters 1938/39; BArch R55/247 Erläuterungen zu den Einnahmen, 1937-38

59 ibid.

60 BArch 197 BPhO Bericht des kaufmännischen Leiters 1938/39

61 ibid.

62 BArch R55/247 Erläuterungen zu den Einnahmen, 1940-41

63 BArch R55/246 Rechnungshof des Deutschen Reichs, Einnahmen und Ausgaben der Berliner Philharmonischen Orchester GmbH für die Rechnungsjahre 1938 und 1939, 15.4.42

64 BArch 197 BPhO Bericht des kaufmännischen Leiters 1938/39

65 ibid.

66 BArch R55/245 BPhO to RMVP Betr. Prüfung der Jahresrechungnen, 31.5.39

67 BArch R55/246 RMVP to Deutsche Arbeitsfront NS-Gemeinschaft *Kraft durch Freude*, 9.2.43

68 BArch R55/247 Erläuterungen zu den Einnahmen, 1939

69 BArch R55/245 Zuschüsse des Ministeriums für Volksaufklärung und Propaganda für das Geschäftsjahr 1934/35

70 BArch R55/247 Erläuterungen zu den Einnahmen, 1939; 1940; 1941; 1943-44

71 BArch R55/1146 Bericht über die Prüfung der Bilanz der BPhO 31.3.31

72 BArch R55/247 Erläuterungen zu den Einnahmen, 1939; 1940; 1941

73 BArch R55/247 Erläuterungen zu den Einnahmen, 1940

74 BArch R55/245 BPhO Bemerkungen zur Gewinn- und Verlustsrechung zum 31.3.35

75 BArch R55/247 Bericht des künstlerischen Leiter, 1940/41

76 BArch R55/246 Rechnungshof des Deutschen Reichs, Einnahmen und Ausgaben der Berliner Philharmonischen Orchester GmbH für die Rechnungsjahre 1938 und 1939, 15.4.42

77 BArch R55/245 BPhO Bemerkungen zur Gewinn- und Verlustrechnung zum 31.3.35; R55/247 Bericht des künstlerischen Leiters 1939/40

78 GStA, IB 2281/27.10, Der Reichsminister für Volksaufklärung und Propaganda to den Herrn Preussischen Finanzminister, 20.10.36

79 BArch R55/951 BPhO Stegmann to RMVP Kohler, 8.10.38

80 BArch R55/245 RMVP Greiner to Reichsminister der Finanzen, 16.12.36

81 PJB BPhO Philharmonische Blätter 1936/37, Nr.1

82 BArch R55/951 BPhO Stegmann to RMVP, 27.10.38

83 BArch BArch R55/197 RMVP Abteilung M, 12.7.39

84 BArch R55/245 RMVP to Präsident des Rechnungshofs des Deutschen Reichs, 22.10.38

85 BArch R55.951 Reichsminister der Finanzen to RMVP, 15.11.39

86 BArch R55/198 Erklärung betr. Den Hilfsfond des Berliner Philharmonischen Orchesters, 17.3.37

87 ABPhO Hauptbuch Hilfsfonds

88 ibid.

89 BArch R55/198 Erklärung betr. Den Hilfsfond des Berliner Philharmonischen Orchesters, 17.3.37.

90 ABPhO Hauptbuch Hilfsfonds

91 ibid.

92 ibid.

93 BArch R55/1147 Abschrift an den Herrn Reichsfinanzminister, 2?.6.34

94 ibid.

95 BArch R55/245 Deutsche Revisions und Treuhand-Aktiengesellschaft, 14.10.35

96 BArch R55/951 Gesellschaftsvertrag des BPhO GmbH, 21.10.35

97 BArch R55/245 BPhO Stegmann to RMVP, 31.5.39

98 BArch R55/247 Abschrift BPhO to RMVP Abt. Haushalt, 5.8.40: "Die Dresdner Staatsoper hat eine grosse Anzahl von Stradivari-Geigen in ihrem Besitz. Die Wiener Philharmoniker besitzen ein grosses Orchester-Archiv, worin Briefe, Bilder, Bücher etc. gesammelt werden, die sie irgundwie von Dirigenten, Komponisten und Solisten, die mit ihnen zusammen gearbeitet haben erhielten."

99 ibid.

100 ibid.

101 ABPhO Pensionskasse Hauptbuch

102 BArch R55/245 Deutsche Revisions und Treuhand-Aktiengesellschaft, 14.10.35

103 BArch R55/951 RMVP Kohler Vermerk, 2.11.38

104 BArch R55/245 Zuschüsse des Ministeriums für Volksaufklärung und Propaganda für das Geschäftsjahr 1934/35

105 BArch R55/246 Rechnungshof des Deutschen Reichs to RMVP, 15.4.42

106 ibid.

107 ibid.

108 BArch R55/247 BPhO Stegmann to RMVP Yum Prüfunungsbericht des Rechnungshofes des Detuschen Reichs, 23.6.42

109 BArch R55/247 BPhO Stegmann to RMVP re: Umkleideräume des Orchesters, 24.5.38

110 BArch R55/246 Gewinn und Verlustrechnung am 31.3.43

111 PCH Dienstvertrag Carl Höfer, 3.1.35

112 BArch (BDC) RK O0024 RMVP dem Herrn Staatssekretär, 14.7.38

113 BArch (BDC) RK O0024 RMVP to Stegmann, ?.5.34

114 BArch R55/197 BPhO to RMVP re: Konzertmeister Siegfried Borries, 24.3.25

115 PJB Gehaltsnachweis über das Herrn Hans Bastiaan, 1.10.44

116 BArch (BDC) RK O0024 RMVP dem Herrn Staatssekretär, 14.7.38

117 ibid.

118 ibid.

119 ibid.

120 ibid.

121 BArch (BDC) RK O0024 BPhO Stegmann to RMVP, 17.2.39

122 ibid.

123 BArch R55/247 Accounting, 1941

124 BArch R55/198 RMVP Vermerk, 29.1.43

125 BArch R55/19? Liste der Orchestermitglieder, 1942

126 BArch R55/1147 BPhO Vertrag v. Schmidtseck, 1.4.34

127 BArch (BDC) RK O0024 RMVP dem Herrn Staatssekretär, 14.7.38

128 BArch R55/247 Accounting, 1941

129 BArch (BDC) RK WO002 Vermerk über die Besprechung in Sachen Dr. Wilhelm Furtwängler, 9.12.46

130 BArch R55/197 RMVP Kohler Vermerk, 3.10.

131 ibid.

132 BArch R55/1148 Furtwängler re: Reichssparkommisar, ?.3.34

133 ibid.

134 BArch (BDC) RK WO002 Furtwängler contract, 3.7.34

135 ZBZ Furtwängler Nachlass B 0:10, Furtwängler to BPhO Busch, 27.1.39

136 BArch R55/1145 Furtwängler contract, 1929

137 BArch R55/1147 Bedarfs-Anmeldung, 30.6.33

138 BArch R55/245 Zuschüsse des Ministeriums für Volksaufklärung und Propaganda für das Geschäftsjahr 1934/35

139 BArch R55/246 Rechnungshof des Deutschen Reichs, 15.4.42

140 BArch R55/247 BPhO to RMVP 12.5.38

141 ibid.

142 BArch R55/246 BPhO Stegmann to RMVP, Zum Prüfungsbericht des Rechnungshofes, 23.6.42

143 BArch R55/245 RMVP to BPhO Örtliche Prüfung des Rechnungshofes des Deutschen Reichs, 22.10.38

144 BArch R55/247 BPhO to RMVP 12.5.38

145 BArch R55/246 Rechnungshof des Deutschen Reichs, 15.4.42

146 ibid.

147 BArch R55/199 Liste der Orchestermitglieder, 1942

148 ZBZ Furtwängler Nachlass, B O:23, Abrechung, 10.5.39

149 ZBZ Furtwängler Nachlass, B O:13, 4.2.39

150 BArch R55/245 Verlust-Vortrag 1933/34

151 BArch R55/247 RMVP Zu dem Geschäftsbericht des BPhO, 26.10.40

152 BArch R55/246 Rechnungshof des Deutschen Reichs, 15.4.42

153 BArch R55/246 Gehälter der Orchestermitglieder, 1.2.42

154 ZBZ Furtwängler Nachlass B O:24, Stegmann to Furtwängler, 6.6.39

155 ZBZ Furtwängler Nachlass B O:87, BPhO Sonaten—Abend, 20.2.40

156 PJB Nachweis über das Herrn Hans Bastiaan Gehalt ab 1.10.44

157 BArch R55/246 Gehälter der Orchestermitglieder, 1.2.42

158 BArch R56 I/66 Havemann Bericht über die am 13.3.33 stattgefundene Besprechung betreffend die zukünftige Gestaltung des Philharmonischen Orchesters; in Prieberg: " Prof. Havemann verlangt, daß das Existenzminimum des einzelnen Orchestermusikers fest gelegt werden muß. Das Philharmonische Orchester kann nur die gleiche Subvention erhalten wie das Kampfbund- Orchester. Weitere Einnahmen kann sich das Philharmonische Orchester dann durch gute Leistungen, auf Reisen etc. verschaffen. [...] Das Spitzengehalt soll für den einzelnen Musiker Mk. 650.- pro Monat betragen und für die ersten Stimmen bis Mk. 800.-. Er bekundet sein Einverständnis, daß Herr Höber

Vorstand bleibt, jedoch werden zwei Mitglieder des Orchesters, die zugleich Mitglieder der N.S.D.A.P. sind, in den Vorstand delegiert. Prof. Havemann spricht dann weiter den Wunsch aus, daß das Philharmonische Orchester unter Furtwängler in allernächster Zeit ein Konzert zu Gunsten des "Kampfbundes für Deutsche Kultur" geben möge und erbittet Antwort möglichst innerhalb 48 Stunden." Havemann was militant, but ultimately powerless. He harassed the Philharmonic endlessly in the early years of the Third Reich, but his ideological fervour rendered the majority of his insistences untenable. Putting the Berlin Philharmonic on the same level as his third class Kampfbund-Orchester was laughable, as much for his orchestra as for the Philharmonic. His proposals would have destroyed the orchestra—the precise opposite of Goebbels' intentions.

159 PCH BPhO Anstellungs- und Besoldungsordnung, 1.8.34

160 BArch R55/197 BPhO to RMVP 5.11.34

161 BArch R55/197 BPhO Stegmann to RMVP, 24.3.36

162 BArch R55/197 BPhO Stegmann to RMVP Betr. Erhöhung des Gehaltes unseres Solo-Cellisten, 23.10.37

163 BArch R55/197 BPhO Stegmann, von Benda, RMVP Betr. Gehalt unseres Konzertmeisters, 2.6.38

164 BArch R55/197 RMVP Leiter der Personalabteilung, Betr. Erhöhung der Bezüge der Konzertmeister, 18.7.41

165 BArch R55/197 RMVP Vermerk 16.3.43

166 ibid.

167 GStA IB 2281/4.9 Preussische Finanzminister to RMVP Goebbels, 29.9.36

168 BArch R55/197 BPhO von Benda, Stegmann to RMVP, 20.4.36

169 ibid.

170 BArch R55/197 BPhO von Benda, Stegmann to RMVP, 20.4.36

171 ibid.

172 ibid.

173 ibid.

174 ibid.

175 GStA IB 2281/4.9 Preussische Finanzminister to RMVP Goebbels, 29.9.36

176 ibid.

177 ibid.

178 GStA IB 2281/5.10 Der Preussische Ministerpräsident gez. Tietjen to RMVP Goebbels, 5.10.36

179 GStA IB2281/27.10 Goebbels den Herrn Preussischen Finanzminister, 27.10.36

180 BArch R55/951 BPhO Stegmann to RMVP, 25.11.38

181 BArch R55/199 Dem Reichsminister Aktennotiz, 8.8.38

182 ibid.

183 BArch R55/951 BPhO Stegmann to RMVP, 25.11.38

184 ibid.

185 BArch R55/951 BPhO Stegmann to RMVP, 27.10.38

186 BArch R55/951 BPhO Stegmann to RMVP Kohler, 8.10.38

187 BArch R55/951 BPhO Stegmann to RMVP, 25.11.38

188 ibid.

189 BArch R55/245 BPhO Stegmann to RMVP, 31.5.39

190 BArch R55/951 BPhO Stegmann to RMVP, 25.11.38

191 BArch R55/951 RMVP Kohler memo, 15.12.38

192 BArc R55/197 Preussische Ministerpräsident to RMVP, ?.8.38

193 ibid.

194 BArch R55/199 Dem Reichsminister, Aktennotiz 8.8.38

195 BArch R55/951 Dem Herrn Reichsminister, 15.12.38

196 BArch R55/951 RMVP Kohler, Vermerk, ?.4.39

197 ibid.

198 BArch R55/951 Einkommen der Orchestermitglieder nach der bisherigen und nach der neuen Reglung Mitgliederstand von 1.12.38

199 PJB Gehaltsnachweis über das Herrn Hans Bastiaan, 1.10.44

200 BArch R55/199 Der Sondertreuhändler to RMVP, 9.1.40

201 PCH BPhO Anstellungs- und Besoldungsordnung, undated

202 ibid.

203 BArch R55/197 BPhO Stegmann an RMVP, 8.12.37

204 ibid.

205 BArch R55/199 Kulturorchester der Ostmark, undated

206 BArch R55/200 Goebbels to München Gauleiter Wagner, 3.5.41

207 ibid.

208 R55/199 RMVP Vermerk, 10.10.41

209 ibid.

210 ibid.

211 BArch R55/199 RMVP Sondertreuhänder to Hitler, undated 1941

212 BArch R55/199 RMVP An den Herrn Staatssekretär, 15.10.41

213 BArch R55/199 RMVP Entwurf, "Mein Führer!", undated

214 BArch R55/199 Aufstellung über die Eingruppierung der deutschen Kulturorchester 1.10.44

215 ibid.

216 BArch R55/951 BPhO von Benda, Stegmann to RMVP, 1.6.38

217 BArch R55/246 BPhO Stegmann to RMVP Ott, 17.10.41

218 BArch R55/247 RMVP memo Betr. Etat unserer Gesellschaft, 22.9.44

Chapter 4

1   BArch R55/197 BPhO Projektierter Inhalt des Vertrages mit Konzertmeister Kolberg, 5.11.34

2   PCH BPhO Anstellungs-und Besoldungsordnung, 1.8.34

3   BArch R55/245 Bemerkungen zur Gewinn- und Verlustrechnung zum 31.3.35

4   PJB Philharmonische Blätter 1936-37, Nr.1

5   BArch R55/197 Bericht des künstlerischen Leiters 1938/39

6   BArch R55/247 Erläuterung zu den Einnahmen, 1938/39

7   BArch R55/197 BPhO Stegmann to RMVP Betr. Leistungs-Zulage für die Berliner Philharmoniker, 20.4.36

8   PCH BPhO Anstellungs-und Besoldungsordnung, 1.8.34

9   BArch R55/1148 Furtwängler re:Reichssparkommissar, ?.3.34

10 BArch R55/951 BPhO Stegmann to RMVP, 1.6.38

11 BArch R55/245 BPhO History, undated 1935

12 PJB BPhO Diensteinteillung 11.42

13 PJB BPhO Dienstplan 8.3.40

14 BArch R55/951 BPhO Stegmann to RMVP Kohler, 8.10.38

15 ibid.

16 BArch R55/951 BPhO to dem Reichsminister, 15.12.38

17 PJB BPhO Dienstpläne 1942-43

18 PJB BPhO Dienstplan 21.1.42: "Die Tage 4., 5., 6. März sind für Proben mit Dr. Furtwängler (neues Werk) reserviert"; Dienstplan 10.4.42: "18.4. 10Uhr Philh. Probe Furtwängler (Durchspielen der Sinfonie von Wilhelm Furtwängler)

19 BArch R55/245 Bemerkungen zur Gewinn- und Verlustrechnung zum 31.3.35

20 BArch (BDC) RK O002 Vormerkung, Gauleiter Paul Giesler München, 1.5.43

21 BArch (BDC) RK O002 Hermann Giesler to Gauleiter des Gaues München/ Oberbayern, Paul Giesler, 28.7.43

22 BArch R55/1148 BPhO Stegmann to RMVP Funk, 17.4.35

23 ibid.

24 PJB Clipping „Der Führer beim Furtwängler-Konzert", 10.2.37

25 "Abends beim Führer. Mit ihm zum Konzert von Thomas Beecham mit den Londoner Philharmonikern in der Philharmonie: ein gesellschaftliches, aber kein künstlerisches Ereignis. Fast das ganze Kabinettda. Beecham dirigiert sehr eitel und unangenehm, dabei nichts dahinter. Sein Orchester in den Streichern ganz dünn, ohne Präzision und Klarheit. Ein schleppender Abend. Und peinlich, da man aus Anstand klatschen muß. Auch der Führer ist sehr unzufrieden. Wie hoch steht doch die musikalische Kultur in Deutschland! Und was haben wir an den Berliner Philharmonikern und Furtwängler." Goebbels Tagebuch II, Eintrag vom 14/XI/36; (2) "Abends zum Konzert des Augusteums-Rom unter Molinari in derPhilharmonie. Das Orchester ist gut, besser als das Londoner, aber nicht so gut wie die Berliner Philharmoniker. Herrliche Cellos und Geigen, zu lautes Schlagzeug. Die Pastorale spielt es nicht ganz nach unserem Niveau. Aber gut Strauß >Eulenspiegel<, Respighis >Pinien von Rom<, ein handfestes Bravourstück,und als Zugabe wunderbar und hinreißend die Meistersinger- Ouvertüre." Goebbels Tagebuch III, Eintrag vom 9/X/37

26 Goebbels Tagebuch, 2.9.33: "Das Adamsche Orchester spielt sich einen Mist zusammen."

27 ibid.

28 Aktennotiz der NSKG, Abt. Musik, Friedrich W. Herzog, 28/VIII/34. Quelle: ACDJC, Document CXLV-533 in Prieberg, Handbuch, p. 1780

29 Alfred Rosenberg, Bemerkung, 28/VIII/34. Quelle: ACDJC, Document: CXLV-533; in Prieberg, Handbuch, 1781

30 ibid.

31 The NSRSO in fact appeared at every Reichsparteitag, specialising in processional accompaniments such as Beethoven overtures and the Meistersinger and Rienzi Vorspiele.

32 Furtwängler and his apologists make much ado about the fact the Nürnberg performance took place the night before the infamous rallies began. This argument is specious as everyone of Nazi prominence was already there. Still, there is nothing to mitigate the view Furtwängler appeared unhappily and under duress. Just half a year after Furtwängler's reconciliation in the aftermath of the Hindemith debacle, it was probably prudent for the conductor to accept an invitation to Nürnberg as a gesture of goodwill, in order to restore favour with the Nazi leaders.

33 Prieberg, Handbuch, 5374; Raabe conducted the Gewandhausorchester in a Beethoven programme surrounding a big speech by Hitler 11.9.35

34 PJB Philharmonische Blätter 1936/37, Die Berliner Philharmoniker in Nürnberg

35 BArch RMVP Gutterer, an Furtwängler, 11/VI/37, in Prieberg, Handbuch, p. 1813

36 PJB BPhO Rundschreiben No.1/39-40, 26.7.39

37 BArch (BDC) RK NO002 von Benda betr. Rücktritt, undated 1939

38 PJB An die Herren Mitglieder des Berliner Philharmonischen Orchesters, 11.8.39: "Wir bitten dabei zu berücksichtigen, dass der Parteitag ausserordentliche Schwierigkeiten betr. Der Bahnverbindungen mit sich bringt [...] Die Quartierfrage wird vom Büro aus in Verbindung mit der betreffenden parteiamtlichen Stelle in Nürnberg geregelt. Wir werden uns bemühen, die Quartierfrage zur Zufriedenheit aller Herren zu regeln. Wir bitten aber zu berücksichtigen, dass die Quartierfrage bei der ausserordentlichen Fülle in Nürnberg anlässlich des Parteitages grosse Schwierigkeiten macht. Es ist auf jeden Fall mit einer grossen Anzahl von Doppelzimmern zu rechnen."

39 Goebbels Tagebuch, 20.6.36

40 Prieberg, Handbuch, p. 1309

41 see Muck, P, Einhundert Jahre, Band III

42 BArch R 55/ 206 RMVP to BPhO, 16.4.42

43 PJB An die Herren Mitglieder des BPhO, 7.7.39

44 ibid.

45 Prieberg, Handbuch, p. 5507

46 BArch R55/247 Bericht des künstlerischen Leiters 1939/40

47 Muck, P, Band III

48 BArch R55/247 Bericht des künstlerischen Leiters über die Spielzeit 1940/41

49 BArch R55/247 Bericht des künstlerischen Leiters 1941/42

50 BArch R55/246 Bericht des künstlerischen Leiters 1942/43

51 Muck, P., Band III

52 ibid.

53 BArch (BDC) RK WO002 Vermerk über die Unterredung mit Herrn v. Westerman bei Herrn Schmidt am 7.12.46

54 PJB Rundschreiben, 26.5.39

55 PJB Rundschreiben, 23.11.39

56 PJB BPhO, 23.11.39

57 PJB An die Herren Mitglieder des BPhO, 23.12.41

58 PJB Philharmonische Blätter 1936/37, "Das Berliner Philharmonische Orchester im Mittelpunkt des Kulturaustauchs"

59 Muck, Band III

60 PJB Philharmonische Blätter 1936/37, "Das Berliner Philharmonische Orchester im Mittelpunkt des Kulturaustauchs"

61 BArch R55/247 Bericht des künstlerischen Leiters über die Spielzeit 1940/41

62 PJB BPhO Besetztungsplan ?.12.41

63 Avgerinos, G., 70 Jahre einer GmbH, p.31

64 BPM Furtwängler Bericht, 25.3.47

65 BArch R55/1148 RMVP-Reichfinanzministerium Betr. Reichssparkommissar, 22.2.34

66 ibid.

67 ibid.

68 BArch R55/1146 Bericht über die Prufung der Bilanz der BPhO, 31.3.31

69 ibid.

70 BArch R55/1148 RMVP-Reichfinanzministerium Betr. Reichssparkommissar, 22.2.34

71 BArch R55/1148 Furtwängler to RMVP Betr. Reichssparkommissar, 22.2.34

72 ibid.

73 ibid.

74 ibid.

75 PPM Furtwängler Bericht, .47

76 BArch Namensakte Vedder, 28.11.33: "Louise Wolf ist angeblich Christin, die Töchter Halbjüdinnen. Gegen die Beschäftigung der Töchter wird von allen Seiten Widerstand gezeigt, vor allem vom Geschäftsführer des Philharmonischen Orchesters (Herrn Höber). Der Vertrag mit dem Philharmonischen (10 Furtwänglerkonzerte) ist in dieser Saison gekündigt. Die Verlängerung des Vertrages ist unklar. Furtwängler will Frau Wolf unterstützen und die Konzerte bei der Firma lassen. Der Geschäftsführer HÖBER wünscht keine Verlängerung des Vertrages falls in der Inhaberschaft und in der Frage der Töchter keine Änderung erfolgt". These remarks are insightful, but ought to be read with the knowledge that Rudolf Vedder was a powerful Berlin concert agent with designs on co-opting the *Philharmonischen Konzerte* for himself

77 ABPO A Flesch 1, Carl Flesch to Louise Wolff, 19.5.35

78 BArch R55/245 BPhO Gewinn- und Verlust-Konto, 3.35

79 BArch (BDC) RK WO002 Furtwängler Vertrag,

80 BArch R55/1148 BPhO Stegmann to RMVP Greiner, 2.1.35

81 PJB Philharmonische Blätter 1936/37, Nr.1

82 Muck, P., Einhunder Jahre BPhO, Vol. II, p.123

83 Geissmar, p.119

84 BArch R55/197 BPhO Stegmann to RMVP 13.10.39

85 PKS Furtwängler to Westerman, 4.7.44

86 BArch R55/197 Bericht des künstlerischen Leiters 1938/39

87 BArch R55/247 Bericht des künstlerischen Leiters 1939/40

88 BArch R55/246 Bericht des künstlerischen Leiters 1942/43

89 Muck, P., Einhundert Jahre BPhO, Vol. II, p.169

90 BArch (BDC) RK NO002 von Benda betr. Rücktritt, undated 1939

91 BArc (BDC) RK O002 Furtwängler to Hitler, 24.4.36

92 PJB Philharmonische Blätter 1936/37, Nr.1

93 BArch (BDC) RK NO002 von Benda betr. Rücktritt, undated 1939

94 ibid.

95 ibid.

96 PKS Furtwängler to Westerman 4.7.44

97 PKS Furtwängler to Westerman 10.8.44

98 BArch R55/1148 BPhO Stegmann to Vorsitzenden des Aufsichtsrates der BPhO Funk, 19.12.34

99 BArch (BDC) RK O002 Vermerk über die Besprechung in Sachen Dr. Wilhem Furtwängler, 9.12.46

100 BArch R55/1148 BPhO Stegmann And die Abonnenten der 10 Philharmonischen Konzerte, 3.1.35

101 ibid.

102 BArch R55/1148 Dr. Adolf Kraetzer to BPhO, 21.1.35

103 BArch R55/1148 BPhO Stegmann to RMVP von Keudell, 30.1.35

104 BArch R55/1148 RMK Ihlert to RMVP Funk, 4.1.35

105 ibid.

106 BArch R55/245 BPhO Stegmann to RMVP Betr. Prüfung der Jahresrechnungen, 31.5.39

107 BArch R56I/109 Hinkel speech "Es muss der Künstler mit dem Volke gehen!", undated, 1938

108 BArch R56I/109 Hinkel speech "Er gehört zu uns", undated, 1936

109 BArch R56I/109 Hinkel speech "Es muss der Künstler mit dem Volke gehen!", undated, 1938

110 PJB Concert poster NSG "Kraft durch Freude" Meisterkonzert, 13.12.36

111 BArch R55/245 BPhO Stegmann to RMVP Betr. Prüfung der Jahresrechnungen, 31.5.39

112 ibid.

113 ibid.

114 ibid.

115 PJB Concert poster NSG "Kraft durch Freude" Meisterkonzert 13.12.36

116 BArch R55/245 BPhO Stegmann to RMVP Betr. Prüfung der Jahresrechnungen, 31.5.39

117 BArch R55/197 Bericht des künstlerischen Leiters 1938/39

118 Muck, Band III

119 PWK Philharmonische Blätter Nr. 1937/38

120 ibid.

121 ibid.

122 ibid.

123 BArch R55/247 Bericht des künstlerischen Leiters 1941/42

124 BArch R55/247 Bericht des künstlerischen Leiters 1940/41

125 Avgerinos, G., 70 Jahre einer GmbH, p. 54

126 PWK Philharmonische Blätter 1935/36, Nr.6

127 BArch R55/197 Bericht des künstlerischen Leiters 1938/39

128 BArch R55/247 Bericht des künstlerischen Leiters 1941/42; BArch (BDC) RK O002 Vermerk über die Besprechung in Sachen Dr. Wilhem Furtwängler, 9.12.46

129 ABPhO Kameradschaft der BPhO Hauptbuch; for the Winterhilfswerk concert in 1940, the orchestra donated RM 3 000, to the Deutsche Rotes Kreuz, the Philharmonic contributed RM 500 in 1940, RM 1 347 in 1941, and at least RM 900 in 1944.

130 Furtwängler ibid.

131 ZBZ Furtwängler Nachlass B O:81, BPhO Stegmann to Furtwängler, 4.3.40

132 BArch R55/247 Bericht des künstlerischen Leiters 1941/42

133 BArch R55/247 Bericht des künstlerischen Leiters 1940/41

134 PWK Philharmonische Blätter Nr. 6 1937/38

135 BArch R55/247 RMVP memo Betr. Etat unserer Gesellschaft, 22.9.44

136 ibid.

137 BArch R55/1148 Der Präsident der Reichskulturkammer Schmidt-Leonhardt, 20.3.35

138 Prieberg, Handbuch, p. 7349

139 BArch R55/1148 BPhO Stegmann to RMVP Betr. Konzert aus Anlass der Papst-Feier, 17.1.35

140 BArch ZSg. 115/16 RPA, 18.12.42; Im Auftrag des RPA Berlin leitet Karajan in Borsigwalde ein
Werkkonzert des BPhO in der Firma Alkett (Altmärkische Kettenwerk GmbH) in Prieberg, Handbuch, p. 3563

141 PJB BPhO Rundschreiben Nr. 7, 9.11.39

142 BArch R55/247 Bericht des künstlerischen Leiters 1939/40

143 BArch R55/197 Bericht des künsterlischen Leiters 1938/39

144 BArch R55/247 Vertrag zwischen der RRG und der BPhO, GmbH, undated

145 BArch R55/197 Bericht des künstlerischen Leiters 1938/39

146 BArch R55/247 Vertrag zwischen der RRG und der BPhO, GmbH, undated

147 ibid.

148 Prieberg, Handbuch, p. 608: 19. April 1941, Das BPhO, Dgt. Böhm, bietet am Vorabend von Hitlers Geburtstag die musikalische Umrahmung einer Rede von Dr. Goebbels

149 Prieberg, Handbuch, p. 3554

150 BArch R55/246 Bericht des künstlerischen Leiters 1940/41

151 BArch R55/247 Bericht des künstlerischen Leiters 1941/42

152 PKS Furtwängler to von Westerman, 10.8.44

153 PKS Furtwängler to von Westerman, 4.7.44

154 BArch R55/247 Bericht des künstlerischen Leiters über die Spielzeit 1939/40

155 PJB BPhO Rundschreiben Nr. 34, 18.11.41: „Reise nach Hamburg. Nur durch besonders Eingreifen des Herrn Verkehrsministers ist die Beförderung des Orchesters nach Hamburg zugesagt worden."

156 BArch R55/246 Bericht des Künstlerischen Leiters 1942/43

157 Avgerinos, G., 70 Jahre GmbH, p.66

158 PHW Memoirs

159 PJB Programme 13.3.42, 18h30

160 Muck, Band III

161 BArch R55/197 BPhO Stegmann to RMVP, 13.12.43

162 see E. Hartmann, Stunde Null

163 Muck, Band III

164 BArch R55/246 BPhO to RMVP, 15.3.44

165 ibid.

166 Muck, Band III

167 BArch R55/247 Büro Staatssekretär, 2.2.44

168 already at a performance of the Mozart Requiem on November 26th, 1944, 26.11.44, the Kittel and Lamy Chors joined forces to muster enough voices for the performance, Muck, Band III

169 Muck, Band III

170 see Hartmann, die BPhO in der Stunde Null; Wiewieorra memoires from PHW Nachlass

171 BArch R55/245 BPhO Statistik im Geschäftsjahr 1934/35, 14.6.35

172 BArch R55/247 Bericht des künstlerischen Leiters 1940/41

Chapter 5

1 BArch R 56 I/126 Hinkel to Böhm. Das BPhO, Dgt. Böhm, bietet Werke von Wagner und das Violinkonzert von R. Schumann (UA) zur Jahrestagung der RKK im Dt.Opernhaus. Solist: G. Kulenkampff (Violine).

2 ZBZ BF 55, Vormerkung Gauleiter Paul Giesler München, 31.5.43

3 BArch R55/245 BPhO Annual Report, 31.3.35

4 ABPhO Philharmonischen Blätter, Ausgabe 8, 1935

5 PKW clipping "Nur weige Musik erschöpft sich nicht"

6 There were also three Mahler songs programmed on January 15th, 1932

7 cf. Grove Dictionary, Dohnanyi, Braunfels, Erdmann, Korngold

8 Prieberg Handbuch, p. 4719

9 M. Kater, Composers, p. 216-217

10 Prieberg Handbuch, p. 4720

11 Goebbels, Tagebuch III. Eintrag vom 17/IV/37. S. 116

12 Kater, Composers, p.17

13 see Kater, Composers; Prieberg Musik im NS-Staat

14 BArch (BDC) RK WO002 Furtwängler Bericht, Blatt 1516

15 see Kater, Composers; Prieberg Musik

16 see Kater

17 E. Schmierer, Lexicon der Oper, Band II, p.144

18 ABPhO Dr. Fritz Stege in Berliner Westen, 18.11.34 Komponisten, die man nicht mehr aufführt, Völkischer Beobachter, 18.11.34: „Hindemith wird verboten. Rassenfremde Musik aber, wie Igor Strawinskys „Frühlingsweihe" darf dagegen von Berliner Staatskapellmeistern ohne Widerspruch auf das Konzertprogramm gesetzt werden, unbeschadet der Tatsache, dass Strawinsky sich abfällig über deutsche Meister der Tonkunst geäußert, dass er deutsche Musik verspottet hat. Es ist mit Sicherheit damit zu rechnen, dass dieser Entschluss noch einmal überprüft wird, ehe das Ausland zu dieser Selbstverstümmelung des deutschen Musiklebens Stellung nimmt."

19 BArch R55/197 Bericht des Künstlerischen Leiters 1938/39

20 Muck, Band III

21 BArch R55/197 Bericht des Künstlerischen Leiters 1938/39

22 Muck, Band III

23 BArch R55/1148 RMVP to RMK Ihlert, 17.1.35

24   ABPhO Westerman an die Reichsmusikkammer Fachschaft Komponisten 11.9.42: „im Auftrage des Sekretariats Furtwängler überreichen wir Ihnen beiliegend Partitur und Orchestermaterial des obigen Werkes. Herr Dr. Furtwängler lässt Sie bitten, die Partitur dort durchzusehen und dem Komponisten einen Bescheid zu geben."

25   Prieberg Handbuch, p. 5729

26   ibid., p. 5711

27   Ibid., p. 1301

28   BArch R 55/ 197 RMVP von Borries an Leiter Pers, Aktenvermerk, 25.8.39

29   Telefunken E 1824/27 Mendelssohns Konzert E-moll für Violine und Orchester; Solist: Georg Kulenkampff. Tondokument im DRA: B006205313., in Prieberg Handbuch, p.4559

30   Telefunken E 1056, den Hochzeitsmarsch aus der "Sommernachtstraummusik" von Mendelssohn. Tondokument im DRA: B005005663, in Prieberg Handbuch, p. 490

31   Interview with Johannes Bastiaan, 6.2.05

32   Berlioz, who even in his own time was more beloved in Germany than in France, remained an occasional visitor to the Philharmonie.

33   BArch R55/695, Hinkel Protokoll der Programmsitzung, 25.3.42

34   PJB BPhO Rundschreiben Nr. 7, 9.11.39

35   Muck, P. Band II

36   BArch R55/20585 RMVP Hadamowsky an Leiter M, Dr. Drewes, 27.11.41

37   PKS Furtwängler to Westerman 4.7.44

38   Ryding, E., and R. Pechefsky, Bruno Walter: A World Elsewhere, p. 221

39   Aus Deutsche Allgemeine Zeitung Nr.161, 5.4.33

40   Ryding, E., and R. Pechefsky, Bruno Walter: A World Elsewhere, p. 221

41   ibid.

42   Ibid.

43   These letters were printed in German newspapers, but the originals have never been found.

44   F. Trenner, Richard Strauss Chronik, p.536

45   Aus Deutsche Allgemeine Zeitung Nr.161, 5.4.33

46   Prieberg, Handbuch, p. 5745; 5073; 1683; 7628; 6847

47   BArch R 55/ 197 RMVP von Borries an Leiter Pers, Aktenvermerk, 25.8.39

48   BArch R55/246 Bericht des künstlerischen Leiters 1940/41

49   Muck, P., Band III; Prieberg, Handbuch; ABPhO Programmsamlung

50   Konzert für Sibelius am 19.3.41 gegeben, also als der Komponist schon 76 war.

51   Osborne, Karajan, Anhang A, S.925

52   BArch (BDC) NO002 Benda Bericht, 1939

53   Tristan was not von Karajan's debut at the Staatsoper. His previous Fidelio was received with only moderate praise. see Osborne, R. Herbert von Karajan, Leben und Musik.

54   BArch (BDC) RK WO002, Furtwängler Ent-Nazifizierung, 17.12.46: Diese Kritik ist meines Erachtens absolut beeinflusst von höherer Stelle […] Das kann nur Göring gewesen sein, Goebbels ist unmöglich."

55   BArch (BDC) RK NO002 Benda Bericht, 1939

56   Dr. Gerhart von Westermann, Exposé. Ohne Datum = Frühjahr 1942. Quelle: NL Furtwängler, in Prieberg, Handbuch, p. 7352

57 ibid.

58 ibid.

59 BArch (BDC) RK WO002, Vermerk über die Unterredung mit Herrn v. Westerman, 7.12.46

60 BArch R 55/ 197 RMVP von Borries an Leiter Pers, Aktenvermerk, 25.8.39

61 PKS Furtwängler Brief an Freda von Rechenberg, 28.7.44: „Soeben erfahre ich aus absolut informierter Quelle (die nicht genannt sein will), dass Staatssekretär Naumann den Vertreter von Hinkel, Dr. Schrade (Generalsekretär der Reichskulturkammer) beauftragt hat, den Fall Vedder erneut aufzugreifen mit dem Ziel einer Rehabilitierung des Beklagten. Die Aktion ist anscheinend zugleich gegen Dr. Drewes [unlesbar]. Ich bitte, erkundigen Sie sich auf vorsichtige Weise, wie die Sache liegt und teilen Sie vor allem Westerman, respektive Drewes (aber nicht telefonisch, nur persönlich) diese absolut authentische Information mit."

62 BArch (BDC) RK WO002 Furtwängler Vertrag, 1.4.34

63 BArch R55/1147 Vertrag Furtwängler, 1.4.34

64 Geissmar, B. p.121; BArch (BDC) RK WOO2 Meldung Fachgruppe Kleinmusikbühnen, 17.8.33

65 from here stems the famous quote (ZBZ Furtwängler archive) on behalf of Schoenberg, etc. debate between Kater and Prieberg.

66 BArch (BDC) RK WOO2 an Herrn Staatskommissar Hinkel, 20.7.33

67 ZBZ BF 47, Fachgruppe Kleinkunstbühnen Meldung, 17.8.33

68 New Grove, Kreisler

69 Kreisler an Furtwängler 1/VII/33. Abdruck, gekürzt, in: Louis P. Lochner, "Fritz Kreisler". Wien, 1957. S. 228, in Prieberg, p. 1753

70 Geißmar, B., Taktstock und Schaftstiefel, Hubermann Brief, p. 128-130

71 PPM, Furtwängler Bericht, p.13

72 BArch (BDC) WO002 Furtwängler de-Nazification, 9.12.46

73 Muck, P., Band III

74 Prieberg, Handbuch, p. 3613

75 ibid.

76 Friedrich Lambart (Hrsg.): Tod eines Pianisten: Karlrobert Kreiten und der Fall Werner Höfer, 1988

77 Prieberg, Handbuch, p. 3678

78 BArch (BDC) WO002 Vermerk Furtwängler, 7.12.46

Chapter 6

1 GstA, BPhO Höber to Preussischer Finanzministerium, 27.1.31

2 ABPhO Stegmann to Rechenberg 12.12.42

3 BArch R55/951 BPhO von Benda, Stegmann to RMVP, 1.6.38

4 PJB Philharmonische Blätter Nr.X 1937, „Musik als Propagandamittel" by Werner Buchholz

5 PJB Philharmonische Blätter Nr.7 1936/37, "Das Berliner Philharmonisches Orchester im Mittelpunkt des Kulturaustausches"

6 BArch R55/246 BPhO Stegmann to RMVP, 21.8.41

7 PJB BPhO Programme für Frankreich, Spanien, Portugal, 17.4.42

8 ABPhO Programm für die Warschauer kulturellen Veranstaltungen, 17. bis 24. Oktober, 1943

9 BArch R55/247 Bericht des künstlerischen Leiters 1941/42

10 PJB poster collection

11 ibid.

12 BArch R55/1147 RMVP, Schmidt-Leonhardt, Vermerk, 11.12.34

13 PPM Furtwängler Bericht

14 BArch (BDC) RK WO002 Vermerk über die Besprechung in Sachen Dr. Wilhelm Furtwängler, 9.12.46

15 Festkonzert auf der Prager Burg. "Prager Abend" VI/65, 17/III/44, in Prieberg, Handbuch, p. 1856: "[...] an der Spitze der Gäste aus Partei, Staat und Wehrmacht sah man die Gauleiter Henlein und Eigruber, den Wehrmachtbevollmächtigten beim Reichsprotektor und Befehlshaber im Wehrkreis Böhmen und Mähren, General der Panzertruppen Schaal, und die Protektoratsregierung. Als Ehrengäste wohnten der Veranstaltung zahlreiche Vewundete aus den Prager Lazaretten bei."

16 BArch (BDC) RK NO002 Hans von Benda Erklärung, 18.9.39

17 ibid.

18 BArch (BDC) RK WO002 Vermerk über die Besprechung in Sachen Dr. Wilhelm Furtwängler, 9.12.46

19 BArch R55/197 Bericht des Künstlerischen Leiters 1938/39

20 BArch (BDC) RK NO002 Hans von Benda Erklärung, 18.9.39

21 ABPhO Telegram von Westerman to Knappertsbusch, 6.9.42

22 PJB Rundschreiben Nr.1 Stegmann and die Herren Mitglieder des BPhO, 30.7.42

23 BArch (BDC) RK WO002 Vermerk über die Unterredung mit Herrn v. Westermann bei Herrn Schmidt Betr. Dr. Furtwängler, 7.12.46

24 BArch R55/246 BPhO Stegmann to RMVP Abt. Haushalt, 27.7.42

25 Muck

26 BArch (BDC) RK NO002 von Benda Bericht, 1939

27 BArch R55/197 Bericht des künstlerischen Leiters 1938/39

28 ABPhO BPhO Stegmann to Kormann, Hauptabt. Propaganda (Abt. Kultur) der Regierung des Generalgouvernements, Krakau, 25.9.43

29 BArch R55/247 Erläuterung zu den Einnahmen, 1941/42

30 BArch R55/1148 BPhO Stegmann to Vorsizenden des Aufsichtsrates, Staatssekretär Funk, 19.12.34

31 BArch R55/246 RMVP Stellungsnahme der Haushaltabteilung, 3.8.42

32 ABPhO Der Reichswirtschaftsminister an das BPhO, 15.9.43

33 BArch R55/197 Bericht des kaufmännischen Leiters 1938/39

34 BArch R55/247 Erläuterung zu den Einnahmen, 1944

35 GStA B 2281/27.10.36 Der Reichsminister für Volksaufklärung und Propaganda an den Herrn Preussichen Finanzminister

36 ibid.

37 BArch R55/246

38 BArch R55/246 BPhO Stegmann to RMVP Betr. Tagesgelder, 30.7.42

39 BArch R55/246 BPhO Stegmann to RMVP Ott, 28.6.41

40 PJB Rundschreiben Nr.39, Stegmann to BPhO, 28.1.42

41 BArch R55/246 BPhO Stegmann to RMVP Betr. Ausgaben während meines Aufenthalts in Athen, 3.9.42

42 BArch R55/246 BPhO Stegmann to RMVP Betr. Tagegelder Spanien-Portugal-Frankreich Reise Mai 1942, 30.7.42

43 BArch R55/246 BPhO Stegmann to RMVP Ott, 28.6.41

44 BArch R55/246 BPhO Stegmann to RMVP Ott, 17.10.41

45 BArch R55/246 BPhO Stegmann to RMVP Ott, 28.6.41

46 ibid.

47 BArch R55/246 BPhO Stegmann to RMVP Ott, 17.10.41

48 ibid.

49 Ibid.

50 BArch R55/247 RMVP Büro Staatssekretär, Betr. Gastspiel der BPhO in Spanien und Portugal, 20.4.44

51 ABPhO BPhO Stegmann an die Philharmonische Gesellschaft Budapest, 16.7.43

52 ABPhO Harmonia von Fischer to BPhO Stegmann, 7.8.43

53 BArch R55/247 Erläuterung zu den Einnahmen, 1939

54 Prieberg, Handbuch, p. 2338

55 BArch (BDC) RK O0024 BPhO Stegmann to RMVP Müller, 3.6.39

56 PJB Reisepass, Befristeter Ausweis, Der Kommandant von Gross Paris

57 PJB Rundschreiben Nr.6, von Westerman to BPhO, 26.11.42

58 PJB Rundschreiben Nr.38 Stegmann to BPhO, 9.1.42: „Aufgrund neuer Bestimmungen sind alle vor dem 1.1.40 ausgestellten Pässe ungültig."; Rundschreiben Nr.35 Stegmann to BPhO, 15.12.41: Wir bitten, die Reisepässe genauestens zu prüfen und festzustellen, ob ihre Gültigkeit für das Inland besteht. Alle Reisepässe, die vor dem 15. Februar 1942 für das Inland ungültig werden, müssen erneut werden."

59 PJB RMVP an das zuständige Polizeirevier, 11.8.42

60 PJB Rundschreiben 1. 30.7.42

61 ABPhO Heinemann

62 PJB Rundschreiben Nr.35 Stegmann to BPhO, 15.12.41

63 ABPhO Itinerary and orchestra list, Balkan tour, 1942

64 PJB Rundschreiben Nr.38 Stegmann to BPhO, 9.1.42

65 ABPhO private photos

66 PJB Schweizer Konzertreise, 1942

67 PJB Süd-Ost Konzertreise, 1942

68 ABPhO BPhO Stegmann to Reichsbahnrat Schober, 19.10.43

69 BArch R55/246 BPhO Stegmann to RMVP Ott, 17.10.41

70 PJB BPhO travel itinerary Süd-Ost Konzertreise, September 1942

71 PJB MER-Direktion (Paris) to BPhO Stegmann, Spanien/Frankreich Reise, 23.8.43: "MITROPA-Betten von Paris nach Berlin/München für einige Persönlichkeiten

reserviert werden müssen. Für diese Bestellungen benötigen wir eine 'kriegswichtige Dienstreise-Bescheinigung' des Propaganda-Ministeriums oder von KDF."

72 ABPhO BPhO Stegmann to Reichsbahnrat Schober, 19.10.43

73 PJB Rundschreiben Nr.37 Stegmann to BPhO, 6.1.42

74 BArch R55/246 BPhO Stegmann to RMVP Ott, 28.6.41

75 PJB Rundschreiben Stegmann an die Herren des BPhO, 12.3.42

76 interview with Johannes Bastiaan, 2.2004

77 ABPhO Stegmann an Furtwängler 15.8.42

78 PJB Rundschreiben Nr.6 von Westerman to BPhO, 26.11.42

79 ABPhO Westerman to Furtwängler 27.3.44: „Die Wahrscheinlichkeit, dass die Spanienreise noch durchgeführt wird, ist äußerst gering. Das Orchester, das morgen nach Dänemark abreist, ahnt natürlich noch nichts von diesem Schlag."

80 PJB Rundschreiben Stegmann an die Herren des BPhO, 12.3.42

81 ABPhO BPhO Stegmann to Oberbereichsleiter Schmonsees, Regierung des G.Gouvernements Warschau, 2.11.43

82 BArch (BDC) RK O0024, Stegmann BPhO to RMVP Müller, 3.6.39

83 PJB clipping „Triumph deutscher Musik im Paris: Furtwängler und die Berliner Philharmoniker in Paris", 193?

84 PJB clipping, „Die Philharmoniker in Lissabon, Begeisterungsstürme" by Gerhard Timm, 1942

85 Muck, P, Band II, p.104

86 ibid, p.125

87 ibid., p.151

88 ibid., p.152

89 BArch R55/198 BPhO von Westerman to RMVP, 21.5.42

90 ibid.

91 Prieberg Handbuch

92 Muck, P., Band II, p.168

93 ibid., p.155

94 PJB Philharmonische Blätter Nr.6, 1936/37, „Musik als Propagandamittel"

95 interview with Johannes Bastiaan, 6.2.2004

96 Muck, P., Band II, p.157

97 ibid., p.162

98 Interview with Johannes Bastiaan, 2.2004

99 ABPhO BPhO Stegmann an Schmonsees, 2.11.43: »Mein Sohn, Leutnant Helmut Stegmann, ist verwundet und liegt im […] Brestlitowsk. Er hat zuletzt am 23. Oktober geschrieben und sollte in ein Heimatlazarett überführt werden. Meine Frau und ich möchten ihn nun gern möglichst bald in dringenden Angelegenheiten sprechen bzw. aufsuchen. Vielleicht besteht die Möglichkeit, dass Sie von dort aus in dem genannten Lazarett [in Brestlitowsk] anrufen, um von meinen Jungen persönlich zu erfahren, wann sein Abtransport nach Deutschland durchgeführt wird.«

100 Goebbels Tagebuch IV, Eintrag vom 27/V/41. S. 661

Epilogue

1 BArch R55/1148 Oberbürgermeister Sahm to RMVP, 14.12.33

2 Friedrich Fischer, a violinist who had been wounded in the leg during the First World War

3 BArch R55/1148 Oberbürgermeister Sahm to RMVP, 14.12.33

4 BArch (BDC) PK T0051 RMVP Vermerk, 26.7.39

5 BArch (BDC) RK O0024 RMVP Leiter der Personalabteilung to Herrn Staatssekretär, 3.5.39

6 BArch (BDC) RK O0024 RMVP Naumann to Herrn Leiter Pers. 11.5.39

7 BArch (BDC) RK O0024 BPhO Stegmann to RMVP Müller, 3.6.39

8 BArch (BDC) RK WO002 Vermerk Unterredung mit Herrn Höber Betr. Furtwängler, 4.12.46

9 Hartmann, E., Die Berliner Philharmoniker in der Stunde Null, p.49-50

10 BArch R55/246 RMVP Leiter R an Herrn Ministerialrat Dr. Getzlaff, 3.1.44

11 Hartmann, E., Die Berliner Philharmoniker in der Stunde Null, p.16

12 Muck, P., Band II, p.178

13 Avgerinos, G., Künstler Biographien

14 Ibid., Prieberg Handbuch, p. 6344

15 Hartmann, p.35

16 Hartmann, p.36

17 Muck, P., Band II, p.187

18 see Sträßner, Matthias, Der Dirigent Leo Borchard, 1999

19 Hartmann, p.38

20 Hartmann, p.37

21 Interview with Dieter Gerhard, 12.06

22 PKS Furtwängler to von Westerman, 25.6.44

23 ibid.

24 Avgerinos, G., Künstler Biographien

25 ibid.

26 Muck, P., Band II, p. 190

27 ABPhO D Bor 5, Bescheinigung des Magistrats der Stadt Berlin 2.6.45

28 ABPhO list, 1947

29 PJB Bastiaan to Branch Military Government, American Sector, 1945

30 Hartmann, p.9

31 ABPhO G Thie 1, Ernst Fuhr to G. Thiele, 29.5.46:
"auf Anweisung der amerikansichen Militärbehörde teilen wir Ihnen mit, dass Ihnen mit sofortiger Wirkung jede kulturelle Tätigkeit im amerikanischen Sektor untersagt ist. Wir bitten daher, Ihre Zugehörigkeit zum Berliner Philharmonischen Orchester per sofort als beendet zu betrachten. Sie können Ihren Fall dem Deutschen Prüfungsausschuss, Berlin W.15, Schlüterstr. 45 zur Untersuchung und Rehabilitierung vorlegen."

32 Avgerinos, Künstler Biographien

33 ibid.

34 ibid.

35 Former Philharmonic violist Dieter Gerhard, who joined the orchestra in 1955 recalls encountering Wolfram Kleber in the 1950s when Kleber was frequently recruited by his old friend Karl Rammelt (also Pg.) as an „Aushilfe" during Berlin Philharmonic recording sessions. Recordings were closed functions, made under the auspecies of the private Berliner Philharmoniker GmbH. They were therefore not subject to either sectoral public performance restrictions, or personnel bans applied to the *Berliner Philharmonisches Orchester GmbH*.

36 BArch (BDC) RK WO002, Vermerk über die Besprechung in Sachen Dr. Wilhelm Furtwängler, 9.12.46, p.3

37 Avgerinos, G., Künstler Biographien

38 ibid.

39 ibid.

40 ibid.

41 BArch (BDC) RK D20 PRSC Branch Military Government, British Troops Berlin A.M.P. Lynch to Lorenz Höber, 25.6.47

42 BArch (BDC) RK D20 Intelligence Section ISC Branch Case Report, Lorenz Höber, 5.47

43 ABPhO Die Philharmoniker, Entwurf, M V 1943

44 Muck, P., Band II, p.192

45 Hartmann, p.43

46 Approaching anyone higher profile, any other German, or another conductor whose repertoire conflicted with Furtwängler's would have most assuredly permanently severed the orchestra's relationship with Furtwängler, regardless the outcome of his de-Nazification proceedings.

47 see Lang, K., Lieber Herr Celibidache…: Wilhelm Furtwängler und sein Statthalter : ein philharmonischer Konflikt in der Berliner Nachkriegszeit, p. 27, 47.

48 Muck, P., Band II, p.272

49 Muck, P., Band II, p.290.

50 ibid., p.151

51 ABPhO Fur 4 VIII, 1955 3 & 4

Index

Strauss, Richard 1, 25, 119, 123,
126, 128, 135, 155, 157,
158, 160, 162, 167, 169, 170,
174, 189, 190, 192, 219
Stravinsky, Igor Fiodorovitch 157,
164, 165, 173

Tallich, Vaclav 183
Taschner, Gerhard 69, 71, 177,
192, 219, 223, 224
Tchaikovsky, Peter 146, 155, 163, 223
Teubner, Herbert 226
Thiele, Heinz-Walter 226, 227
Thierfelder, Helmuth 120
Thomas, Kurt 119
Tiessen, Heinz 165
Tietjen, Heinz 105, 175, 176
Toscanini, Arturo 180, 184, 211
Traeder, Willi 151
Trapp, Max 157, 160
Troester, Arthur 99, 224

Ulrich, Kurt 219

Varese, Edgar 157
Vedder, Rudolf 175, 176, 177
Vondenhoff, Bruno 139

Wagner, Richard 117, 120, 124, 135, 147,
152, 154, 155, 162, 167, 189, 219
Walter,, Bruno 46
Walter, Bruno 96, 133, 167, 168,
169, 170, 171, 179, 180,
183, 184, 190, 231
Watzke, Rudolf 183
Weber, Carl Maria von 135,
155, 163, 219
Webern, Anton von 157
Wehe, Paul 20
Weisbach, Hans 118, 172
Westerman, Gerhart von 10, 34, 35, 36,
37, 65, 71, 74, 75, 95, 132, 139,
147, 148, 149, 162, 176, 177, 192,
204, 210, 222, 223, 224, 233

Winkelsesser, Paul 156
Wolf, Hugo 118
Wolf, Reinhard 57, 183, 223, 224
Wolf, Winifried 183
Wolff, Hermann 126, 128
Wolff, Louise 126, 128, 169
Wolff, Richard 42, 51, 53, 57, 66, 67, 232
Woywoth 213, 225
Woywoth, Hans 58, 224

Yamada, Kazuo 123
Yamada, Kosaku 119

Ziller, Martin 68, 105

Selected Bibliography

Avgerinos, Gerasrassimos Avgerinos, 1972.

Avgerinos, Gerassimos, *Künstler-Biographien die Mitglieder im Berliner Philharmonischen Orchester von 1882-1972*, Berlin, 1972

Avgerinos, Gerassimos. *Eulenspiegelein, Narreteien. Drei und fünfzig der schönsten Geschichten aus dem Dasein des Berliner Philharmonischen Orchesters, gesammelt und nacherzählt von Gerassimos Avgerinos.* Berlin: Gerassimos Avgerinos, 1971.

Briner, Andres. *Paul Hindemith*, Atlantis Musikbuch-Verlag, 1988.

Burleigh, Michael. *The Third Reich: a new history*, London: Macmillan, 2000.

Cuomo, Glenn R. (ed.) *National Socialist cultural policy*, New York: St. Martin's Press, 1995.

Dümling, Albrecht, *Entartete Musik : Dokumentation und Kommentar zur Düsseldorfer Ausstellung von 1938*. Düsseldorf: DKV, 1993.

Evans, Richard J., Das *Dritte Reich: Diktatur/The Third Reich in Power, 1933-1939*, London: Allen Lane, 2005.

Evans, Richard J., *Das Dritte Reich: Aufstieg/The Coming of the Third Reich*, London: Allen Lane, 2003.

Fetthauer, Sophie, *Deutsche Grammophon: Geschichte eines Schallplattenunternehmens im „Dritten Reich"*, Hamburg: von Bockel, 2000.

Furtwängler, Elisabeth. *Über Wilhelm Furtwängler*, Wiesbaden: Brockhaus, 1980.

Geissmar, Berta. *Musik im Schatten der Politik. Erinnerungen.* Zürich, 1945.

Gerstberger, Walter (ed.), *Der legendäre Geiger Gerhard Taschner*, Augsburg: Bernd Wissner, 1998.

Goebbels, Joseph, *Tagebücher 1924-1945*, München : Piper, 1992.

Goldsmith, Martin, *The Inextinguishable Symphony : a true story of music and love in Nazi Germany*, New York : J. Wiley & Sons, 2000.

Haffner, Herbert. *Furtwängler, Berlin* : Parthas, 2003.

Hartmann, Erich, *Die Berliner Philharmoniker in der Stunde Null: Errinerungen an die Zeit des Untergangs der alten Philharmonie*, Berlin: Musik-und-Buchverlag Werner Feja, 1996

Hellsberg, Clemens, *Demokratie der Könige : die Geschichte der Wiener Philharmoniker*, Wien : Kremayr & Scheriau, 1992

Herzfeld, Friedrich. *Wilhelm Furtwängler. Weg und Wesen.* Leipzig: Wilhelm Goldmann Verlag, 1941.

Jäckel, Eberhard. *Hitlers Weltanschauung/Hitler's world view : a blueprint for power.* Cambridge: Harvard Univesity Press, 1981.

Kater, Michael H. *The Twisted Muse : musicians and their music in the Third Reich*, New York, Oxford: Oxford University Press, 1997.

Kater, Michael H. *Composers of the Nazi Era : eight portraits*, New York; Oxford: Oxford University Press, 2000.

Kater, Michael, Albrecht Reithmüller (eds.) *Music and Nazism : art under tyranny, 1933-1945*, Laaber : Laaber, 2003.

Kershaw, Ian. *Popular opinion and political dissent in the Third Reich: Bavaria 1933-1945*, Oxford: Clarendon, 1983.

Friedrich Lambart (Hrsg.): *Tod eines Pianisten : Karlrobert Kreiten und der Fall Werner Höfer.* - Berlin: Hentrich, 1988

Lang, Klaus, *Lieber Herr Celibidache…: Wilhelm Furtwängler und sein Statthalter : ein philharmonischer Konflikt in der Berliner Nachkriegszeit.* Zürich : M & T Verlag, 1988.

Levi, Erik. *Music in the Third Reich,* Basingstoke; Macmillan, 1994.

Meyer, Michael. *The politics of music in the Third Reich,* New York : Peter Lang, 1993.

Muck, Peter, *Einhundert Jahre Berliner Philharmonisches Orchester: Darstellung in Dokumenten,* Tutzing: Hans Schneider, 1982

Osborne, Richard, *Herbert von Karajan: a life in music,* London: Chatto & Windus, 1998.

Permoser, Manfred, *Die Wiener Symphoniker im NS-Staat,* Frankfurt-am-Main: Peter Lang Europäischer Verlag der Wissenschaften, 2000

Prieberg, Fred K., *Handbuch Deutscher Musiker 1933-45,* CD-ROM, www.fred-prieberg.de

Prieberg, Fred K., *Kraftprobe : Wilhelm Furtwängler im Dritten Reich,* Wiesbaden : F.A. Brockhaus, 1986.

Prieberg, Fred K., *Musik im NS-Staat, Frankfurt am Main* : Fischer Taschenbuch Verlag, 1982.

Ryding, Erik. *Bruno Walter : a world elsewhere,* New Haven; London: Yale University Press, 2001.

Shirakawa, Sam H., *The Devil's Music Master: The Controversial Life and Career of Wilhem Furtwängler,* Oxford: Oxford University Press, 1992

Speer, Albert, *Spandauer Tagebücher,* Frankfurt/M: Propyläen, 1975.

Speer, Albert, *Erinnerungen*. Berlin : Propyläen Verlag, 1969.

Strässner, Matthias, *Der Dirigent Leo Borchard : eine unvollendete Karriere*, Berlin: Transit, 1999.

Strauss, Richard, *Der Strom der Töne trug mich fort. Die Welt um Richard Strauss in Briefen*, Tutzing, 1967.

Stresemann, Wolfgang. *Philharmonie und Philharmoniker*, Berlin: Stapp, 1977.

Vries, Willem de. *Sonderstab Musik : music confiscations by the Einsatzstab Reichsleiter Rosenberg under the Nazi occupation of Western Europe*, Amsterdam : Amsterdam University Press, 1996.

Wackernagel, Peter, *Wilhelm Furtwängler. Die Programme der Konzerte mit dem Berliner Philharmonischen Orchester 1922-1954*, Wiesbaden, 1965.

Walter, Michael, *Richard Strauss und seine Zeit*, Laaber : Laaber, 2000.

Weissweiler, Eva, *Ausgemerzt! : das Lexikon der Juden in der Musik und seine mörderischen Folgen*, Köln : Dittrich-Verlag, 1999.

Berliner Philharmonisches Orchester (BERLIN) *50 Jahre Berliner Philharmonisches Orchester.* [mit Alfred Einstein und Wilhelm Furtwängler] (Charlottenburg, 1932.)

The musical migration: Austria and Germany to the United States ca 1930-1950 (International conference) *Driven into paradise: the musical migration from Nazi Germany to the United States*, Berkeley, Calif. : University of California Press, 1999.

200 Jahre Staatsoper im Bild. Aus Anlass des 200jährigen Jubiläums der Berliner Staatsoper im Auftrage der Preussischen Staatstheater herausgegeben von Julius Kapp, Berlin, 1942.